STRUCTURED PROGRAMMING USING PL/1 AND SP/k

J.N.P. Hume

R.C. Holt

Department of Computer Science
University of Toronto

RESTON PUBLISHING COMPANY, INC., Reston, Virginia

A Prentice-Hall Company

Library of Congress Cataloging in Publication Data

Hume, J   N   P
    Structured Programming using PL/1 and SP/k.

    Bibliography: p.
    Includes index
        1. PL/I (Computer program language) 2. Electronic
digital computers—Programming. I. Holt, Richard C.,
1941-   joint author. II. Title
QA76.73.P25H85   001.6'424   75-23350
ISBN: 0-87909-793-0
ISBN: 0-87909-792-2 (PBK)

© 1975 by
RESTON PUBLISHING COMPANY, INC.
Reston, Virginia 22090
A Prentice-Hall Company

16   15   14   13   12   11

Printed in the United States of America.

PREFACE

This book is intended to form the basis of an introductory course in computing. No particular mathematical background beyond basic arithmetic is assumed; examples are taken largely from everyday life. In this way, the focus is on programming and problem solving, rather than on mathematics. It is our strong conviction that the foundation of computer programming must be carefully laid. Bad habits once begun are hard to change. Even for those who do not continue to study computer science, an experience in the systematic analysis of problems from the statement of "what is to be done" to the final algorithm for "doing it" can be very helpful in encouraging logical thinking.

The programming language presented here is PL/1, a high-level language that permits good programming. This language is introduced in a series of subsets that we call SP/1, SP/2, SP/3, and so on. The SP stands for structured programming and that is what we hope a student will be learning by following this step-by-step presentation of PL/1 subsets.

Just as a program provides a list of instructions to the computer to achieve some well-defined goal, the methodology of structured programming provides a list of instructions to persons who write programs to achieve well-defined goals. The goals of structured programming are to get a programming job done correctly and in such a form that later modifications can be done easily. This means that programs must be understood by people other than their authors.

As each PL/1 subset is learned, new possibilities open up. Even from the first subset SP/1, it is possible to write programs that do calculations and print. By the time the subset SP/4 is reached, a student has learned how to handle alphabetic information, as well as to do numerical calculations and structure the control flow of the program.

Structured programming is especially important when working on larger programs; a detailed discussion of the techniques of modular programming and top-down design accompanies the introduction of PL/1 procedures in SP/6.

Many examples in the book are from data processing, and in SP/8 the ability to handle files and records is introduced. General concepts of data structures, searching, and sorting fit well into this important area that touches all our lives.

The book ends with examples of scientific calculations and the translation of a high-level programming language into machine language.

At all times we have tried to present things in easy to understand stages, offering a large number of program examples and exercises to be done by the student. Each chapter has a summary of the important concepts introduced in it.

The subsets SP/1, SP/2, SP/3, . . . , referred to as a group by the name SP/k, were designed by Richard Holt and David Wortman. These subsets are supported by an SP/k compiler, developed at the University of Toronto, that provides high-speed diagnostic processing of student jobs on either the IBM 360/370 computers or the DEC PDP-11 computers. But this book can be used with other PL/1 compilers, such as the PL/C compiler, because SP/k is a compatible subset of PL/1.

The research leading to the design of the SP/k language was supported by the Onrario Ministry of Education; Tom Hull, Ric Holt, Corley Phillips and Julie Fischette conducted this research. Tom Hull suggested to the authors that they should write this book.

This book was prepared using a text editing system on a computer. Each program was tested using both the SP/k and PL/C compilers. The job of transcribing the authors' pencil scrawls into the computer was done with great care and patience by Inge Weber. The book has been class tested. We are indebted to the many people who offered constructive criticism. In particular we would thank Jim Horning, Bob Cherniak, Brian Clark, Dave Barnard, Les Mezei, Rudy Schild, and Laurie Johnston for their detailed critiques. We have sprinkled through the book names of other people who have helped us.

The time taken to write a book comes at the expense of other activities. Since most of the time was in the evenings or weekends we must end with grateful thanks to our wives Patricia and Marie.

J.N.P. Hume
R.C. Holt

CONTENTS

9 STRUCTURING YOUR ATTACK ON THE PROBLEM — 117

10 THE COMPUTER CAN READ ENGLISH — 129

11 SP/6: PROCEDURES — 141

12 MODULAR PROGRAMMING — 161

CHAPTER 1

WHAT IS IN A NAME?

The name of this book is somewhat of a mouthful! Perhaps it would help if we took it piece by piece and introduced you to the name slowly. We hope that it is no secret that the book has to do with <u>computers</u> and particularly with the <u>use</u> of computers rather than their design or construction. To use computers you must learn how to speak their <u>language</u> or a language that they can understand. We do not actually speak to computers yet, although we may some day; we write messages to them. The reason we write these messages is to instruct the computer about some work we would like it do for us. And that brings us to <u>programming</u>.

WHAT IS PROGRAMMING?

Programming is writing instructions for a computer in a language that it can understand so that it can do something for you. You will be learning to write programs in one particular <u>programming language</u> called PL/1. When these instructions are put on to some medium that a computer can <u>read</u> such as <u>punched cards</u> then they can be fed into the machine. They go into the part of the computer called its <u>memory</u> and are recorded there for as long as they are needed. The instructions could then be <u>executed</u> if they were in the language the computer understands directly, the language called machine language. If they are in another language such as PL/1 they must first be <u>translated</u>, and a program in machine language <u>compiled</u> from the original or <u>source</u> program. After compilation the program can be executed.

Computers can really only do a very small number of different basic things. For example, an instruction which says, STAND ON YOUR HEAD, will get you nowhere. The repertoire of instructions that any computer understands usually includes the ability to move numbers from one place to another in its memory, to add, subtract, multiply, and divide. They can, in short, do all kinds of arithmetic calculations and they can do these operations at rates of up to a million a second. Computers are extremely fast calculating machines. But they can do more; they can also handle alphabetic information, both moving it around in their memory and comparing different pieces of information to see if they are the same. To include both numbers and alphabetic information we say that computers are data processors or more generally information processors.

When we write programs we write a sequence of instructions that we want executed one after another. But you can see that the computer could execute our programs very rapidly if each instruction were executed only once. A program of a thousand instructions might take only a thousandth of a second. One of the instructions we can include in our programs is an instruction which causes the use of other instructions to be repeated over and over. In this way the computer is capable of repetitious work; it tirelessly executes the same set of instructions again and again. Naturally the data that it is operating on must change with each repetition or it would accomplish nothing.

Perhaps you have heard also that computers can make decisions. In a sense they can. These so-called decisions are fairly simple. The instructions read something like this:

    IF JOHN IS OVER 16 THEN PLACE HIM ON THE HOCKEY TEAM;
        ELSE PLACE HIM ON THE SOCCER TEAM

Depending on the condition of John's age, the computer could place his name on one or other of two different sports teams. It can decide which one if you tell it the decision criterion, in our example being over sixteen or not.

Perhaps these first few hints will give you a clue to what programming is about.

WHAT IS STRUCTURED PROGRAMMING?

Certain phrases get to be popular at certain times; they are fashionable. The phrase, "structured programming" is one that has become fashionable recently. It is used to describe both a number of techniques for writing programs as well as a more general methodology. Just as programs provide a list of instructions to the computer to achieve some well-defined goal, the methodology of structured programming provides a list of instructions to persons who write programs to achieve some well-defined goals. The goals of structured programming are, first, to get the job done. This deals with how to get the job done and how to get it done correctly. The second goal is concerned with having it done so that other people can see how it is done, both for their education and in case these other people later have to make changes in the original programs.

Computer programs can be very simple and straightforward but many applications require that very large programs be written. The very size of these programs makes them complicated and difficult to understand. But if they are well-structured, then the complexity can be controlled. Controlling complexity can be accomplished in many different ways and all of these are of interest in the cause of structured programming. The fact that structured programming is the "new philosophy" encourages us to keep track of everything that will help us to be better programmers. We will be cataloguing many of the elements of structured programming as we go along, but first we must look at the particular programming language you will learn.

WHAT IS PL/1?

The name PL/1 is short for "Programming Language One" and is a language that has been developed to be independent of the particular computer on which it is run and oriented to the problems that persons might want done. We say that PL/1 is a high-level language because it was designed to be relatively easy to learn. As a problem-oriented language it is concerned with problems of numerical calculations such as occur in scientific and engineering applications as well as with alphabetic information handling required by business and humanities applications.

PL/1 is a very extensive language, so that although each part is easy to learn, it requires considerable study to master. Many different computer installations have the facilities to accept programs written in PL/1. This means that they have a PL/1 compiler that will translate programs written in PL/1 into the language of the particular machine that they have. Also many programs have already been written in PL/1; in some installations a standard language is adopted, and PL/1 is often that standard language.

It has been the experience over the past years that a high-level language lasts much longer than machine languages, which change every five years or so. This is because once an investment has been made in programs for a range of applications, an installation does not want to have to reprogram when a new computer is acquired. What is needed is a new compiler for the high-level language and all the old programs can be reused.

Because of the long life-span of programs in high-level languages it becomes more and more important that they can be adapted to changes in the application rather than completely reconstructed.

A high-level language has the advantage that well-constructed and well-documented programs in the language can be readily modified. It is our aim to teach you how to write such programs. To start your learning of PL/1 we will study subsets of the full PL/1 language called SP/k. SP/k was developed at the University of Toronto.

WHAT IS SP/k?

The name SP/k stands for "<u>S</u>tructured <u>P</u>rogramming <u>subset</u> k". There really is a series of subsets beginning at SP/1, then SP/2, and going on up. The first subset contains a small number of the language features of PL/1, but enough so that you can actually write a complete program and try it out on a computer right away. The next subset, SP/2, contains all of SP/1 as well as some additional features that enlarge your possibilities. Each subset is nested inside the next higher one so that you gradually build a larger and larger vocabulary in the PL/1 language. At each stage, as the special features of a new subset are introduced, examples are worked out to explore the increased power that is available.

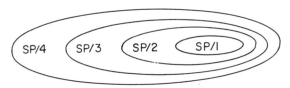

THE SP/k SUBSETS

In a sense, the step-by-step approach to learning PL/1 is <u>structured</u> and reflects the attitude to programming that we hope you learn.

There is no substitute for practice in learning to program, so as soon as possible and as often as possible, submit your knowledge to the test by creating your own programs.

WHY LEARN JUST A SUBSET?

The PL/1 language is very extensive; some features are only used rarely or by a few programmers. If you know exactly what you are doing, then these features may provide a faster way to program; otherwise they are better left to the experts. A beginner cannot really use all the features of the complete PL/1 language and will get lost in the complexity of the language description. With a small subset it is much easier to pick up the language and then get on with the real job of learning programming.

A compiler that can handle the full PL/1 language must, of necessity, be much slower than a compiler that handles only a subset. For learners we need a fast compiler because, for many programs, compiling is nearly all that happens; the execution is sometimes omitted or is very short because there are errors in the program. A compiler capable of translating only a subset can be very much smaller in size and will require less memory space in the computer. A special compiler can be used for the SP/k language and this can be small enough to run on some very inexpensive computers often called minicomputers. SP/k compilers are also available for large computers and provide fast compilation. But it is not necessary to have an SP/k compiler to use the SP/k language since it is a subset of PL/1. Any PL/1 compiler will do. SP/k programs will also work on another popular PL/1 subset compiler called PL/C. The reverse is not true, since the subset offered by PL/C is a larger one. Another suitable compiler is the PLUTO compiler.

But perhaps most important, the SP/k language has been selected from the PL/1 language so as to provide features that encourage the user to produce well-structured programs. This is why it is so appropriate as a means of learning structured programming.

CORRECTNESS OF PROGRAMS

One of the maddening things about computers is that they do exactly what you tell them to do rather than what you want them to do. To get correct results your program has to be correct. When an answer is printed out by a computer you must know whether or not it is correct. You cannot assume, as people often do, that because it was given by a computer it must be right. It is the right answer for the particular program and data you provided because computers now are really very reliable and rarely make mistakes. But is your program correct? Are your input data correct?

One way of checking whether any particular answer is correct is to get the answer by some other means and compare it with the printed answer. This means that you must work out the answer by hand, perhaps using a slide rule or hand calculator to help you. When you do work by hand you probably do not concentrate on exactly how you are getting the answer but you know you are correct (assuming you do not make foolish errors). But this seems rather pointless. You wanted the computer to do some work for you to save you the effort and now you must do the work anyway to test whether your computer program is correct. Where is the benefit of all this? The labor saving comes when you get the computer to use your program to work out a similar problem for you. For example, a program to compute telephone bills can be checked for correctness by comparing the results with hand computation for a number of representative customers and then it can be used on millions of others without detailed checking. What we are checking is the method of the calculation.

We must be sure that our representative sample of test cases includes all the various exceptional circumstances that can occur in practice, and this is a great difficulty. Suppose that there were five different things that could be exceptional about a telephone customer. A single customer might have any number of exceptional features simultaneously. So the number of different types of customers might be 32, ranging from those with no exceptional features to those with all five. To test all these combinations takes a lot of time, so usually, we test only a few of the combinations and hope all is well.

Because exhaustive testing of all possible cases to be handled by a program is too large a job, many programs are not thoroughly tested and ultimately give incorrect results when an unusual combination of circumstances is encountered in practice. You must try to test your programs as well as possible and at the same time realize that with large programs the job becomes very difficult. This has led many computer scientists to advocate the need to prove programs correct by various techniques other than exhaustive testing. These techniques rely on reading and studying the program to make sure it directs the computer to do the right calculation. Certainly the well-structured program will be easier to prove correct.

CHAPTER 1 SUMMARY

The purpose of this book is to introduce computer programming. We have begun in this chapter by presenting the following programming terminology.

1. Program (or computer program) - a list of instructions for a computer to follow. We say the computer "executes" instructions.

2. Programming - writing instructions telling a computer to perform certain data manipulations.

3. Programming language - used to direct the computer to do work for us.

4. PL/1 - a popular programming language. Fortran, Cobol, Basic and APL are some other popular programming languages.

5. SP/k - the programming language used in this book. SP/k is a subset of the PL/1 programming language, meaning that every SP/k program is also a PL/1 program, but some PL/1 programs are not SP/k programs. SP/k is itself composed of subsets SP/1, SP/2 and so on. This book teaches SP/1, then SP/2, and so on up to SP/8.

⑥ High-level language - a programming language that is designed
   to be convenient for writing programs. PL/1 is a high-
   level language.

⑦ Structured programming - a method of programming that helps
   us write correct programs. The SP/k language has been
   designed to encourage structured programming. This book
   teaches a structured approach to programming.

CHAPTER 2

YOU AND THE COMPUTER

"The time has come," the walrus said, "to talk of many things" - Lewis Carroll.

And the things we want to talk about in this chapter have to do with getting to know a little bit about computers and how they are organized. A computer is a complex object composed of wires, transistors, and so on, but we will not be trying to follow wiring diagrams and worrying about how to build a computer. What we will be interested in is the various main parts of a computer and what the function of each is. In this way your programming will be more intelligent; you will understand a little of what is going on inside the computer.

PARTS THAT MAKE THE WHOLE

We have already mentioned a number of things about computers. They have a memory where numbers and alphabetic information can be recorded. They can add, subtract, multiply, and divide. This means they have a part called the arithmetic unit. They can read information off certain media, like punched cards, and print results on printers. The printer may print a whole line at a time or just one character at a time, like a typewriter. We say they have an input (for example, a card reader) and an output (a printer). The input-output unit is often referred to as the I/O. Computers execute instructions in sequence. The part of the machine that does this is called the control unit. The arithmetic unit and the control unit are usually grouped together in a computer and called the central processing unit or CPU. So then the computer is thought of as having three parts, memory, I/O and CPU.

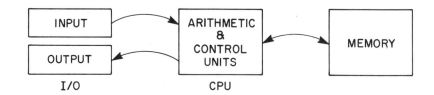

I/O   CPU

MAIN PARTS OF A COMPUTER

We will look at these different parts in turn and see how they
work but first we must see how numbers and alphabetic information
can be represented in a computer.

CODED INFORMATION

    You are all familiar with the way that information used to
travel over telegraph wires in the form of Morse Code. Perhaps
you know that each letter or number is coded as a pattern of dots
and dashes. For example, the letter A is a dot followed by a
dash, E is one dot, V is three dots and a dash. The letters are
separated from each other by a pause with no dots or dashes. The
famous signal SOS is

              ... --- ...

This is an easy one to remember in emergencies. The Morse Code
was designed so that the signal could activate some noise-making
device and the listener could then translate the coded message
back into letters. Modern teletype machines can send messages
much faster because the machines themselves can be used to decode
the messages. For these, a character is represented by a pattern
of pulses, each pattern being of the same length. Instead of
dots and dashes, which are two different lengths of electric
pulses, they use one basic time interval and in that time
interval have either a pulse or a pause. Each character requires
5 basic time intervals and is represented by a sequence of pulses
and pauses. We often write down a pulse as a 1 and a pause as 0,
and then the pattern for B is 10011, I is 01100, L is 01001. The
word BILL would be transmitted as

        10011011000100101001

Strings of ones and zeros like this can be associated with
numbers in the binary system. In the decimal system the number
342 means

        $3 \times 10^2 + 4 \times 10^1 + 2 \times 10^0$

where 10^2 stands for 10 squared, 10^1 for 10 to the first power, that is 10, and 10^0 for 10 to the power zero, which has a value 1. In the binary system of numbers 1101 means

$$1x2^3 + 1x2^2 + 0x2^1 + 1x2^0$$

In the <u>decimal</u> <u>system</u> this binary number has a value 8+4+0+1=13. We say that this number in the decimal system requires 2 <u>decimal</u> <u>digits</u> to represent it. In the binary system it requires 4 <u>binary</u> <u>digits</u>. We call a binary digit a <u>bit</u>. So the binary number representing the word BILL has 20 bits, each letter requiring 5 bits. Sometimes we take the number of bits required to represent a character as a group and call it a <u>byte</u>. Then the word representing BILL has four bytes. In a computer we must have a way of recording these bits, and usually the memory is arranged into <u>words</u>, each capable of holding a whole number of bytes.

In some machines a single letter is represented by a byte of six bits and the word length is 6 bytes or 36 bits. There are many different combinations of byte length and word length in different computers. This is something the machine designer must decide.

MEMORY

Most machines record letters and numbers in the binary form because it is possible to have recording devices that can record, read, and hold such information. Most recording devices involve a recording something like that on the tape of a magnetic tape recorder. There is a big difference, though, in the recording. On audio tape we have a magnetic recording that varies in intensity with the volume of the sound recorded. The frequency of the variations gives the pitch of the sound. For a computer, the recordings vary between two levels of intensity which you might think of as "on" and "off". If in a particular region there is an "on" recording it could indicate the binary digit one and if "off" the digit zero. So on a strip of magnetic tape there would be designated areas that are to hold each bit of information.

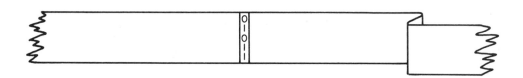

BITS RECORDED ON MAGNETIC TAPE

Binary digits can thus be recorded on reels of magnetic tape. In a similar way they can be recorded on tracks of a magnetic

disk and these disks can be stacked one above the other on a
spindle that is kept constantly spinning. To read or record
information on a magnetic disk the recording/reading head moves
to the correct track of the correct disk.

MAGNETIC DISK MEMORY

This kind of memory is called a magnetic disk pack and is
commonly used when large amounts of information are to be stored
in the computer and requested randomly. If information is to be
retrieved in a particular sequence or order then a magnetic tape
reel can be used to store it. Tape reels and disk packs can be
removed from the machine and stored if you need to keep
information for long periods of time.

Neither tape nor disks are as fast to read and write as
another type of magnetic recording on the surface of a constantly
spinning cylinder called a drum.

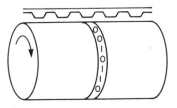

MAGNETIC DRUM MEMORY

All these devices require the movement of objects, a reel of
tape, a spinning disk or drum, and sometimes read/write heads.
These mechanical devices can never give really high-speed access
to information. We need memory devices with no moving parts so
we can perform operations at rates of the order of a million a
second. The only things that move in a really high-speed memory
device are the electric signals in the wires. As you know,
electric signals can move very rapidly, at nearly the speed of
light. A very common form of high-speed memory is the magnetic
core memory. A magnetic core is a tiny doughnut-shaped piece of
material that can be magnetized. When magnetized it is like a
bar magnet bent around in a circle.

MAGNETIC CORE

There are two directions in which a core can be magnetized, clockwise and counter-clockwise, and these can represent the two binary digits.   To form a memory the cores are threaded on to wires in two directions just like a fly screen, with a core around every intersection of the wires.   When signals pass through the wires thay can record information in the cores or read out information from the cores, and it can all happen extremely rapidly.

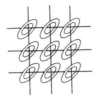

MAGNETIC CORE MEMORY

The main memory of the computer can be made of magnetic cores grouped into words. To find any particular word you need to know where it is located in the array of cores. You need to know its address. Every word (which, remember, is just a group of bits, one bit in each core) has its own address which is a number. An address may, for example, be 125. Words that are neighbors in the array have consecutive addresses, such as 125 and 126, just like houses on a street. The addresses themselves do not have to be stored in the computer. You can tell what address a word has from its location in the array. This is not always possible for houses on the street because the numbering is not completely systematic.

THE CONTENTS OF WORDS IN MEMORY

ARITHMETIC UNIT

All computers have a part where arithmetic can take place. This is the arithmetic unit. When a new number is written in a memory location, the old number stored there is automatically erased, just as any old recording is erased as a new recording is made on a magnetic tape recorder. Just reading a number, like playing an audio recording, does not damage the recording no matter how often you do it. If you want to combine numbers, say add them, it must be done in a special location in the arithmetic unit called the accumulator. On some machines, the size of the accumulator is the same as the size of a word in memory.   Words,

or rather the information stored in memory locations, can be
loaded into the accumulator. In a simple machine language, the
instruction

                    LOAD 125

would cause the number recorded in location 125 to be placed in
the accumulator. Whatever was recorded in the accumulator before
would be erased before the load takes place. If we want to add
another number we would write

                    ADD 126

This would add the number stored in 126 to what was already in
the accumulator and the sum of the two numbers would then be in
the accumulator. This total could be recorded in the memory for
later use by the instruction

                    STORE 127

The result of the addition would now be in location 127 but would
also remain in the accumulator.

    The accumulator can also be used for subtraction,
multiplication, and division. In a high-level language like PL/1
you never need to think about the accumulator. You merely
indicate that you want numbers in two locations, say A and B, to
be added and name the location, say C, where you want the answer
to be stored. You write this all in one statement, namely

                    C=A+B

This PL/1 statement says: add the number stored in location A to
the number stored in location B and place the result in location
C. In the machine all location addresses are numbers. In PL/1
we give the locations names which are called <u>identifiers</u>. The
compiler changes these names to numerical locations and changes
the single instruction

                    C=A+B

to the three machine instructions.

                    LOAD   A
                    ADD   B
                    STORE C

CONTROL UNIT

You have just seen examples of machine language instructions. They each consist of two parts: the operation part, for example LOAD, and the address part, A. Each part can be coded as a binary number, then the whole instruction will just be a string of bits. Suppose that you have a machine with a word length of 36 bits. Then an instruction might be itself stored in such a word with, say, 18 bits for the operation part and 18 bits for the address part. With 18 bits you can represent binary numbers that go from 1 to 2 to the power 18, which is 262,144. You can refer to any one of over a quarter of a million different memory locations.

Consecutive instructions in a machine language program are stored in consecutive locations in the memory and are to be executed one after the other. The control unit does two things. It uses a special location called the <u>instruction pointer</u> to keep track of what instruction is currently being executed. It places the instruction to be executed in a special location called the <u>control register</u>. In the control register the instruction is decoded and signals are issued to the different parts of the computer so that the operation requested is actually carried out. As each instruction is executed, the instruction pointer is increased by one to give the address of the next instruction in the program. This next instruction is then fetched from the memory, placed in the control register, and executed. This process continues, with instructions being executed sequentially unless a special instruction is encountered, which resets the instruction pointer and causes a <u>jump</u> from the normal sequence to a different part of the program.

In brief, the control unit controls the sequence of execution of instructions and determines the effect that execution has on the information stored in the memory.

Computers were originally referred to as <u>stored program calculators</u> because the instructions as well as the numbers or characters they operate on are stored in the memory. They were also referred to as <u>sequential machines</u>, because normally they followed a sequence of instructions one after another unless a jump instruction directs them to do otherwise.

INPUT AND OUTPUT

We have spoken of having both data and instructions in the
memory of the machine and changing the data by the execution of
instructions. But how do we get data or instructions into the
computer, and how do we get data out of the machine after it has
been operated on? That is the function of the input and output
units. We must have instructions that cause the machine to read
information into its memory and to print information out from its
memory. And we must have parts of the computer, the input and
output units, that respond to these instructions. One reading
device commonly used is a punched card reader. You are all
familiar with the standard punched card with 80 columns in which
punching can take place.

80-COLUMN PUNCHED CARD

For digits, a single hole is made in a column in the position
corresponding to the digits 0 to 9. Each alphabetic character
requires two holes in a column, one in a digit position and the
other in one of the three positions at the top of the card called
the 0,11, and 12 positions. Special characters like dollar signs
require that three holes be punched in a column. The actual
representations in terms of punched holes for each character or
digit can be fixed into a card punch keyboard so that when the
key on the keyboard for the character is pressed, the correct
punching occurs on the card. Many keypunches also interpret the
punching by printing the corresponding characters at the top of
the card above the column where the punching is. This is so that
you can read what is punched on the card. The machine can only
read the punching.

Sometimes cards are prepared by marking them with a soft
black pencil in certain designated areas. These marks are then

read by a reader that senses their presence, just as the punched
card reader senses holes. On mark sense cards digits require a
single mark, alphabetic characters and special characters require
two marks in the same column. Some keywords in the PL/1 language
can be obtained by marks in the first column or at the top of
other columns.

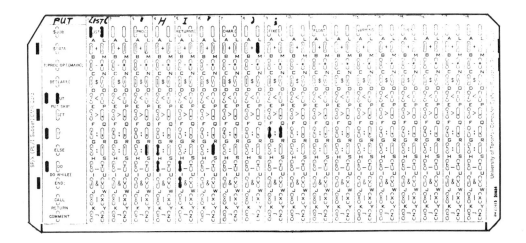

MARK SENSE CARD

For some input units there is no medium, like cards, outside
the computer where information is first recorded.   Instead, a
keyboard is attached directly by a line, such as telephone line,
to the input unit. This eliminates the card and the card reader
but the result is similar.

When a mistake is made in punching cards, the card is to be
ejected from the punch and removed. A second attempt is then
made to produce a correctly punched card. One of the good things
about cards is that they can individually be replaced or removed
and new cards inserted in a card deck without having to repunch
the entire deck. Since instructions are placed in sequence,
usually one to a card, this sequence must be maintained. If you
drop a deck of cards they can get out of sequence and it is
difficult to get them arranged correctly again. Keep an elastic
band around your card decks to prevent accidents. The elastic is
removed as they are placed into the card reader then replaced
immediately after they are read.

The keyboard of a card punch or online computer input
terminal is similar to that of a standard typewriter, so it helps
if you can type. But hunt-and-peck methods will get you there
too. In addition to the ordinary typewriter keys, there are

special keys for indicating the end of the input for that card or
line.

The output units can be line-at-a-time printers or
typewriters. The typewriters are the same as those used for
input with online terminals. When card decks are the form of
input, the output usually comes on the fast printers. Printers
can have very high speeds. A speed of 1000 lines a minute is
common, but some printers go faster. Most printers are slower.

Across a printed page there are often positions to print 120,
132 or more characters although some printers print only 72
characters on a line. The paper is continuous but may be divided
by perforations into pages, each capable of holding about 60
lines of printing. Your output will probably be limited to a few
pages for each run on the computer. Because users' jobs are run
one after another each must be careful to put an identification
on the program so that the appropriate output can be claimed.
You have to tear the pages apart by hand as the machine feeds
paper continuously, piling the printer output on the other side
of the printer from the blank paper supply.

PROGRAM TRANSLATION

We have said that three machine language instructions,
namely,

        LOAD A
        ADD   B
        STORE C

correspond to what is written in PL/1 as

        C=A+B

Instructions in the high-level language PL/1 are very much
simpler to write than instructions in machine language. For one
thing, you do not have to be aware of the accumulator; for
another, the notation is very similar to the one used in simple
mathematical expressions and should be easy for you to get used
to. The PL/1 language is more powerful in that a single PL/1
instruction can correspond to many machine language instructions.
We will see later that if you are working in a high-level
language, the machine can detect when you make certain kinds of
mistakes in your program.

In short, high-level languages are designed to suit you
rather than suit a computer. And in being that way they make the
job of programming less difficult.

A PL/1 program cannot execute directly on a computer but must
be translated into the language for the particular computer you
have. This is accomplished after the PL/1 program has been read

in, or loaded into, the memory. The translation is performed by
another program, called the compiler, that is already stored in
the computer memory. The compiler reads your PL/1 program and
forms the appropriate sequence of machine language instructions
from your PL/1 statements. After compilation, execution of the
machine language program begins automatically, provided you have
not made any errors in your PL/1 program that the compiler can
detect but cannot repair. The kind of errors that are detectable
are mostly in the form of the statements. If they are not proper
or grammatical statements in the PL/1 language the compiler will
report an error to you in your printout. Errors in grammar are
called syntax errors. In English you know there is an error in
the sentence,

THE BOYS IS WALKING.

A machine can spot this kind of error but it cannot easily spot
an error in meaning. It might never determine that the sentence,

THE HOUSE IS WALKING.

is not a meaningful sentence; it would accept it as syntactically
correct.

Well, that is enough of an introduction now; let us get down
to actually writing programs.

CHAPTER 2 SUMMARY

In this chapter we presented the main parts of a computer and
showed how information is stored in the memory. We explained
briefly how a high-level language such as PL/1 is translated, or
compiled, to machine language before being executed by a
computer. The following important terms were introduced.

Memory – the part of a computer that stores information, such
        as data or a program. Magnetic tapes, disks, and drums
        are called secondary memory; they require mechanical
        motion to access information stored on them. Main
        memory can be immediately accessed by the computer; main
        memory may be composed of magnetic cores. The computer
        can transfer information between secondary memory and
        main memory.

CPU (central processing unit) – composed of the arithmetic
        unit and the control unit. The arithmetic unit carries
        out operations such as addition and multiplication. The
        control unit directs other parts of the computer,
        including the arithmetic unit, to carry out a sequence
        of instructions that is in the main memory.

Input and Output – ways of getting information into and out
        of a computer. The punch card, or IBM card, can be used

to prepare input for a computer. An input device called a card reader is used to sense the holes in punch cards and transmit the encoded information to the main memory. An output device called a printer takes information from main memory and prints it on paper.

Coded information - before information can be entered into a computer, it must be coded in a convenient form for the computer's circuitry. The circuitry recognizes "off" and "on" which we can think of as 0 and 1. The smallest unit of information is a binary digit, 0 or 1, called a bit. Letters are represented in a computer by a sequence of bits, called a byte. Bytes are arranged into words, typically four bytes to the word. The main memory of the computer is a sequence of words. These words can hold data and programs.

Translation (or compilation) - before a program written in a language like PL/1 can be executed by a computer, it must be translated into machine language. The program as written in PL/1 is called the source program. The translated program is placed in words in the main memory and is executed by the computer's CPU.

CHAPTER 3

SP/1: PROGRAMS THAT CALCULATE AND PRINT

This is the chapter where we set the stage for programming and you meet the cast of characters in the play. Nothing very much is going to happen in this first subset, SP/1, but you will be able to go through the motions of writing a complete program, submitting it to a computer and having it executed. This will let you get used to the mechanics of handling cards, learn how to arrange a card deck, and find out what you must do with it to get it read by the computer. Also you will see what kind of printed output to expect. Things will happen, though what the computer is actually doing for you will not be very exciting yet. But remember you will go through the same motions as are necessary when your programs do have more content.

CHARACTERS

We will be learning the programming language PL/1 a little bit at a time. Any language consists of words and the words are made up of <u>symbols</u> that we call <u>characters</u>. These characters are put together in <u>strings</u>. In English the word

ELEPHANT

is a string of characters of length eight. It contains only seven different characters, the character E being used twice. We can tell that it is a word because it has a blank in front of it and one at the end. In a way the <u>blank is also a character</u>, but a <u>special</u> <u>character</u> for separating words. We sometimes <u>denote</u> <u>the blank by b</u> when we print programs in this book so that you can see how many blanks are present.

blank = b

In English, we group words into sentences and we can tell the end of a sentence because of a special mark, the period. We also

21

have a different kind of sentence that ends with a question mark, don't we? In addition to periods and question marks, we have other <u>punctuation</u> <u>marks</u> which serve to make sentences in the language easier to read. They also serve to remove ambiguity in a sentence. There is some doubt about the meaning of the sentence,

      THE STUDENT CLAIMS THE TEACHER UNDERSTANDS.

The doubt is removed if it is written with commas, as,

      THE STUDENT, CLAIMS THE TEACHER, UNDERSTANDS.

It is important that statements in a programming language be <u>unambiguous</u>, so punctuation is used a great deal. Instead of a sentence, the basic unit in the main part of a program is a <u>statement</u>. Statements end with a semicolon. This serves to separate them just as periods separate sentences in English. The comma is used to separate items in any list of similar items, and parentheses are used to enclose things that belong together.

We will have words in PL/1 that are made up of letters of the alphabet and might also have digits in them. Although there are definite rules governing the way that PL/1 statements are formed, we want them to be understandable. This means the words should be like English words. We use words like NAME, COST, INCOME, TAX, INVOICE, SUM, or words like PAGE1, TABLE6, ITEM35, and so on. Most of these words are invented by you. You are not allowed to use words that do not at least have one letter at the beginning. If the PL/1 compiler sees a digit at the beginning of a word it assumes that it is a <u>number</u>. For example, the word 317 is taken as a number. This means that words like 3RD_PAGE are illegal and will not be accepted by the PL/1 compiler.

Before we leave characters we should perhaps list them all. A <u>character</u> is a letter, or a digit, or a special character. The <u>letters</u> are

      A B C D E F G H I J K L M N O P Q R S T U V W X Y Z $ # @

Perhaps you are surprised to see $ # @ in this list. But you should not be, because we do not have to stick exactly to the normal definition of letters. We do want to stick to our rule that words that are not numbers should begin with a letter and yet we want some special words that begin with characters that are not letters in English. We will, for instance, use the words $DATA and $JOB. You could also have an acceptable word that begins with a letter, according to our definition, that is #2 or @10B. The <u>digits</u> are the normal ones

      0 1 2 3 4 5 6 7 8 9

The <u>special characters</u> are

   + - * / ( ) = < > . : ; ? , % & | ¬
   b blank
   ' (apostrophe or single quote)
   _ (break character or underscore)

NUMBERS

    Computers can do arithmetic calculations and they can do them
extremely rapidly. When you learned arithmetic you first learned
to handle numbers that are whole numbers, or integers. You
learned that 5+6=11 and 2x3=6. In PL/1 numbers like 2, 3, 512,
809, and 46281 are called <u>fixed</u> constants. <u>Any string of digits</u>
<u>is a fixed constant</u>. You will remember that we will be <u>storing</u>
<u>numbers in the computer and representing them as a string of bits</u>
in some <u>coded representation</u>. The largest number we can
represent will be limited by the length of the string of bits
that are in a word in our computer. Word lengths vary from one
computer to another and different PL/1 compilers have different
maximum lengths for the digit strings that represent fixed
numbers. You will probably be safe in expecting at least five
decimal digits to be within the maximum.

    If you have integers requiring longer digit strings, say for
instance the population of the world, you must use the other form
of numbers which is the <u>float</u> form.

    If you have a large number like

   635,642,000

you can write it as

   6.35642×10^8

Perhaps you recognize this as what is called scientific notation.
In PL/1 the form of a <u>float</u> constant such as our example is

   6.35642E8

The first part is called the <u>fraction part</u>, the second part the
<u>exponent</u>. The exponent is the letter E followed by the power of
10 that is to multiply the fraction part. Maybe you learned this
notation before in a science course where very big numbers, like
the mass of the moon, often occur. <u>Float</u> notation is also used
for numbers that are not integers. These are either <u>fractions</u> or
<u>mixed numbers</u>. We write either of these in decimal notation
where a point called the decimal point separates the integer from
the fraction part. Examples of fractions are

   .5   .0075   .0000023

Mixed numbers are

        5.27   889.6   6.0216

When we write fractions in float notation we usually standardize the form by putting the first non-zero digit followed by a decimal point followed by the remaining digits. Then the power of 10 is computed to make it right. The fraction .0000023 is written as 2.3×10^{-6}. In PL/1 this then is 2.3E-6. It could also be written as .23E-5, or 23.E-7, or even as 23E-7.

fixed Constant

float Constant

A fixed constant must **not** have a decimal point; a float constant usually has a decimal point (with exceptions like the very last example) and **must** have an exponent. The exponent is proceded by the letter E and consists of an optional plus or minus sign followed by one or more digits. Most compilers allow up to six digits in the fraction of a float number, and exponents up to 38 and down to -38.

CHARACTER STRINGS

We have said that computers can handle both numbers and strings of characters. We have seen that there are two forms for numbers, the fixed and the float.

A character string can consist of any of the characters that we have specified: letters, digits and special characters. Very often, when printing the results of a computer calculation, we want the results labeled. What we want is to print a string of characters on the page. In the statement that specifies what we want the computer to print, we include the actual string that we want printed enclosed in single quotation marks. These strings enclosed in quotation marks are called literals or character string constants.

Literals

Examples of literals are

    'BILL JONES', 'BALANCE IN ACCOUNT', 'X='

×

If the literal you want to give contains a quotation mark or an apostrophe, which is the same character, then you must put two quotes rather than a single quote. For example, the literal corresponding to the short form of 'CANNOT' is 'CAN''T'.

We will see how to use these literals in a program when we learn what the instruction is that causes printing.

EXPRESSIONS

One of the important concepts we have in PL/1 is that of an
expression. The way that we explain what a word like expression
means is basically to give examples and then generalize these
examples.

First of all 32, 5, 6.1E2 and 58.1E6 are all expressions. So
the general statement is that fixed constants and float constants
are expressions. So are literals like

'THIS IS AN EXPRESSION'

Any expression may be enclosed in parentheses and still be an
expression. For example (32), (6.1E2) and ('TOM') are also
expressions. The expressions that are fixed or float constants
can be combined into compound expressions using the signs of
arithmetic for adding, subtracting, multiplying, and dividing.
These expressions are called arithmetic expressions. We use the
standard signs for adding and subtracting, namely the plus and
minus. For multiplication we use the asterisk (*) because there
is no times sign. For division we use the slant or slash symbol
(/). Examples of arithmetic expressions are

   2+3, 5.2E1*7.8E5, 6E0/2E0, 10-15

Fixed and float values may be combined in a single expression,
and when they are the result is a float value. For example,
2+3.0E1 has the value 3.2E1.

If two numbers are to be divided, one of them must be a float
number. Instead of writing 13/2 you write 13/2E0 and get the
correct result 6.5E0. Always make a habit of using E0 in any
integer division and all will be well.

Division

A very complicated arithmetic expression is

   2*5+8-3*5/2E0+6

In evaluating this you have to know what to do first because you
really can only add, subtract, multiply or divide numbers two at
a time. The rule is to do the multiplications and divisions
first, then the additions and subtractions. Also you start at
the left-hand side of the expression and work to the right. We
are using here rules of precedence, that the operations multiply
and divide have precedence over add and subtract. Parentheses
can be used to guide the sequence of evaluation. For example,
you write 3*(5+8) instead of 3*5+8 if you want the addition to
take place before the multiplication. Expressions in parentheses
take precedence.

In a later chapter you will see how character strings may be
combined, but it is clear that they cannot be used in arithmetic
operations.

EXAMPLES OF ARITHMETIC EXPRESSIONS

The following examples illustrate the rules for performing arithmetic in the PL/1 programming language.

72+16   Value is 88.

8*5+7   Value is 47. Note that * means multiply.

2+10*4   Value is 42. Note that multiplication is done before addition.

(2+10)*4   Value is 48. The parentheses cause the addition to be done before the multiplication.

1/3   This division is not allowed because neither 1 nor 3 is a float number. Instead, you could write 1/3E0 (3E0 is the float equivalent of 3).

1/3E0   Value is .333333E0, which is approximately one third. Note that the result of combining a fixed number, such as 1, and a float number, such as 3E0, is a float number. The value .333333E0 can be written in other forms such as 3.33333E-1 and 3.33333E-01.

72E0+16E0   Value is 88E0, which can be written in other forms such as 8.8E1 and 8.80000E+01.

(9.83E0+16.82E0)/2.935E0

                This expression is equivalent to the following
                $$\frac{9.83+16.82}{2.935}$$
                The exponent parts (E0) must be introduced because float numbers must have an exponent part. The parentheses were used so the division would apply to the sum of 9.83E0 and 16.82E0 (and not just to 16.82E0).

PRINTING

Our main purpose in subset number one is to introduce you to the main characters in PL/1 and to get you to write your first program. The program is not going to do very much but it has to do something so that you can see that it is working. The most it can do is to print numbers or character strings on the printer. Then you can see that some action is taking place.

The statement that we will use in the program is like this

```
PUT LIST (3, 5.1E1, 'BILL');
```

Printing produced by the PUT LIST statement is placed in successive fields across the print line. The print line has spaces for a certain number of characters. This line is divided into 5 equal fields. If the line has 120 characters then the width of the field is 24 character spaces. If it is 70 a field width of 14 character spaces is used. The items that are in parentheses after the PUT LIST are placed one to a field going from left to right. Literals are printed, without the quotation marks, beginning at the left-hand side of the field. When float numbers are printed, their exponents are given, for example 2.53000E+01.

If two PUT LIST instructions are given one after another then the printing continues in the same line until all five fields have been used, then goes to a new line. If you want to start a new line with a PUT LIST you write instead PUT SKIP LIST. If you want to start a new page before printing you use PUT PAGE LIST. A blank line can be left by using

```
PUT SKIP LIST(' ');
```

since here the literal consists of a blank. This is also useful for skipping fields. If a literal is longer than the width of the field it spills over into the next field and the following item will be printed beginning in the next field. Strings of characters are limited to a maximum length of 127.

Expressions other than fixed and float constants and literals may also be placed in a PUT LIST statement. The statement

```
PUT LIST(2+3, 4/2E0);
```

will result in a 5 being printed in the first field and 2.00000E+00 in the second. An interesting statement might be

```
PUT LIST('2+3=',2+3);
```

it would print

```
2+3=     5
```

There would be a number of spaces between the equal sign and the 5 in the actual printing. You can move the 2+3= over to the right by putting blanks in the literal

```
PUT LIST('       2+3=',2+3);
```

but you cannot move the 5 over to the left. Note that the quotes around the literal are not printed.

※ Can move literals, but not numbers

THE PROGRAM

Now that you know a statement that will give some action, you must learn what is necessary to make a complete program. Then you can try the computer for yourself. The shortest program you can write consists of one statement preceded by a line like this:

    OPUS1:PROCEDURE OPTIONS(MAIN);

and followed by

        END;

You will note that every line we write is concluded by a semicolon, even the last line in the program. The name OPUS1 is one we made up to describe the very first complete program. (OPUS is Latin for "work".) You must make up an identifier you like yourself. It must start with a letter and have no special characters other than the break character. Some compilers such as PL/C allow a program's identifier to be at most 7 characters long; other compilers allow at most 31. The rest of the first line, beginning with the colon, is rigidly fixed for all PL/1 programs. Take a good look at it. Note the letter S on OPTIONS and the parentheses around MAIN. It helps also to remember how to spell PROCEDURE.

Now comes the big moment for a complete program.

```
OPUS1:PROCEDURE OPTIONS(MAIN);
   PUT SKIP LIST('2+3=',2+3);
   END;
```

There it is, our opus number one, a complete PL/1 program. But wait, one little thing is still needed, namely, two control cards. On one you identify yourself, so that the output printing can be returned to you, and not someone else, and also you tell the computer what compiler to use.

CONTROL CARDS

The beginning control card that is used is different in different installations. The one we use is of the form

    $JOBK ID='PAT HUME'

The $ sign is punched in column 1 of the card followed immediately, starting in column 2, by the word JOB and the letter K which stands for the SP/k compiler. If we wanted the PL/C compiler we would have $JOBC. Inside the quotation marks you put your own name, which then appears on your output exactly as you wrote it. The letters ID stand for identification. Often control cards are prepunched with things like $JOBK on them and you must add your own ID. In our examples we will just use $JOB and you can find out what is required by your own compiler.

When you punch the cards for the program use columns 2-72 of the card. Column 1 is reserved for the special $ sign which indicates control cards. Punching beyond column 72 is ignored by some PL/1 compilers. An SP/k compiler accepts punching in all 80 columns. You need not start the punching of a statement in column 2. Any number of blanks can be left before the first word or between words. Later on we will be showing you how to indent the statements in your program to make it easier to read.

There is another control card required at the end. It has $DATA in the first five columns.

AN EXAMPLE PROGRAM

The following is a complete job for the computer. This job illustrates the use of the PUT LIST statement.

```
1   $JOB ID='RIC HOLT'
2    T:PROCEDURE OPTIONS(MAIN);
3       PUT LIST('Z    G','Z    G');
4       PUT SKIP LIST(' I  A',' I  A');
5       PUT SKIP LIST('  GZ','  GZ');
6       END;
7   $DATA
```

The program causes the following pattern to be printed.

```
Z    G        Z    G
 I  A          I  A
  GZ            GZ
```

As you can see, the top line of the pattern is printed by the PUT LIST statement numbered 3. This statement causes its first literal, 'Z   G', to be printed in the first field of the print line and its second literal, again 'Z   G', to be printed in the second field of the print line. Statements 4 and 5 cause the printing of the second and third lines of the pattern. Statement 3 did not contain the word SKIP because it produces the first print line. If SKIP were omitted from statement 4, the zigzag pattern would be spoiled because the two literals ' I A' and ' I A' would then appear to the right of (and on the same print line as) 'Z   G' and 'Z   G'. Line 5 could be replaced by the following two statements without changing the printed pattern:

```
    PUT SKIP LIST('  GZ');
    PUT LIST('  GZ');
```

The two statements are equivalent to statement 5 because the second one does <u>not</u> contain the word SKIP. If you want the printing to begin on a new page you use PUT PAGE LIST.

You may think that you cannot do very much with this subset of PL/1, but here is another program.

```
$JOB ID='RIC HOLT'
 OPUS2:PROCEDURE OPTIONS(MAIN);
    PUT PAGE LIST('L',' OO OO','V     V','EEEEE');
    PUT SKIP LIST('L','O  O  O','V     V','E');
    PUT SKIP LIST('L','O     O',' V   V','EEE');
    PUT SKIP LIST('L',' O   O',' V V','E');
    PUT SKIP LIST('LLLLLLL','  O O');
    PUT LIST('   V','EEEEEEE');
    PUT SKIP LIST(' ',' O');
    END;
$DATA
```
Why don't you try putting this program on cards and running it to see what happens. Do you see the difference between PUT LIST and PUT SKIP LIST?

CHAPTER 3 SUMMARY

In this chapter, we explained how to write very simple computer programs. These programs are written in a small subset of the PL/1 language which is called SP/1. The following important terms were presented.

Character - is a letter (ABC...), digit (012...9) or special character(*/.;:, etc).

Fixed constant - is an integer (whole number) such as 78 and 2931. There may be a minus sign in front of the integer. A fixed constant should not be preceded by a dollar sign and must not contain commas or a decimal point. The following should <u>not</u> be used: $25 25,311 125.00.

Float constant - is a number such as 3.14159E0 (equal to 3.14159×10^0 or simply 3.14159). Float constants consist of a fraction (3.14159) and an exponent part (E0).

Literal (or character string constant) - is a sequence of characters enclosed in quotes, such as 'WHY NOT?'.

Arithmetic expression - composed of either a single number or a collection of numbers combined using addition, subtraction, multiplication and division (+,-,* and /). Parentheses may enclose parts of the expression.

Rules of precedence - specify the order for applying +,-, * and / to find the value of an arithmetic expression. Parenthesized expressions are evaluated first. Proceeding from left to right, * and / are applied first and then + and -.

PUT - means "print". The PUT LIST statement prints a list of expressions (literals or arithmetic expressions).

PUT LIST statement - this statement is of the form:

        PUT LIST(list of expressions separated by commas);

   Optionally, SKIP or PAGE can be inserted between PUT and
   LIST.

Field - the PUT LIST statement causes printing in five equal
   fields across a line.

SKIP - when used in PUT SKIP LIST, this causes printing to begin
   on the next line. If SKIP is omitted, printing by PUT LIST
   continues to the next field of the current line.

PAGE - when used in PUT PAGE LIST, causes printing to begin on a
   new page.

Output (or printout) - printing which the computer does at your
   request. The PUT LIST statement produces output from the
   computer.

                        CHAPTER 3 EXERCISES

1. What will the following program cause the computer to print?

```
T:PROCEDURE OPTIONS(MAIN);
  PUT SKIP LIST('*   *');
  PUT SKIP LIST('** **');
  PUT SKIP LIST('* * *');
  PUT SKIP LIST('*   *');
  END;
```

Can you rearrange the lines in this program to print a different
letter?

2. Consider the following program.

```
T:PROCEDURE OPTIONS(MAIN);
  PUT SKIP LIST('H   H',' A','L');
  PUT SKIP LIST('H   H',' A A','L'):
  PUT SKIP LIST('HHHHH','AAAAA');
  PUT LIST('L');
  PUT SKIP LIST('H   H','A   A','L');
  PUT SKIP LIST('H   H','A   A','LLLLL');
  END;
```

   (a) What will the program cause the computer to print?
   (b) Which lines do <u>not</u> cause any printing?
   (c) What is the difference between PUT SKIP LIST and PUT LIST?

3. Write programs to print the following:

(a)

```
  SEESEE          YOU   YOU        PEAPEAPEA
 SEE   SEE        YOU   YOU        PEA    PEA
 SEE              YOU   YOU        PEA    PEA
 SEE              YOU   YOU        PEAPEAPEA
 SEE              YOU   YOU        PEA
 SEE              YOU   YOU        PEA
 SEE   SEE        YOU   YOU        PEA
  SEESEE          YOUYOUYOU        PEA
```

(b)

```
 T
 TR                   M          SQUARE
 TRI                 A O         Q    R            A
 TRIA               I   N        U    A         R  M
 TRIAN              DIAMOND      A    U         Y   I
 TRIANG             I   N        R    Q         PYRAMID
 TRIANGL             A O         ERAUQS
 TRIANGLE             M
```

(c)

```
  T  T
  I  I
  C  C                                            PLUS
 TICTACTOE      Z   G   Z   G                      PLUS
  A  A            I  A   I  A                   PLUSPLUSPLUS
  C  C             GZ      GZ                   PLUSPLUSPLUS
 TICTACTOE                                         PLUS
  O  O                                             PLUS
  E  E
```

(d)

```
  H            STAIR          CH  EC  KE  RS
 O P             S              CH  EC  KE  RS
  S              T            CH  EC  KE  RS
  C              E              CH  EC  KE  RS
 O T             P            CH  EC  KE  RS
  C            STAIR            CH  EC  KE  RS
  H               S           CH  EC  KE  RS
                  T             CH  EC  KE  RS
                  E
                  P
```

4. What do the following cause the computer to print?

```
(a) PUT SKIP LIST(2,'PLUS',3,'IS',2+3);
(b) PUT SKIP LIST('23424+19872+36218=',
         23424+19872+36218);
(c) PUT SKIP LIST('2 FORMULAS:',2+3*5,(2+3)*5);
(d) PUT SKIP LIST('SUBTRACTION',20-10-5,20-(10-5));
```

5. Write   statements to calculate and print the following:

   (a) The sum of 52181 and 10032.
   (b) 9213 take away 7918.
   (c) The sum of 9213, 487, 921, 2013 and 514.
   (d) The product of 21 times the sum of 816, 5 and 203.
   (c) 343 plus 916 all multiplied by 82.
   (f) 3.14159 (pi) times 8.94 divided by 2.
   (g) 3.14159 times the square of 8.94 (Note: X^2 can be written
       as X*X).

CHAPTER 4

SP/2: VARIABLES AND ASSIGNMENTS

In this subset you will learn how to read numerical information into the computer, how to perform arithmetic calculations on the numbers you read in, and how to print the answers out. You will learn, as well, how to make your programs understandable to others (as well as to yourself) by careful choice of words that you can make up and by comments that you can add to your program. The principal concept to learn in this subset is the idea of a <u>variable</u>.

VARIABLES

We have said that a computer has a memory and that in the memory there are locations where information can be stored. Each location has its own unique address. In a high-level language like PL/1 we do not ever refer to an actual machine address. Instead we use a name to identify a particular location. It is like referring to a house by the name of the owner rather than by its street address. We use the word <u>variable</u> to stand for the memory location. It is named by an <u>identifier</u>.

The identifier for a variable must begin with a letter and contain no blanks or special characters, other than the break character. If you think of the variable as the store location and its name as the identifier then you will realize that the <u>value</u> of the variable will be the actual information that is stored in the memory location. Locations are arranged to <u>hold</u> only one type of information or data. We speak of the <u>data type</u> of a variable. A variable may hold integers, in which case we say it is a <u>fixed</u> <u>variable</u>. It could also be a <u>float</u> <u>variable</u> or a character <u>variable</u>. If a variable is a <u>fixed</u> variable its value can be any integer. The value may be changed from time to

time in the program but its <u>type</u> <u>attribute</u> can never change; once
a fixed variable, always a fixed variable.

Examples of variable identifiers are

ACCT_NO, TAX, TOTAL, MARK

They are similar to the identifier we used in the PROCEDURE
OPTIONS(MAIN), but that identifier was not identifying a
variable; it labeled a PROCEDURE. Identifiers for variables can
be up to 31 characters long.

It is <u>very</u> important to choose identifiers that relate to the
kind of information that is stored in the corresponding
locations. Well-chosen identifiers make a program easier to
understand.

DECLARATIONS

We must make the words we want to use as variable identifiers
known to the compiler and associate them with memory locations
suitable for the particular data type they will hold. This is
accomplished by means of "declarations" that are placed in the
program immediately following the PROCEDURE OPTIONS(MAIN).

We will not, at the moment, show how character variables can
be declared but look only at fixed and float variables. To
declare that SUM is to be a fixed variable we write

DECLARE(SUM)FIXED;

The identifier is enclosed in parentheses after the <u>keyword</u>
DECLARE and followed by the keyword FIXED, then a semicolon.
This establishes SUM as having the type attribute FIXED. To
declare DISTANCE to be a float variable use

DECLARE(DISTANCE)FLOAT;

If a number of fixed variables are required they can all be
listed inside the one set of parentheses, separated by commas,
for example

DECLARE(SUM,MARK,NUMBER)FIXED;

Both <u>fixed</u> and <u>float</u> variables can be put into a single
declaration as in the following

DECLARE(SUM)FIXED,
    (DISTANCE,SPEED)FLOAT;

Putting declarations in a program is like phoning ahead for hotel
reservations; when you need it, the space is there with the
right name on it. Also the compiler can substitute the actual

machine address whenever it encounters a variable in the program. It does this by keeping a directory showing variable identifiers and corresponding memory locations. This directory is set up as the declarations are read by the compiler.

You should not use as variable identifiers any of the words that are PL/1 keywords. These are DECLARE, PROCEDURE, FIXED, FLOAT, LIST, MAIN, and so on. Sometimes it would cause no trouble to do this; often it would.

ASSIGNMENT STATEMENTS

In addition to declarations, you will be learning two types of PL/1 statements that cause things to happen as the program is executed. We say that they are executable statements. The PUT LIST statement is an executable statement; it causes printing to take place. One of the two new executable types we will have is the statement that reads cards, the GET LIST statement, but first we will look at the assignment statement.

There are no keywords in an assignment statement but it has a very definite form. The form is

variable identifier = expression;   *assignment statement*

There is an equal sign and on the left of it is a single word, a variable identifier. This identifier must have been declared to be either fixed or float. On the right hand of the equal sign there is an expression. We have looked at expressions that contained fixed or float constants; now expressions can also contain fixed or float variable identifiers. We have expressions like

    5+10/3E0   (8+9)*7

but now we can have expressions like

    SUM+1   TOTAL/1.00E2   SUM-MARK

We will not use variable identifiers in the expression of an assignment statement to begin with but instead use a simple expression, a fixed constant. For example,

    AGE=5;

is an assignment statement. It has the result of storing the number 5 in the memory location identified by the name AGE. If AGE has appeared in the declaration

    DECLARE(AGE)FIXED;

then the number will be stored as an integer and would be printed out by

```
    PUT LIST(AGE);
```

as 5. If, on the other hand, it were declared FLOAT it would be
stored and printed as 5.00000E+00.

    Assignments look like equations and this is misleading. When
we write

```
    AGE=5;
```

we are not stating something that is true when you encounter it
in a program. You mean by the statement that the value 5 is to
be assigned to the variable AGE. Some programming languages try
to keep assignments from looking like equations by using an arrow
pointing left instead of an equal sign, and write

```
    AGE < - 5
```

    This way of writing the assignment indicates the action that
is to take place. We are stuck with PL/1's equal sign and you
must just learn to think of the action.

    So   far the expression on the right-hand side of the
assignment has just been a fixed constant, but we can have more
complicated expressions.

```
    AGE=1980-1966;
```

Here we are subtracting the year of birth, 1966, from the year
1980 to get the age in 1980. This instruction would assign the
value 14 to the variable AGE. We could get the same result as
follows

```
    BIRTH_YEAR=1966;
    THIS_YEAR=1980;
    AGE=THIS_YEAR - BIRTH_YEAR;
```

Here we have two additional variables BIRTH_YEAR and THIS_YEAR
which are given values in assignment statements then used in an
expression on the right-hand side of another assignment
statement. We could have another statement

```
    NEXT_AGE=AGE+1;
```

which would give the age the following year to the variable
NEXT_AGE. Remember, if we use identifiers in a program they must
all appear in declarations. We would need the declaration

```
    DECLARE(AGE,BIRTH_YEAR,THIS_YEAR,NEXT_AGE)FIXED;
```

A variable may be assigned values over and over during a program.
For example, we might have

```
SUM=2+3;
PUT LIST(SUM);
SUM=3+4;
PUT LIST(SUM);
```

and so on. Now we come to perhaps the most confusing type of assignment statement. Suppose in a program you were making calculations year by year and needed to keep a variable AGE that held the value of the current age for the calculation. We might change the value at the end of the year by the assignment:

```
AGE=AGE+1;
```

Now you can see that the assignment statement is certainly not an equation, or this would be nonsense. What happens when this statement is executed is that the value stored in the variable AGE is added to the integer 1 and the result of the addition stored back in the same location.

In machine language, if the memory location of AGE is 336 and if there is a constant 1 stored in location 512, then the PL/1 assignment statement

```
AGE=AGE+1;
```

could be translated as

```
LOAD   336
ADD    512
STORE  336
```

TRACING EXECUTION

We have seen that variables are associated with locations in the memory of the computer. We can assign values to variables and, during a program, we can change the values as often as we want. The values can vary and that is why the locations are called variables. The location stays the same but the value can change.

Sometimes it is helpful when getting used to writing programs, to keep track of values stored in the memory locations corresponding to each variable. This can help us to understand the effect of each statement. Some statements change a value; others do not. We call this tracing the execution of instructions.

We do not need to know the numerical, or machine address of the locations. As far as we are concerned the identifier is the address of the variable. For example, if before execution of

```
AGE=AGE+1;
```

```
we had
      AGE is 9
then after
      AGE is 10
```

We will trace now a slightly more complicated program by
writing the values of all the variables involved after each
instruction is executed. Here we will use some meaningless names
like X,Y, and Z because the program has no particular meaning.
We just want to learn to trace execution. We will write the
tracing on the right-hand side of the page and the program on the
left. The labels over the right-hand side give the names of the
locations; their values are listed under the names, opposite each
instruction. When the value of a particular variable has not yet
been assigned we will write a dash.

LINE		X	Y	Z
1	TRACE:PROCEDURE OPTIONS(MAIN);			
2	DECLARE(X,Y,Z)FIXED;	-	-	-
3	X=5;	5	-	-
4	Y=7;	5	7	-
5	Z=X+Y;	5	7	12
6	X=X+5;	10	7	12
7	X=Z;	12	7	12
8	Y=Z;	12	12	12
9	X=X+Y+Z;	36	12	12
10	Y=Y*Z;	36	144	12
11	Z=(X+Y)/12E0;	36	144	15
12	X=X/5E0;	7	144	15
13	PUT LIST(X,Y,Z);	7	144	15
14	END;	7	144	15

The lines of the program are numbered so that we can make
reference to them. You will have found that the computer numbers
the lines in your program so that it can refer to errors in
specific lines.

First notice that the locations X,Y, and Z do not get
established until the DECLARE. They have no values assigned at
this point though. All is straightforward until line 6 when X
appears on both sides of the assignment statement. The values
shown at the right are, remember, the values after execution of
the statement on that line. In line 11 note that since a
division is not possible unless either the divisor or dividend
has a float value, we add E0 to the integer 12. When the
division yields an integer the answer is exact but in line 12 you
can see that the fractional part of the division is dropped. We
say it is truncated. The true answer is 7.2 but the integer 7 is
stored in location X because it is of the type FIXED. To always
get the fractional part of the result in a division we must store
the answer in a FLOAT variable location.

The output statement in line 13 is different from the output statements in SP/1 because now we can include the names of variables in the list. We have

    PUT LIST(X,Y,Z);

The machine can tell the difference between variable identifiers and literals because identifiers have no quotes. There is no possible confusion between numbers and identifiers because an identifier may not begin with a digit. You can see now why PL/1 has this rule.

In this example we showed a division with truncation. Sometimes we want to round off the results of a division, say in determining costs to the nearest cent. If COST is the value in cents of a 2-kilogram package of soap flakes then the cost of one kilogram to the nearest cent KG_COST is produced by

    KG_COST=COST/2E0+.5E0;

The variable KG_COST has been declared to be fixed so it will accept only whole number values. This method of rounding is to add .5 to the answer, which is computed with the proper fractional part. Then, after addition, the fractional part is truncated because the value is assigned to the fixed variable KG_COST. Adding .5 has the effect that if the right answer has a fractional part below .5 then it is rounded by truncation of the fraction. If it is .5 or over , it is rounded up to the next integer. Try it yourself for 88.3 and 88.7. When rounding off a negative number, you must subtract .5 instead of adding it.

rounding off, for fixed variables (positive, negative)

                            INPUT OF DATA

Now we will learn how to read data from cards into the computer. We did not learn this at the same time as we learned to print data because the idea of a variable is essential to input. It is not essential to output because we can have numbers and literals, that is, fixed and float constants and constant character strings. If we write

    GET LIST(X,Y,Z);

we will read three numbers off a card and store them in the three variables X, Y, and Z. The card with the three numbers is called a data card and is placed in the card deck immediately following the $DATA control card. We need to have a $DATA control card whether or not there are any data cards. On the data card, the numbers need not be arranged in any set fields, but must be separated from each other by at least one blank. Here is a sample program, including control cards, that reads information in and prints it out.

entering data

```
$JOB ID='PAT HUME'
 IN_OUT:PROCEDURE OPTIONS(MAIN);
    DECLARE(X,Y,Z)FIXED;
    GET LIST(X,Y);
    Z=X+Y;
    PUT LIST(Z,Y,X);
    END;
$DATA
 5  7
```

The printed output for this program would appear in the first three fields and would be

     12   7   5

On input, the first number on the data card, namely 5, is associated with the first variable X and stored in that location. The number 7 is stored in location Y.

When punching float numbers for input, you do not have to put any more significant figures than necessary in either the fraction or exponent; you need not punch

    2.00000E00

You can have only 2.E0 or 2E0. On input, if the exponent is zero, you may omit it completely. Thus numbers like

    35.8   3.14159   0.025

are all acceptable as float numbers. We call numbers in this form non-integer fixed constants. These are acceptable on data cards but are not used as an alternative for float constants in a program.

CONVERSION BETWEEN FIXED AND FLOAT

Conversions between fixed and float form will occur automatically whenever required by the attribute of the variable that is to hold the number. If a data item is on a card as an integer and is read into a location defined by a variable that has been declared as FLOAT, then it will be converted to float. If a float constant or a non-integer fixed constant is read into a location defined by a variable that has been declared as FIXED, any fractional part will be truncated and the integer part kept. For example:

```
$JOB ID='RIC HOLT'
 CONVERT:PROCEDURE OPTIONS(MAIN);
    DECLARE(X,Y)FIXED,
       (Z)FLOAT;
    GET LIST(X,Y,Z);
    PUT LIST(X,Y,Z);
    GET LIST(X,Y,Z);
    PUT SKIP LIST(X,Y,Z);
    END;
$DATA
 22.5    36    25    2    18.16E1    5E4
```

The output for this program will have two lines with the printing

```
    22       36       2.50000E+01
     2      181       5.00000E+04
```

FIXED ⟷ FLOAT

Within a program it is often necessary to convert between fixed and float. This can be accomplished by assigning the fixed value to a float variable and vice versa. For example, suppose that AVERAGE_MARK is a float variable holding the average mark in a term examination. You would like the average to the nearest mark. Declare another variable AVERAGE as fixed and write in the program

    AVERAGE = AVERAGE_MARK+.5E0

AVERAGE will then be an integer, the rounded average mark.

COMMENTS

One of the main aims of structured programming is that your programs be easily understood by yourself and by others. Choosing variable names that suggest what is being stored is an excellent way to make programs readable. We have shown several programs with just X,Y, and Z as variable names. This is because these are meant to show you what happens in assignment statements and GET and PUT LIST statements and are not about real applications. It is not advisable to use such meaningless names. We want your programs to look more like English than like algebra when you are finished.

One other thing that you can do to make a program understandable is to include comments in English along with the program. We have been providing comments to some of our examples in the accompanying text but you can write comments right into the program. To accomplish this, simply enclose the comments inside a pair of symbols that will act like brackets; in that way the comment is not mistaken for a program statement. The symbols you use are /* to begin and */ to end the comment. For example

    /* THIS IS A COMMENT */

could be placed <u>anywhere</u> in the program where blanks can occur. You could have one between GET and LIST if you wanted. To be sensible it is best to have comments occur at the ends of lines or on separate lines.

Comments should not be split between cards, have */ in them, or be put in the data. Otherwise anything goes. From now on we will be including comments in our examples.

AN EXAMPLE JOB

We now give a job(control cards, program and data values) which illustrates the use of variables, assignment statements, GET LIST statements, and comments. The program reads in the length, width and height of a box (as given in inches) and then prints the area of the base of the box (in square centimeters) and the volume of the box (in cubic centimeters). Lines 1 and 18 are control cards, lines 2-17 are the program and line 19 gives the data.

```
 1  $JOB ID='MARIE GUINDON'
 2    EXAMPLE:PROCEDURE OPTIONS(MAIN);
 3      /* READ BOX LENGTH, WIDTH AND HEIGHT IN INCHES */
 4      /* THEN CONVERT TO CENTIMETERS AND CALCULATE */
 5      /* THE BOX'S BASE AREA AND VOLUME. */
 6      DECLARE(LENGTH,WIDTH,HEIGHT,AREA,VOLUME,CM_PER_INCH)FLOAT;
 7      CM_PER_INCH=2.54E0;
 8      GET LIST(LENGTH,WIDTH);
 9      LENGTH=CM_PER_INCH*LENGTH;
10      WIDTH=CM_PER_INCH*WIDTH;
11      AREA=LENGTH*WIDTH;
12      PUT LIST('AREA=',AREA);
13      GET LIST(HEIGHT);
14      HEIGHT=CM_PER_INCH*HEIGHT;
15      VOLUME=HEIGHT*AREA;
16      PUT SKIP LIST('VOLUME=',VOLUME);
17      END;
18  $DATA
19     2.6    1.2    6.92
```

This program will print the following

```
AREA=        2.01290E+01
VOLUME=      3.53803E+02
```

where the area is in square centimeters and the volume is in cubic centimeters. The area and volume printed depend on the three values on the data cards; the data values 2.6, 1.2 and 6.92 could be replaced by the dimensions of a different box.

Line 2 simply marks the beginning of the program; it causes no action on the part of the computer. Lines 3, 4 and 5 are intended for you, the reader of the program, and are ignored by the computer.

Line 6 of the program sets up memory locations for variables called LENGTH, WIDTH, HEIGHT, AREA, VOLUME and CM_PER_INCH. These variables have the FLOAT attribute, instead of the FIXED attribute, because they have non-integer values (such as 2.6). Line 7 sets the value of CM_PER_INCH to 2.54E0; notice that the exponent (E0) is required. Line 8 causes the data values 2.6 and 1.2 to be read into variables LENGTH and WIDTH. Since 2.6 and 1.2 are data values (they do not appear inside the program), we need not give them an exponent part.

Line 9 takes the value 2.6E0 from the LENGTH variable, multiplies it by CM_PER_INCH and then returns the result to LENGTH. The multiplication sign (*) is required; we could <u>not</u> write simply

    LENGTH=2.54E0 LENGTH;

Line 10 is similar to line 9.

Line 11 takes the values in LENGTH and WIDTH, multiplies them together, and places the result in AREA. Line 12 then prints:

        AREA=   2.01290E+01

As of line 11, the variables HEIGHT and VOLUME have not been used. An attempt to print HEIGHT or VOLUME in line 11 would be an error because those variables have not yet been given a value.

Since the GET LIST statement of line 8 uses up the first two data values, 2.6 and 1.2, the GET LIST statement of line 13 reads the value 6.92 into HEIGHT. The computer does not know that 6.92 represents the height of a box. It only knows that it is instructed to read the next data value into the variable named HEIGHT.

Line 14 converts to centimeters, line 15 computes the volume and line 16 prints the volume. Line 17 is the end of the program and tells the computer to stop working on this program.

This job would print the same thing if we made the following changes.

(1) Replace line 8 by the two assignment statements:

    LENGTH=2.6E0;
    WIDTH=1.2E0;

(2) Replace line 12 by the assignment statement:

HEIGHT=6.92E0;

(3) Delete line 19, the data values.

These three changes result in a program which is given the dimensions of the box by assignment statements rather than by input statements (GET LIST statements). The advantage of the original program, which uses GET LIST statements, is that the program will work for a new box simply by replacing the data card, line 19.

LABELING OF OUTPUT

Just as comments help to make a program more understandable, output that is properly identified by labels is self-explanatory. What you are trying to do is to prepare documents that need no further explanation from you when you show your computer printout to others.

The compiler always lists your program, including comments, but the output data should also be labeled so the reader is in no doubt about what the numbers are, without reading the program. Very often you present results without showing how you got them, that is, you do not include the program.

There are two basic ways to label results. If different values of the same set of variables are listed in columns on the output, then a label can be placed at top of each column. For example, the output for comparing costs of boxes of soap flakes might be

COST IN CENTS	WEIGHT IN KGS	COST PER KG
125	1	125
200	2	100
260	3	87

There is no reason to use exactly the same labels as the variable names, since the literals printed at the top of the columns can be longer and contain blanks. They are printed independently. The program that produces this table might be

```
$JOB ID='DICK SWENSON'
 SOAP:PROCEDURE OPTIONS(MAIN);
    /*COMPUTE AND TABULATE COST PER KG*/
    DECLARE(COST,WEIGHT,COST_KG)FIXED;

    /*PRINT HEADINGS OF TABLE*/
    PUT LIST('COST IN CENTS','WEIGHT IN KGS','COST PER KG');

    /*PROCESS DATA FOR FIRST BOX*/
    GET LIST(COST,WEIGHT);
    COST_KG=COST/(WEIGHT*1E0)+.5E0;
    PUT SKIP LIST(COST,WEIGHT,COST_KG);

    /*PROCESS DATA FOR SECOND BOX*/
    GET LIST(COST,WEIGHT);
    COST_KG=COST/(WEIGHT*1E0)+.5E0;
    PUT SKIP LIST(COST,WEIGHT,COST_KG);

    /*PROCESS DATA FOR THIRD BOX*/
    GET LIST(COST,WEIGHT);
    COST_KG=COST/(WEIGHT*1E0)+.5E0;
    PUT SKIP LIST(COST,WEIGHT,COST_KG);
    END;
$DATA
     125    1
     200    2
     260    3
```

You can see how comments can be inserted, how the column headings are printed, and how each line of the table is calculated and printed. The SKIP in the output statement ensures that each starts on a new line. In the program we have repeated three statements, without change, one set of three for each box. If we had 100 boxes, this would have been a little monotonous. When we want to repeat statements we do not do it this way; a more convenient way is possible with a new PL/1 statement that will cause this kind of repetition. But that comes in the next subset, SP/3.

A second kind of output labeling was already used in the previous example but can be illustrated by a program segment

```
    COST=5;
    PUT LIST('COST=',COST);
```

This would result in the printing

```
    COST=       5
```

This method is easier when just a few numbers are being printed.

PROGRAM TESTING

It is easy to make mistakes in programming. The first thing
you should do to test a program is to read over your program
carefully to spot errors. It is valuable to trace the execution
yourself before you submit it to the computer. Your goal should
always be to produce programs that you <u>know</u> are correct without
testing, but this is not always possible. You could ask someone
else to read it too. If he cannot understand your program it may
show that your program is poorly written or has errors. Next you
put your program on cards and proofread your cards to see that
they match your intentions. Check that the control cards are
present. Next you submit your deck.

If you have made errors in your program that involve the form
of statements, the compiler spots these during compilation and
reports them on the output. It refers to an error of a certain
type in line so and so of the program. It has been careful to
give numbers to each line so that it can make these references.
Errors in form are called <u>syntax</u> <u>errors</u>. Examples of common
syntax errors are

   1. leaving out the semicolon at the end of a statement
   2. forgetting the END
   3. forgetting to declare a variable
   4. misspelling PROCEDURE or any other keyword

In a way, a syntax error is a good error since it is detected for
you by the computer. But it is frustrating to have to correct it
and resubmit the deck. It wastes time. Some people say that
having syntax errors is a symptom of sloppy programming and a
sure indication that there are other errors.

When there are simple syntax errors, most compilers attempt
to repair them and go on. Their repairs are just guesses at what
you intended and some of the guesses are pretty wild. They
always give the programmer a warning if a repair has been
attempted. Some errors cannot be repaired and, as a result, no
execution takes place. Your printout has only the program
listing and error messages. Very sad! Back to the drawing board.
Be sure to proofread the entire listing of your program, looking
for unreported errors.

If there are no unrepairable syntax errors, execution takes
place right after compilation. This does not, however, mean that
all is well.

If answers are printed, they should be checked against hand
calculated answers. If they agree, it is possible that your
program is correct. If they disagree it is possible that your
hand calculations are incorrect or that your program has errors.
The errors now are usually of a kind called <u>semantic</u> <u>errors</u>. You
are asking for a calculation that you did not mean to ask for.

It has a different <u>meaning</u> from your intentions. For instance,
you are adding two numbers and you meant to subtract them.

To find semantic errors you must look at the program again
and try to trace what it must be doing rather than what you
thought it would do. <u>To help in the tracing it is often good to</u>
<u>insert additional PUT LIST instructions between other statements</u>
<u>and print out the current value of variables that are changing.</u>
In this way you can follow the machine's activity. These extra
PUT LIST instructions can be removed after the errors have been
found.

tracing:
additional
PUT LIST

Sometimes there is no output printing from the PUT LIST
instructions that give the final results. This might happen in
many ways, for instance, if you ask in the GET LIST statements
for more data items than you have on the data cards. The
computer will tell you it reached the END OF FILE so the error is
spotted. It is important that the data items match the variables
in the GET LIST statements, or answers can be ridiculous.

Care must be taken about the FIXED and FLOAT distinction
between numbers as the computer converts automatically and will
not warn you if things are going wrong.

COMMON ERRORS IN PROGRAMS

When you try running a program on a computer, the computer
may detect <u>errors</u> in your program. As a result, <u>error</u> <u>messages</u>
will be printed. Since the computer does not understand the
purpose of your program, its error messages are limited to
describing the specific illegalities which it detects.
Unfortunately, the computer's error messages usually do not tell
you how to correct your program so that it will solve the problem
you have in mind.

In order to help you avoid such errors, we list some of the
errors which commonly occur in students' programs.

① Missing semicolons - Do not forget to put semicolons at the end
    of every statement.

② Missing parentheses - Do not forget the parentheses required
    around MAIN and following LIST.

③ Missing first card of program - Every PL/1 program must have a
    card of the form

        identifier:PROCEDURE OPTIONS(MAIN);

④ Missing END; at the end of the program.

⑤ Missing $DATA

6. Missing quotes, especially the last quote. Consider the following erroneous statement:

        PUT LIST('INVOICE);

This statement is missing a quote between the E and the right parenthesis. After printing an error message, the compiler may try to repair the error by concluding that you want it to print
        INVOICE);
rather than
        INVOICE

7. Uninitialized variables - When a variable is declared, a memory location, or cell, is set aside, but no special value is placed in the cell. That is, the cell is not yet initialized. A variable must be given a value, via an assignment statement or a GET LIST statement, before an attempt is made to use the value of the variable in a PUT LIST statement or in an expression.

8. Undeclared variables - Before a variable is used in a statement (assignment, GET LIST or PUT LIST) the variable must be declared. All declarations must precede all other statements.

9. Mistaking I for 1 - The characters I and 1 look similar, but are entirely different to the computer.

10. Mistaking O for 0 - The characters O(oh) and 0(zero) look similar, but are entirely different to the computer.

11. Mistaking 1 (one) for | (the "or bar") or l (the letter "ell").

12. Mistaking - (minus sign) for _ (underscore).

13. Attempt to read beyond end-of-file - Sometimes a program reads all of its data, and then tries to read more (non-existent) data. That is, GET LIST statements consume all the data values following $DATA, and then a GET LIST statement tries to read another (non-existent) data value. Either the program or the data is in error.

CHAPTER 4 SUMMARY

This chapter introduced variables, as they are used in programming languages. Essentially, a variable is a memory location, or cell, which can hold a value. Suppose X is the name of a variable; then X denotes a cell. If X is a variable having the FIXED attribute, then the cell for X can hold an integer value such as 9, 291, 0 or -11.

The following important terms were discussed in this chapter.

Identifier   - can be used as the name of a variable. An
   identifier must begin with a letter; this letter can be
   followed by additional letters, digits or underscores (_).
   The following are examples of identifiers: X, I, WIDTH,
   INCOME_TAX and A1.

Attribute (or type) - Each variable has an attribute; in this
   chapter we introduced the FIXED and FLOAT attributes.   The
   attribute of a variable is determined by its declaration.

Declaration - establishes variables for use in a program. For
   example, the declaration

        DECLARE(I)FIXED;

   creates a variable called I which can be given fixed values.
   Declarations occur immediately after PROCEDURE OPTIONS(MAIN);
   and before any PUT LIST, GET LIST or assignment statements.

DECLARE   - the word instructing the computer to create variables.
   A declaration can be of the form:

   DECLARE(list of identifiers separated by commas)attribute;

   The "attribute" must be FIXED or FLOAT for the SP/2 subset.
   Optionally, the declaration can be extended for further
   variables, for example:

        DECLARE(I)FIXED,
           (X,Y)FLOAT,
           (J,K)FIXED;

   This declaration is exactly equivalent to the following:

        DECLARE(I)FIXED;
        DECLARE(X,Y)FLOAT;
        DECLARE(J,K)FIXED;

Assignment - means a value is assigned to a variable. For
   example, the following is an assignment statement which gives
   the value 52 to the variable I:

        I=52;

Truncation - throwing away the fractional part of a number. When
   a float number is assigned to a variable with the FIXED
   attribute, the variable is given the truncated value.

Number conversion - changing a fixed number to a float number or
   vice versa. Conversion from float to fixed causes truncation
   of the result.

Data (or input data) - values which a program can read. The data
   values follow the $DATA card.

GET - means "Read data." The GET LIST statement reads data values into a list of variables.

GET LIST statement - this statement is of the form:

GET LIST(list of variable names separated by commas);

Optionally, SKIP may be inserted between GET and LIST to cause the reading to begin on the succeeding data card. If SKIP is omitted, reading will automatically proceed to the next data card when the values of one card have all been read.

Comments - information in a program which is intended to assist a person reading the program. The following is a comment which could appear in a PL/1 program:

/* THIS PROGRAM PRINTS GAS BILLS */

Comments do not affect the execution of a program.

Documentation - written explanation of a program. Comments are used in a program to document its actions.

Keyword - a word, such as PROCEDURE or LIST, which is an inherent part of the programming language. Keywords must not be used as identifiers.

Errors - improper parts of, or actions of, a program. For example, the statement

PUT LIST('HELLO';

has an error in that a right parenthesis is missing. If the computer detects an error in your program, it will print an "error message".

CHAPTER 4 EXERCISES

1. Suppose that I, J and K are variables with the fixed attribute and they presently have the values 5, 7 and 10. What will be printed as a result of the following statements?

```
    PUT SKIP LIST(I,I+1,I+J,I+J*K);
    K=I+J;
    PUT SKIP LIST(K);
    J=J+1;
    PUT LIST(J);
    I=3*I+J;
    PUT LIST(I);
```

2.   RADIUS, DIAMETER, CIRCUMFERENCE and AREA are FLOAT variables.
A value has been read into RADIUS via a GET LIST statement. Write
statements which do each of the following.

    (a) Give to DIAMETER the product of 2 and RADIUS.
    (b) Give to CIRCUMFERENCE the product of pi (3.14159) and
        DIAMETER.
    (c) Give to AREA the product of pi and RADIUS squared.
        (RADIUS squared can be written as RADIUS*RADIUS.)
    (d) Print the values of RADIUS, DIAMETER, CIRCUMFERENCE
        and AREA.

3.   Suppose I is a variable with the FIXED attribute. I has
already been given a value via an assignment statement. Write
statements to do the following.

    (a) Without changing I, print out twice the value of I.
    (b) Increase I by 1.
    (c) Double the value of I.
    (d) Decrease I by 5.

4.   M, N and P are variables with the fixed attribute. What will
the following statements cause the computer to print?

```
M=43;
N=211;
P=M;
M=N;
N=P;
PUT LIST(M,N);
```

5.(a) What will be printed by the following job?

```
1   $JOB ID='ANN MORLEY'
2    PAIRS:PROCEDURE OPTIONS(MAIN);
3      DECLARE(FIRST,SECOND)FIXED;
4      GET LIST(FIRST,SECOND);
5      PUT LIST(FIRST+SECOND);
6      GET LIST(FIRST,SECOND);
7      PUT LIST(FIRST+SECOND);
8      END;
9   $DATA
10     22   247   -16
11     528
```

(b) Which lines of this job are control cards? Which are program
and which are input data?

6. (a) What will be printed by the following job?

```
1    $JOB ID='FRED LEE'
2    /* CALCULATE TERM MARK */
3    COMBINE:PROCEDURE OPTIONS(MAIN);
4       DECLARE(GRADE1,GRADE2)FLOAT;
5       DECLARE(MARK)FIXED;
6       GET LIST(GRADE1,GRADE2);
7       MARK=(GRADE1+GRADE2)/2+.5E0;
8       PUT LIST(GRADE1,GRADE2,MARK);
9       END;
10   $DATA
11      81.7
12      85.9
```

(b) Which lines of this job are control cards; which are program and which are input data?

7. Trace the execution of the following program. That is, give the values of the variables LENGTH, WIDTH, and ABOUT and give any output after each line of the program.

```
1    $JOB ID='JOE MURPHY'
2     AREA:PROCEDURE OPTIONS(MAIN);
3        DECLARE(SIZE,LENGTH,WIDTH)FLOAT,
           (ABOUT)FIXED;
4        /* READ SIZES AND CONVERT FEET TO YARDS */
5        GET LIST(SIZE);
6        WIDTH=SIZE/3E0;
7        GET LIST(SIZE);
8        LENGTH=SIZE/3E0;
9        ABOUT=WIDTH*LENGTH+.5E0;
10       PUT LIST('LENGTH AND WIDTH ARE',LENGTH,WIDTH);
11       PUT SKIP LIST('AREA IS:',LENGTH*WIDTH,
           'THIS IS ABOUT',ABOUT,'(SQUARE YARDS)');
12       END;
13   $DATA
14      9.60   15.9
```

8. Write a program which reads three values and prints their average, rounded to the nearest whole number. For example, if 20, 16 and 25 follow the $DATA card then your program should print 20. Make up your own data for your program.

9. Write a program which reads a weight given in pounds and then prints out the weight in (1) pounds, (2) ounces, (3) kilograms and (4) grams. Note: 16 ounces equal one pound, 2.2046 pounds equal one kilogram and 1000 grams equal one kilogram.

10. Write a program which reads a distance given in miles and prints the distance in (1) miles, (2) yards, (3) feet, (4) inches and (5) meters. Note: 1760 yards equal one mile and 1 kilometer equals 0.62137 miles.

CHAPTER 5

SP/3: CONTROL FLOW

In the first two subsets of PL/1 we have learned to write programs with statements that cause the computer to read cards and assign values to variables, evaluate arithmetic expressions and assign the values to variables, and print results with labels. In all programs the statements were executed in sequence until the END was reached, at which time the program was terminated. In this subset we will learn two ways in which the sequence of statements may be altered. One involves the repetitious use of statements; the other involves alternate paths in the flow of statements. The first is called a loop, the second a branch. We speak of the flow of control since it is the control unit of the computer that determines which statement is to be executed next by the computer.

COUNTED LOOPS

The normal flow of control in a program is in a straight line. We can, however, give a statement that will cause the statements that follow it to be repeated. In the last chapter, in the example where we were reading information about boxes of soap flakes, we had to write the statements over and over to get repetitions. A statement that will produce repetition is the counted DO loop. For our example we could have written

```
DO I=1 TO 3;
  GET LIST(COST,WEIGHT);
  COST_KG=COST/(WEIGHT*1E0)+.5E0;
  PUT SKIP LIST(COST,WEIGHT,COST_KG);
END;
```

The three statements that we had to repeat three times are prefaced by

```
DO I=1 TO 3;
```

and followed by END;

The variable I is an index, which must be declared as a fixed
variable, and which counts the number of repetitions. First the
index I is set to 1, then the three statements are executed.
When the END is reached, control is sent back to the DO. At this
time the index I is increased by 1, making it 2. The three
statements are again executed and, at END, back we go to the DO.
This time I becomes 3 and a third execution of the three
statements in the DO loop takes place. When control returns to
the DO, this time I has become 4 and this is found to be larger
than the 3 that was specified as the upper limit of the count.
When this happens, control goes out of the loop to the next
statement after the END.

A counted or indexed DO loop is used whenever we know exactly
how many repetitions we want to take place. We do not need to
count by ones or start the count at 1. We could, for example,
have

```
DO COUNT=12 TO 24 BY 2;
```

Here we have called the index COUNT and are starting at 12 and
going by 2s up to, and to include, 24. At the moment there is no
real need to count in any fancy way, but in a higher subset we
will use this feature and sometimes even count backwards by -1.

The other kind of loop statement is the DO WHILE statement
but we cannot introduce it until we look at conditions. The DO
WHILE is a loop statement that causes repetition as long as a
certain condition is true. The condition concerned is written in
parentheses after the word WHILE.

CONDITIONS

There are expressions in PL/1 that are called logical
expressions and these have values that are either true or false.
The following is a list of logical expressions with their value
written on the same line. The symbol > means is greater than, <
means is less than, the equal sign means is equal to, and the
sign ¬ means not.

logical expression	value
5=2+3	true
7>5	true
2<6	true
5+3<2+1	false
6¬=10	true
5>5	false
5>=5	true

You can probably see how these work.

There are compound conditions formed by taking two single conditions and putting either the logical operator & (and) or the logical operator | (or) between them. With & both conditions must be true or else the compound condition is false. For example, (8>7 & 6<3) is false since (6<3) is false. With |, if either or both of the single conditions is true, the compound condition is true. For example, (8>7|6<3) is true since (8>7) is true. It is possible to have multiple compoundings. For example,

    (8>7 & 2=1+1) & (6>7 | 5>1)

is true. The parentheses here show the sequence of the operations. There is a rule of precedence if there are no parentheses, namely, the & (and) operator has higher precedence than the | (or) operator. This means that & operations are done before | operations.

LOGICAL VARIABLES

If you want to assign a logical value to a variable, it must be typed by a declaration as BIT(1). The reason this word is used is because a single binary digit, a bit, is all that is necessary to give the information, true or false. In PL/1 we write '1'B to indicate true, and '0'B to indicate false. You must write these this way so they are not mistaken for the decimal numbers 0 and 1 in a program. Logical variables can be read, assigned logical values, or printed, but cannot be used in arithmetic expressions. For example, if you want a logical variable SWITCH assigned the value true you must include the declaration and the assignment.

    DECLARE(SWITCH)BIT(1);
    SWITCH='1'B;

The variable SWITCH may be used in a condition.

CONDITIONAL LOOPS

We have introduced the notion of a condition; now we will actually use it. One of the major uses of conditions is in the DO WHILE (condition) loop. The repetition is to take place as long as the condition stated in parentheses after the word WHILE is true. Once it is false, the control goes to the statement following the END that terminates the loop.

So far we have discussed only conditions involving fixed constants. These we labelled as true or false. The condition in the DO WHILE loop cannot be like this, because if it is always

true we would loop forever and if always false we would not loop
at all.   The condition must involve a variable whose value
changes during the looping.

   In the following example the DO WHILE is used to accomplish
exactly what the counted DO loop did for the soap flakes boxes.

```
1     I=1;
2     DO WHILE(I<=3);
3        GET LIST(COST,WEIGHT);
4        COST_KG=COST/(WEIGHT*1E0)+.5E0;
5        PUT SKIP LIST(COST,WEIGHT,COST_KG);
6        I=I+1;
7        END;
8     PUT LIST(I);
```

   In statement 1 the value of the variable I appearing in the
condition is set initially to 1, then we enter the loop.   This
stage is called initialization and is always necessary in
conditional loops. In line 2 we begin the loop.   The condition
in parentheses is true since I is 1, which is less than 3. Thus
the next four instructions are executed.   These constitute the
body of the loop. In the body, statement 6 alters the value of
the variable appearing in the condition. This means that it is
changing each time around the loop. At the end of the first loop
it becomes 1+1=2. The END causes control to return to the start
of the loop. The condition is then examined and since it is true
(2<=3) the body is executed a second time. It will be true also
on the third time but on the fourth round, I will be 4 and (4<=3)
is false. When I is printed by statement 8 it is 4.   This
printing is not part of the original example, but was included
here to show you what happens to the index I.

   The various phases of a DO WHILE loop are

   phase 1. initialization, especially of the variable in the
         condition

   phase 2. test condition and if true then continue to next
         statement, if false go to statement following END

   phase 3. execute body of loop which includes altering the
         variable in the condition

   phase 4. return to phase 2 at the END.

   Phase 1 is necessary to give the variable appearing in the
condition an initial value.

READING CARDS

As an example of the two types of DO loops we will look at a very simple example of reading data from cards and printing it out, assuming that each card produces one line of printing. The only real problem will be to stop when you reach the last card. There are two distinct ways of doing this. One is to count the cards by hand, prepare a card with this count on it, and place it in front of the data cards. Then we use a counted DO loop to read them. The other method is to place a card at the end of the data cards with a piece of data that is impossible as a real entry. We call it a dummy card. Sometimes it is called an end-of-file marker. Suppose, to talk specifically, that each data card has on it a student number and a grade received in an examination. To illustrate we will have only three data cards, but you can see how it will work with more.

Method 1. Counting the cards

```
$JOB ID='GORDY PROCTOR'
 MARKS1:PROCEDURE OPTIONS(MAIN);
    DECLARE(STUDENT_NUMBER,MARK,COUNT,I)FIXED;
    PUT LIST('STUDENT NO.','MARK IN COMPUTING');
    GET LIST(COUNT);
    DO I=1 TO COUNT;
       GET LIST(STUDENT_NUMBER,MARK);
       PUT SKIP LIST(STUDENT_NUMBER,MARK);
       END;
    END;
$DATA
    3
    1026    86
    2051    90
    3163    71
```

Notice that we took the trouble to label the output. Perhaps the two ENDs, one after the other, seem strange. The first belongs to the DO loop, the second to the PROCEDURE OPTIONS(MAIN). The machine can keep track of these just as you can tell which right parenthesis goes with which left one in this example:

        (2+5*(2+6))

Both the PROCEDURE and the DO loop must be closed with an END.

In the second method we will place a dummy card with two zeros on it at the end of the deck.

<u>Method 2</u>. Testing for the dummy card

```
$JOB ID='JIM CORDY'
 MARKS2:PROCEDURE OPTIONS(MAIN);
    DECLARE(STUDENT_NUMBER,MARK)FIXED;
    PUT LIST('STUDENT NO.','MARK IN COMPUTING');
    GET LIST(STUDENT_NUMBER,MARK);
    DO WHILE(STUDENT_NUMBER¬=0);
       PUT SKIP LIST(STUDENT_NUMBER,MARK);
       GET LIST(STUDENT_NUMBER,MARK);
       END;
    END;
$DATA
    1026    86
    2051    90
    3163    71
       0     0
```

In this example you will notice that the initialization
involves reading the first card outside the loop, in order to get
a value for the variable STUDENT_NUMBER appearing in the
condition of the DO WHILE. Since the first card has already been
read, it must be printed before a new card is read. This means
that the sequence is PUT LIST then GET LIST, rather than the way
it is in method 1. As soon as the new card has been read, we
return to the DO WHILE where the condition is tested. These two
techniques for dealing with a variable number of items, like
cards, are used again and again in programming. The DO WHILE is
more difficult to program but probably more useful, since if
there are many cards, it is easier for the user to stick in an
end-of-file card than to count cards.

EXAMPLES OF LOOPS

We will now give example programs to illustrate details about
loops. The examples each draw a zigzag. Here is the first
example:

```
1    WIGGLE:PROCEDURE OPTIONS(MAIN);
2       DECLARE(J)FIXED;
3       DO J=1 TO 3;
4          PUT SKIP LIST('*');
5          PUT SKIP LIST(' *');
6          PUT SKIP LIST('  *');
7          PUT SKIP LIST(' *');
8          END;
9       END;
```

This program, appropriately called WIGGLE, prints the following pattern:

```
 *
  *
   *
  *
 *
  *
   *
  *
 *
  *
   *
 *
```

The WIGGLE program causes the body of the loop, statements 4 through 7, to be executed three times. The variable J is 1 during the time the first four stars are printed. J is 2 during the time the next four stars are printed, and J is 3 while the last four stars are printed. After the last star is printed, J is set to 4 and since J then exceeds the limiting value, 3, of the loop, the loop is terminated.

Notice that in this program the variable J is used for only one purpose: to see that the loop is repeated the desired number of times. Line 3 means, essentially, "Repeat this loop three times." If we replaced line 3 by the following line

        DO J=9 TO 13 BY 2;

then the program would still print the same pattern. The only difference is that J would have the values 9,11 and 13 during the printing of the stars and would end up with the value of 15. Similarly, the same pattern would be printed if we replaced line 3 by the line:

        DO J=9 TO 14 BY 2;

Here again, J would be 9,11 and 13 during the printing of the stars and would end with the value 15. In this case the limit value, 14, does not actually match 13, the last value of J within the loop. However, the loop still stops after three times through because when 2 is added to 13, the result of 15 exceeds

the limit of 14. Although our two replacements for line 3 do not
change the pattern printed, they should not be used because they
make the program more confusing for people to understand. This
is because people more naturally think of "repeat this loop three
times" as running through the loop with values 1,2, and 3, rather
than values 9,11, and 13.

Here is one more possible replacement for line 3 which does
not change the printed pattern:

    DO J=3 TO 1 BY -1;

In this case, J will be 3 while the first four stars are printed,
then J will be 2 while the next four stars are printed, and then
J will be 1 while the last four stars are printed. Finally, J
will end up with the value of zero. This illustrates the fact
that if the step size, which is -1 here, is negative, then the
loop will count backwards to smaller values. Again, for this
example program, the original version of line 3 is preferable
because it is easier to understand its meaning at a glance.

As you have seen from these examples, when a PL/1 counted DO
loop completes, the final value of the counting variable is not
equal to the limit value. For example, in the unchanged WIGGLE
program, J ended up as 4 and the limit value was 3. This is
somewhat confusing in that we might have expected J to end up
with the value 3. In fact, in some programming languages other
than PL/1, counted DO loops work differently and would leave J as
3. It is good programming practice to avoid this confusion by
following the advice:

> When a counted DO loop has finished, do not use the
> final value of the counting variable.

There is another possible source of confusion in counted DO
loops. The PL/1 language does not prevent you from changing the
value of the counting variable inside a counted DO loop. For
example, in the loop body we could set J to 15 by an assignment
statement or a GET LIST statement. If this were done in the
WIGGLE program, the next test of the condition J>=3 would
terminate the loop. Then, the meaning of line 3 would no longer
be "Repeat this loop three times." This results in confusion —
not for the computer, but for people trying to read the program.
It is good programming practice to avoid this confusion by
following the advice:

> Inside a counted DO loop, do not alter the value of the
> counting variable.

We will now rewrite our WIGGLE program using DO WHILE instead
of a counted DO. We will call our new program WAGGLE. (Did you
know that in German "wiggle waggle" means "waddle" like a duck?
Well it does.)

```
1     WAGGLE:PROCEDURE OPTIONS(MAIN);
2        DECLARE(J)FIXED;
3        J=1;
4        DO WHILE(J<=3);
5           PUT SKIP LIST('*');
6           PUT SKIP LIST(' *');
7           PUT SKIP LIST('  *');
8           PUT SKIP LIST(' *');
9           J=J+1;
10       END;
11    END;
```

This WAGGLE program works exactly like our previous WIGGLE program. Lines 3,4, and 9 of WAGGLE are equivalent to line 3 of WIGGLE. Since it is easier to see that line 3 of WIGGLE means, "Repeat this loop three times," the WIGGLE version is preferable. We will, however, use WAGGLE to illustrate a few more points about loops.

In the WAGGLE program, consider moving line 9, which is

        J=J+1;

up to between lines 4 and 5. This change does not alter the printed pattern. It simply changes the point at which J has its value increased. J will have the value 2 while the first four stars are printed, then 3 while the next four stars are printed and finally 4 while the last four stars are printed. J ends up with the value of 4. Even though J is set to 4 before the last four stars are printed, the loop is not stopped. This is because J is not compared to the limit value 3 until control returns to line 4. This illustrates the fact that in a DO WHILE loop, the condition is tested only once - at the top - each time through the loop.

Now let us look back at the unchanged WAGGLE program. Suppose that you prepared this program for the computer and mistakenly made line 9 into

        J=J-1;

The mistake is that the plus sign was changed to a minus sign. Such a small mistake! Surely the computer will understand that a plus was wanted! But it will not do so. The computer has a habit of doing what we <u>tell</u> it to do rather than what we <u>want</u> it to do. Given the WAGGLE program, with the mistake, the computer will do the following. With J set to 1 it will print the first four stars. Then, as a result of the erroneous line 9, it will set J to 0 and will print another four stars. Then it will set J to -1 and print four more stars. Then it will set J to -2 and print four more stars and so on and so on. In theory, it will <u>never stop</u> printing stars because the condition J<=3 will always be true. This is called an <u>infinite loop</u>. Luckily, the computer will eventually stop your program when your program has printed too much or when your program has executed too many statements. When it stops your program, it will print an error message complaining about the excessive printing or running of your program. Unfortunately, the error message will not tell you that you should have had a plus sign instead of a minus sign, because the computer will not know what you were thinking when you prepared the program.

BRANCHES IN CONTROL FLOW

We have learned how to change from a flow of control in a straight line, or <u>linear</u> sequence, to flow in a loop, either counted or conditional. Now we must look at a different kind of structure in the sequence of control. This structure is called branching. It is a little like a fork in the road where there are two paths that can be followed. The road branches into two roads. When you come to a fork in a road you must <u>decide</u> which of the two branches you will take. Your decision is based on where you are heading. Suppose one sign at the fork gives the name of your destination and the other road sign gives some other name. Suppose your destination is Toronto; an instruction for deciding which branch to take might be

```
IF(LEFT_BRANCH_SIGN='TORONTO') THEN
    take the left branch;
ELSE
    take the right branch;
```

We have written this decision in exactly the form you use in PL/1 for branching in the sequence of control. The main difference is that the part we have written as "take the left branch" must be replaced by a PL/1 statement to do something. The same is true of the other branch which follows the keyword ELSE.

Suppose that there is a variable called CLASS_A which contains the number of students in a class called A. Students are to be assigned to Class A if their mark in computer science (CS_MARK) is over 80; otherwise they are to be assigned to Class B (CLASS_B). The PL/1 statement which decides which class to place the student in, and counts the number going into each class, is

```
IF CS_MARK>80 THEN
    CLASS_A=CLASS_A+1;
ELSE
    CLASS_B=CLASS_B+1;
```

The IF...THEN...ELSE statement causes control to split into two paths but, unlike forks in roads, you will notice that it immediately comes back together again. This means that we are

never in any doubt about what happens; after the execution of one
or the other of the two branches, the control returns to the
normal sequence. One way of looking at the IF...THEN...ELSE
statement is that it provides two possibilities, only one of
which is to be selected, depending on whether the condition
following the IF is true or false. After one or other path is
executed the normal control sequence is resumed.

If you want to execute two or more statements in either the
THEN branch or the ELSE branch, you must enclose them with DO; in
front and END; afterwards. This use of the DO has nothing
whatever to do with loops. We are already hardened to the use of
END to go with PROCEDURE, DO WHILE, and counted DOs. For
example, consider the program segment

```
IF (X>Y) THEN
    DO;
        X=Y+1;
        Y=5;
        END;
ELSE
    DO;
        Y=X+1;
        X=3;
        END;
```

We will not try to give any meaning to this example. It just
shows how the DO; and END; must be used when more than one
statement follows either the THEN or the ELSE. Notice that in
this example we have put parentheses around the condition X>Y.
Parentheses may be used if you like, but are not essential as
they are in the DO WHILE.

You must always have one statement, or a group of statements
bracketed by DO; END; after the THEN. If there is nothing that
you want to do in the ELSE branch you must leave out the word
ELSE entirely. For instance, you may have the statement which
would eliminate the balance in a bank account if it were less
than 10 cents.

```
IF BALANCE<10 THEN
    BALANCE=0;
```

Here there is no ELSE statement, but this just means that if the
balance is larger than 10 cents we do not make it zero.

THREE-WAY BRANCHES

We have seen how a linear control structure can be split up
into two branches and then brought together again. What do we
write if we have a situation where more than two branches are
required? We will do a three-way branch and then you will see

how any number of branches can be achieved. This can also be
viewed as selecting one of three alternatives.

As an example, we will write a program that counts votes in
an election. Suppose that there are three political parties
called Right, Left, and Middle, and that to vote for one of these
parties you punch a 1, or a 2, or a 3 respectively on a card.
Here is the program that reads the vote cards and counts each
party and the total. The last card has -1 on it.

```
$JOB ID='MARJORIE DUNLOP'
 VOTING:PROCEDURE OPTIONS(MAIN);
    DECLARE(VOTE,RIGHT,LEFT,MIDDLE,COUNT)FIXED;
    RIGHT=0;
    LEFT=0;
    MIDDLE=0;
    GET LIST(VOTE);
    DO WHILE(VOTE¬=-1);
       IF VOTE=1 THEN
          RIGHT=RIGHT+1;
       ELSE
          IF VOTE=2 THEN
             LEFT=LEFT+1;
          ELSE
             IF VOTE=3 THEN
                MIDDLE=MIDDLE+1;
       GET LIST(VOTE);
       END;
    COUNT=RIGHT+LEFT+MIDDLE;
    PUT LIST('RIGHT COUNT','LEFT COUNT','MIDDLE COUNT','TOTAL COUNT');
    PUT SKIP LIST(RIGHT,LEFT,MIDDLE,COUNT);
    END;
$DATA
(vote cards with either 1, or 2, or 3 on them)
-1 (dummy card for end-of-file)
```

In this program we have two different things happening. One
is a three-way branch, which is accomplished by a series of three
IF THEN statements, one for each value of VOTE. This means that
an invalid vote does not get counted anywhere. If we wanted
notification that there was an invalid vote we could have
inserted the following in the program right before GET
LIST(VOTE);

   ELSE PUT SKIP LIST('INVALID VOTE',VOTE);

This then makes it a four-way branch.

The minimum program needed for a three-way branch would be
one IF...THEN...ELSE statement nested inside another:

```
IF VOTE=1 THEN
   RIGHT=RIGHT+1;
ELSE
   IF VOTE=2 THEN
      LEFT=LEFT+1;
   ELSE
      MIDDLE=MIDDLE+1;
```

If there are any invalid votes, they are given to the MIDDLE party.

There is no fixed way of doing the job. Here is another try at it.

```
IF VOTE<3 THEN
   IF VOTE<2 THEN
      RIGHT=RIGHT+1;
   ELSE
      LEFT=LEFT+1;
ELSE
   MIDDLE=MIDDLE+1;
```

Again we have nesting of two IF...THEN...ELSE statements, but in a different sequence. Notice that we put the ELSE that goes with an IF vertically beneath it so that the nesting of the statements is clear.

EXAMPLE IF STATEMENTS

We will now give a series of examples of IF statements which might be used in a government program for handling income tax. Let us suppose that the program is to write notices to people telling them whether they owe tax or they are to receive a tax refund. The amount of tax is calculated and then the following is executed.

```
IF TAX > 0 THEN
   PUT LIST('TAX DUE IS',TAX,'DOLLARS');
ELSE
   PUT LIST('REFUND IS',-TAX,'DOLLARS');
```

Notice that it was necessary to change the sign of "tax" when printing the refund.

Unfortunately, our program, like too many programs, is not quite right. If the calculated tax is exactly zero, then the program will print REFUND IS 0 DOLLARS. We could fix this problem by the following.

```
IF TAX > 0 THEN
   PUT LIST('TAX DUE IS',TAX,'DOLLARS');
ELSE
   IF TAX = 0 THEN
      PUT LIST('YOU OWE NOTHING');
   ELSE
      PUT LIST('REFUND IS',-TAX,'DOLLARS');
```

We have used a <u>nested</u> IF statement to solve the problem, that is,
an IF statement which is inside an IF statement. In general, we
can nest any kind of statement inside an IF statement including
assignment statements, GET LIST and PUT LIST statements, DO
statements and IF statements.

   Now suppose that when tax is due we wish to tell the taxpayer
where to send his check. We can expand the program as follows:

```
IF TAX > 0 THEN
   DO;
      PUT LIST('TAX DUE IS',TAX,'DOLLARS');
      PUT SKIP LIST('SEND CHECK TO DISTRICT OFFICE');
      END;
ELSE
   IF TAX = 0 THEN
      PUT LIST('YOU OWE NOTHING');
   ELSE
      PUT LIST('REFUND IS',-TAX,'DOLLARS');
```

Since we wanted more than one statement to be executed when TAX >
0 we had to group them together using the construct:

```
        DO;...END;
```

This construct acts like a set of parentheses and makes our two
statements appear as one statement. This construct is <u>not</u> a
loop; its only purpose is to group statements which follow THEN
or ELSE in an IF statement.

   We will now change the order of tests and slightly change the
problem in order to illustrate another point. Suppose that when
the "tax" is zero, we do not want to print anything. We can
start out by checking for zero, and if we do not find zero, we
can print an appropriate "tax due" or "refund" message.

```
IF TAX ¬= 0 THEN
   IF TAX > 0 THEN
      PUT LIST('TAX DUE IS',TAX,'DOLLARS');
   ELSE
      PUT LIST('REFUND IS',-TAX,'DOLLARS');
```

Since we did not want to print anything when the tax is zero, we
omitted the ELSE part of the initial IF statement.   There is a
possible point of confusion in that we must be sure that the
computer will consider the single ELSE clause to be part of the

second IF. There is no difficulty, because the rule here is that
an ELSE clause is assumed to be associated with the nearest
preceding IF. Thus, the message about the refund is printed when
the condition TAX > 0 is found to be false. To help people
understand our program, we have indented the ELSE clause to the
level of its corresponding IF statement. However, this
indentation is ignored by the computer.

PARAGRAPHING THE PROGRAM

In order to follow the structure of the nesting of
IF...THEN...ELSE statements we have indented the program so that
the IF and ELSE that belong to each other are lined up
vertically. The statements following the THEN and the ELSE are
indented. This is called paragraphing the program, and is
analogous to the way we indent paragraphs of prose to indicate
grouping of thoughts. Paragraphing makes a valuable contribution
to understandability and is a must in structured programming.

Also, if you examine the programs with DO loops you will see
that the loop has been indented starting right after the DO and
going down to the END that belongs with the DO.

In the next chapter we will be examining the situation where
DO loops are nested, and then we will use two levels of
indentation.

There are no set rules about how much indentation you should
use or exactly how, for instance, an IF...THEN...ELSE statement
should be indented; but it is clear that being systematic is an
enormous help. When you are writing programs, decide how many
blanks you will use for each level of indentation and stick to
this.

Compilers like the SP/k compiler paragraph a program
automatically so that the listing is paragraphed even though the
original cards are not prepared with indentations.

CHAPTER 5 SUMMARY

In this chapter we introduced statements which allow for (a)
repetition of statements and (b) selection between different
possibilities. We introduced conditions which are used to
terminate the repetition of statements and to choose between
different possibilities. Comparisons and logical operators are
used in specifying conditions. The following important terms
were discussed in this chapter.

Loop (or DO loop) - a programming language construct which causes
    repeated execution of statements. In SP/k, loops are either
    counted DO loops or DO WHILE loops.

Counted DO loop - has the following form:

```
                        exp        exp        exp
        DO variable = start TO limit [BY step];
           statements
           END;
```

The variable, called the counting variable, must have the
FIXED attribute. The square brackets are shown around BY
step to indicate that it can be omitted. If it is omitted,
BY 1 is assumed. Each of "start," "limit" and "step" can be
expressions; these expressions are evaluated before the
repetition starts and are not affected by the statements
inside the loop.

DO WHILE loop - has the following form:

```
        DO WHILE(condition);
           statements
           END;
```

The condition is tested at the beginning of each pass through
the loop. If it is found to be true, the statements inside
the loop are executed and then the condition is again tested.
When the condition finally is found to be false, control is
passed to the statement which follows the END. Any variables
which appear in the condition must be given values before the
loop begins. Notice that the condition is in parentheses.

Loop body - the statements that appear inside a loop.

Comparisons - used in conditions. For example, comparisons can
   be used in a condition to determine how many times to execute
   a loop body. The following are used to specify comparisons.

```
        <   less than
        >   greater than
        <=  less than or equal
        >=  greater than or equal
        =   equal
        ¬=  not equal
```

Notice that the equal sign = is used both for testing for
equality and for assigning values, but that there is no
relationship between the two uses. Whether = means
comparison or assignment depends on where it appears in the
program.

Conditions - are either true or false. Conditions can be made up
   of comparisons and the following three logical operators.

```
        &   and
        |   or
        ¬   not
```

End-of-file (or end-of-data) detection - When a loop is reading a series of data items, it must determine when the last data item has been read. This can be accomplished by first reading in the number of items to be read and then counting the items in the series as they are read. It can also be accomplished by following the last data item by a special dummy card which contains special, or dummy data. The program knows to stop when it reads the dummy data.

IF statement - has the following form:

        IF condition THEN
           statement
        [ELSE
           statement]

The square brackets are shown around the ELSE clause to show that it can be omitted. If the condition is true, the first statement is executed. If the condition is false, the second statement, if present, is executed. In either case, control then goes to next statement after the ELSE clause - or if the ELSE clause is omitted, to the next statement after the THEN clause. Any statement, including another IF statement, can appear as a part of an IF statement.

Paragraphing - indenting a program so that its structure is easily seen by people. The statements inside loops and inside IF statements are indented to make the overall program organization obvious. The computer ignores paragraphing when translating and executing programs.

CHAPTER 5 EXERCISES

1. Suppose I and J are variables with values 6 and 12. Which of the following conditions are true?

     (a) 2*I<=J
     (b) 2*I-1<J
     (c) I<=6&J<=6
     (d) I<=6|J<=6
     (e) I>0&I<=10
     (f) I<=12|J<=12
     (g) I>25|(I<50&J<50)
     (h) I¬=4&I¬=5
     (i) I<4|I>5
     (j) ¬(I>6)

2. The following program predicts the population of a family of wallalumps over a 2-year period, based on the assumption of an initial population of 2 and a doubling of population each 2 months. What does the program print?

```
EXPLODE:PROCEDURE OPTIONS(MAIN);
   DECLARE(MONTH,POPULATION)FIXED;
   POPULATION=2;
   PUT SKIP LIST('MONTH','POPULATION');
   DO MONTH=0 TO 24 BY 2;
      PUT SKIP LIST(MONTH,POPULATION);
      POPULATION=2*POPULATION;
      END;
   END;
```

3. Suppose you have hidden away 50 dollars to be used for some
future emergency. Assuming an inflation rate of 12 per cent per
year, write a program to compute how much money, to the nearest
dollar, you would need at the end of each of the next 15 years to
be equivalent to the buying power of 50 dollars at the time you
hid it.

4. Trace the following program. That is, give the values of the
variables together with any output after the execution of each
statement.

```
       $JOB ID='F.G.WONG'
   1   CLASS:PROCEDURE OPTIONS(MAIN);
   2      DECLARE(NUMBER,GRADE,SUM)FIXED;
   3      SUM=0;
   4      GET LIST(GRADE);
   5      NUMBER=0;
   6      DO WHILE(GRADE¬=-1);
   7         IF GRADE>=0 & GRADE<=100 THEN
   8            DO;
   9               SUM=SUM+GRADE;
  10               NUMBER=NUMBER+1;
  11               END;
  12         ELSE
  13            PUT SKIP LIST('**ERROR:GRADE=',GRADE);
  14         GET LIST(GRADE);
  15         END;
  16      PUT SKIP LIST('AVERAGE IS',(1E0*SUM)/NUMBER);
  17      END;
       $DATA
        95  110  85  -1  75
```

5. Write a program that reads the following data cards and
calculates the average of (a) each of the two columns of data,
and (b) each row of the data. You should either precede the data
with a number giving the count of the following data cards or add
a dummy card following these data cards.

92	88
75	62
81	75
80	80
55	60
64	60
81	80

6. Write a program which reads in a sequence of grades (0 to 100) and prints out the average grade (rounded to the nearest whole number), the number of grades and the number of failing grades (failing is less than 50). Assume that a "dummy" grade of 999 will follow the last grade. See that your output is clearly labelled. Answer the following questions:

(a) What will happen if the grade 74 is mispunched as 7 4?

(b) What will happen if the dummy grade 999 is left off? (You can try this.)

(c) What will your program do if there are no grades, i.e., if 999 is the only data item?

(d) What will happen if the two grades 62 and 93 are mispunched as 6293?

Test your program using the following data:

```
85   74   44   62   93
41   69   73  999
```

7. Write a program which determines the unit price (cents per ounce) of different boxes of laundry soap. Round the unit price to the nearest penny. Each box will be described by a card of the form:

pounds	ounces	price in cents
5	0	125

This box of soap has a rounded unit price of 2 cents per ounce. Make up about 10 data cards describing soap boxes; if you like, use real examples from a supermarket. You are to precede these cards with one data card containing a single integer giving the number of soap box cards. Do not use a dummy card to mark the end of the data. Print a nicely labelled table giving weights, prices in cents and unit costs. Answer the following questions:

(a) What would your program do if the above example data card were mispunched as

```
50   125
```

(b) Would it be possible to make your program "smart enough" to detect some kinds of mispunched data? How or why not?

CHAPTER 6

STRUCTURING CONTROL FLOW

In the last chapter we introduced the two kinds of statements that cause an alteration from the linear flow of control in a program. One type caused looping, the counted DO or the DO WHILE; the other caused branching, or selective execution, the IF...THEN...ELSE. Learning to handle these two kinds of instructions is absolutely essential to programming. And learning to handle them in a systematic way is essential to structured programming.

BASIC STRUCTURE OF DO LOOPS

It is hard to appreciate, when you first learn a concept like loops, that all loops are basically the same. They consist of a sequence of statements in the program that:

1. initialize the values of certain variables that are to be used in the loop. These consist of assigning values to

   (a) variables that appear in the condition of a DO WHILE

   (b) variables that appear in the body of the loop on the right-hand side of assignment statements.

2. indicate that a loop is to commence and give the information that is to control the number of repetitions. This is the DO itself. Its form is

   DO control-phrase

The control-phrase may be of two types:

   (a) for the counted DO, it is, for example

        I=1 TO 20 BY 1

    (b) for the conditional DO, it is, for example

        WHILE (I < = 20)

    The condition should contain at least one variable.

3. give the list of statements, called the body of the loop, that
are to be executed each time the loop is repeated. If the loop
is controlled by a conditional DO, then within the body of the
loop there must be some statements that assign new values to the
variables appearing in the condition. Usually there is only one
variable and its value may be changed by either

    (a) an assignment statement or

    (b) a GET LIST statement.

4. indicate the end of the loop. This is the END. At this point
control is returned to the DO.

5. give the next statement to be executed once the looping has
been carried out the required numbers of times. Control goes
from the DO to this statement when

    (a) the condition of the DO WHILE is false or

    (b) the value of the index controlling the counted DO is
    beyond the value indicated after the word TO in the DO.

    It is to be noted very carefully that there is no exit from
the loop, except from the DO itself, and this exit always goes to
the statement immediately after the END. It is never possible to
go somewhere else in a program. In this way we keep track of
control flow and never have the possibility of getting confused
about its path. The complete language PL/1 offers a statement
for altering the path of control called the GO TO statement. It
permits you to send control anywhere in your program. Since
computer scientists came to recognize the importance of proper
structuring in a program, the freedom offered by the GO TO
statement has been recognized as not in keeping with the idea of
structures in control flow. For this reason we will never use
it. It is not a member of any subset of SP/k. If you are using
another compiler such as a PL/1 or a PL/C compiler, you will find
that the GO TO statement is permitted. Even so, you should not
use it.

    For many good programmers it has long become a habit to
restrict the use of the GO TO to that of leaving the body of a DO
loop somewhere in the middle and exiting to the statement
following the END of the loop. We can only exit from the DO
itself. An exit inside the body is usually related to a second
condition. This second condition can be incorporated in the

condition following the DO by having a compound condition. We will look at examples of this later in the chapter.

FLOW CHARTS

A flow chart is a diagram made up of boxes of various shapes, rectangular, circular, diamond and so on, connected by lines with directional arrows on the lines. The boxes contain a description of the statements of a program and the directed lines indicate the flow of control among the statements. The main purpose of drawing a flow chart is to exhibit the flow of control clearly, so that it is evident both to the programmer and to a reader who might want to alter the program.

A method of programming that preceded the present method of structured programming found that drawing a flow chart helped in the programming process. It was suggested that a first step in writing any program was to draw a flow chart. It was a way of controlling complexity.

When we limit ourselves to the two standard forms of altering control flow, the DO loop and the IF...THEN...ELSE, there is little need to draw these flow charts. In a sense, especially if it is properly paragraphed, the program is its own flow chart; it is built of completely standard building blocks.

Perhaps it would be helpful to show what the flow charts of our two basic building blocks would be like in case you wanted to draw a flow chart for your whole program.

The flow chart for an IF...THEN...ELSE statement is shown.

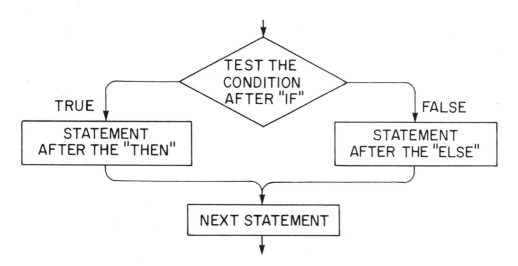

FLOW CHART FOR IF...THEN...ELSE

For the DO WHILE loop that we described, the flow chart would
be as shown. The various phases are numbered.

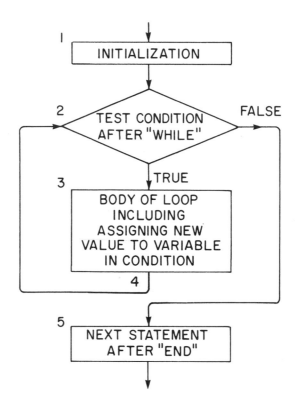

FLOW CHART FOR CONDITIONAL DO

The flow chart for the counted DO would be similar except that
box 2 would initialize the index to its first value, increment it
by the required amount and then test to see if it has gone beyond
the find value.

With these basic diagrams and the ordinary straight line
sequence, flow charts for all SP/k programs can be built. In a
way, because they are so obviously related to the program, they
do not really need to be drawn. Any one of the rectangular boxes
in these diagrams may be replaced by a sequence of rectangular
boxes, or either one of the two basic diagrams themselves.

PROBLEMS WITH LOOPS

Certain errors are very common with loops. With counted
loops the likelihood of errors is much smaller, since the

initialization and alteration of the index are done by the DO itself. You can, however, forget to initialize a variable that is used in the body of the loop. Another problem comes if by chance the index that is used to count the loop is altered in the loop body. The letters I, J, and K are often used as indexes, and you forget to DECLARE them or accidentally use them again. This can happen when one DO loop is nested inside another and the index I is used by mistake for both loops. You might write

```
DO I=1 TO N;
```

and forget to initialize N. You should trace the execution of all loops by hand to see if the first iteration is working alright. Then you should also check the last one.

NESTED LOOPS

We will now look at the more complicated loops. In the following example, subsidiary output has been inserted for testing purposes. You are asked to sum the marks of students in 4 subjects and print these with the average, to the nearest mark. There are a number of cards, one for each student. A card with the total number of students precedes the mark cards.

```
$JOB ID='BOB CHERNIAK'
 CLASS:PROCEDURE OPTIONS(MAIN);
    /* A SAMPLE PROGRAM WITH ERRORS */
    DECLARE(NUMBER_OF_STUDENTS,I,SUM,AVERAGE,
       MARK,STUDENT_NUMBER)FIXED;
    GET LIST(NUMBER_OF_STUDENTS);
    SUM=0;
    DO I=1 TO NUMBER_OF_STUDENTS;
      GET LIST(STUDENT_NUMBER);
      DO I=1 TO 4;
        GET LIST(MARK);
        SUM=SUM+MARK;
        PUT SKIP LIST(MARK,SUM);    ) Test
        END;
      AVERAGE=SUM/4E0+.5E0;
      PUT SKIP LIST(STUDENT_NUMBER,AVERAGE);
      END;
    END;
$DATA
 3
 205    55    60    65    70
 208    83    81    96    90
 209    72    68    78    81
```

In this program there are a number of errors. The program is being tested with the extra printing of

```
PUT SKIP LIST(MARK,SUM);
```

Here is the output produced by the computer in addition to
the usual program listing:

55	55
60	115
65	180
70	250
205	63

What this program demonstrates is the situation of one DO loop
nested inside another. It was intended that the inner DO loop be
repeated 4 times for each time the outer loop is repeated once.
There ought to be 3x4=12 lines of printing, but instead we have 5
lines. The outer loop is being executed only once. The index of
the inner loop should not be the same as the index for the outer
loop.   To fix this error we used DO J=1 TO 4; and declared J.
Also the fact that another error was present was then noticed.
This was that the initialization of SUM=0; belongs to the inner
loop and should be located just prior to the inner loop.   The
card for SUM=0; was moved to follow DO I=1 TO NUMBER_OF_STUDENTS;
and the following printout resulted:

55	55
60	115
65	180
70	250
205	63
83	83
81	164
96	260
90	350
208	88
72	72
68	140
78	218
81	299
209	75

Since we were now satisfied that all was well, we removed the
card with PUT SKIP LIST(MARK,SUM) and ran the program with the
full number of data cards. You will notice that when we have one
DO loop nested inside another we use two levels of indentation to
indicate the control structure. Here is the corrected program.

```
$JOB ID='BOB CHERNIAK'
 CLASS:PROCEDURE OPTIONS(MAIN);
    /* CORRECTED SAMPLE PROGRAM */
    DECLARE(NUMBER_OF_STUDENTS,I,J,SUM,AVERAGE,
       MARK,STUDENT_NUMBER)FIXED;
    GET LIST(NUMBER_OF_STUDENTS);
    DO I=1 TO NUMBER_OF_STUDENTS;
       SUM=0;
       GET LIST(STUDENT_NUMBER);
       DO J=1 TO 4;
          GET LIST(MARK);
          SUM=SUM+MARK;
          END;
       AVERAGE=SUM/4E0+.5E0;
       PUT SKIP LIST(STUDENT_NUMBER,AVERAGE);
       END;
    END;
$DATA
 (data as before)
```

AN EXAMPLE PROGRAM

We will illustrate some details about loops with another program. Like some of our previous examples, this program prints a zigzag. However, our new program is smarter than the old ones in that it can print out different sizes of and numbers of zigs and zags, depending on the input data.

```
$JOB ID='IRA GREENBLATT'
 PICKZIG:PROCEDURE OPTIONS(MAIN);
    DECLARE(MAJOR,MINOR)FIXED;
    DECLARE(HOW_MANY,HOW_BIG)FIXED;
    GET LIST(HOW_MANY,HOW_BIG);
    DO MAJOR=1 TO HOW_MANY;
       PUT SKIP LIST('****');
       DO MINOR=1 TO HOW_BIG;
          PUT SKIP LIST('*');
          END;
       PUT SKIP LIST('****');
       DO MINOR=1 TO HOW_BIG;
          PUT SKIP LIST('   *');
          END;
       END;
    END;
$DATA
 3   2
```

This program, given the data values 3 and 2, prints the following pattern. We have shown in parentheses values of MAJOR and MINOR during the printing of each of the single star lines.

```
                                         (MAJOR,MINOR)
****
*                                            (1,1)
*                                            (1,2)
****
    *                                        (1,1)
    *                                        (1,2)
****
*                                            (2,1)
*                                            (2,2)
****
    *                                        (2,1)
    *                                        (2,2)
****
*                                            (3,1)
*                                            (3,2)
****
    *                                        (3,1)
    *                                        (3,2)
```

The first data value, 3, caused the sub-pattern

```
        ****
        *
        *
        ****
            *
            *
```

to be printed three times. The second data value, 2, was used in
determining the height of this sub-pattern.

    As you can see in the program, there are two separate loops
inside the main DO loop. Both of these loops use the variable
MINOR as a counting variable. There is no difficulty using MINOR
in this way. Each time one of these two loops is entered, MINOR
is set back to have the value 1.

    Our program has a number of ENDs in it. It has one END for
each DO loop plus one END to go with

    PICKZIG:PROCEDURE OPTIONS(MAIN);

Each of these ENDs can be thought of as a right parenthesis; we
can consider that PROCEDURE OPTIONS(MAIN) and DO act like left
parentheses which must be matched to ENDs. When you are writing
a program, you must see that an appropriate END is supplied for
each DO loop as well as for the entire program.

We can change the pattern printed by changing the data card. For example, the following pattern is printed for data values 1 and 1.

	(MAJOR,MINOR)
****	
*	(1,1)
****	
*	(1,1)

In this case, the loops are each executed only once.

We can shrink the pattern down to nothing at all by using the data values 0 and 1. When the first data value is zero, then the limit value HOW_MANY is also zero and is less than MAJOR'S starting value 1. As a result, the main loop is executed zero times. Since the main loop is not executed, the second data value, 1, has no effect. We could supply data values 0 and 2 instead of 0 and 1 and would still get the same pattern, namely, no pattern at all.

Now let us switch things around so the second data value is zero, but the first is not. For data values 2 and 0, the pattern becomes

```
****
****
****
****
```

In this case the main loop is executed twice, but the two inside loops were each executed zero times.

The data values were used by this program to determine the pattern to print. You could write other programs which print different pictures for different data. For example, your program could print a face which is smiling or frowning, or bald or frizzy, depending on the data.

DO LOOPS WITH MULTIPLE CONDITIONS

Sometimes we must terminate a loop if something happens that is unusual. One of the conditions controlling the loop is the standard one; the other is the unusual one. All loops with double-headed conditions must be DO WHILE loops, since the counted loop does not allow for the possibility of a second condition. We have seen that compound conditions can be formed from two or more simple conditions using the & (and) and | (or) operators.

As an example, we will write a program to look for a certain number in a list of numbers on cards. If you find it in the list, print the position it occupies in the list; if it is not in the list, print NOT IN LIST. The list will be positive integers terminated by an end-of-file marker -1.

```
$JOB ID='MARY SEEDHOUSE'
 HUNT:PROCEDURE OPTIONS(MAIN);
    DECLARE(NUMBER,LIST_NO,I)FIXED;
    GET LIST(NUMBER);
    GET LIST(LIST_NO);
    I=1;
    DO WHILE(LIST_NO¬=NUMBER & LIST_NO¬= -1);
       I=I+1;
       GET LIST(LIST_NO);
       END;
    IF LIST_NO=NUMBER THEN
       PUT LIST('I=',I);
    ELSE
       PUT LIST('NOT IN LIST');
    END;
$DATA
 35
 12    16    25    35    40
 51   -1
```

The output for the program with this data is

        I=   4

Notice that in the body of the loop the variable LIST_NO in the condition can be changed by the GET LIST(LIST_NO) statement; it is initialized outside the loop. Since an index I is required to give the position of the number in the list, it must be incremented in the statement I=I+1 and initialized to 1 outside the loop.

IF STATEMENTS WITH MULTIPLE CONDITIONS

Just as DO WHILE can have multiple conditions, so also can IF statements. These can be used very effectively to avoid nesting of IF statements. Suppose you want to count people in a list who fall into a particular age group, say 18-65, as ADULTS. The following program will count the number in the category ADULT in the list. The list of ages is terminated by a -1.

```
$JOB ID='ANGIE BLONSKI'
 WORKERS:PROCEDURE OPTIONS(MAIN);
    DECLARE(ADULT,AGE)FIXED;
    GET LIST(AGE);
    ADULT=0;
    DO WHILE(AGE ¬= -1);
       IF(AGE>=18&AGE<=65) THEN
          ADULT=ADULT+1;
       GET LIST(AGE);
       END;
    PUT LIST('NUMBER OF ADULTS=',ADULT);
    END;
$DATA
 16 25 31 12 28 69 -1
```

The output is NUMBER OF ADULTS= 3. The IF with the compound condition could have been replaced by the more awkward construction with a nested IF statement:

```
IF AGE>=18 THEN
   IF AGE<=65 THEN
      ADULT=ADULT+1;
```

but this is not advisable.

CHAPTER 6 SUMMARY

In this chapter we have taken a closer look at the DO and IF constructs. We discussed flow charts and the GO TO statement as they relate to the SP/k subset of PL/1. We presented more complex examples of loops and conditions. The following important terms were discussed.

Flow chart - a graphic representation of a program. A flow chart consists of boxes of various shapes interconnected by arrows indicating flow of control. SP/k programs can be represented by flow charts.

Exit from a loop - means stopping the execution of a loop. Exit from a DO WHILE loop occurs where the loop's condition is found to be false.

GO TO statement (not in SP/k) - transfers control to another part of a program. The GO TO statement is available in full PL/1 and is sometimes used to exit from a loop by transferring control to the statement following the loop. Careless use of GO TO statements leads to complex program structures which are difficult to understand and to make correct.

Nested statements - means statements inside statements. For example, DO loops can be nested inside DO loops.

Multiple conditions - conditions which use the & (and) or | (or)
  logical operators.

CHAPTER 6 EXERCISES

  We will base all the exercises for this chapter on the same
problem, which we now describe. A meteorologist keeps records of
the weather for each month as a deck of punched cards. The first
card of the deck gives the number of days of the month.

  The following cards give the rainfall, low temperature, high
temperature and pollution count for each day of the month. For
example, the data for a month could be as follows:

```
       31 rain low high  pollution
        0    33   37    3
       1.2   34   39    3
        0    35   40    .5
        0    34   38    2
       etc.
```

Each of the following exercises requires writing a program which
reads one month's weather and answers some questions about the
month's weather. To make things easier for you, answers for the
first two exercises are given.

1. Find the first rainy day of the month. (The following
program finds the required day and is a solution for this
exercise.)

```
WETDAY:PROCEDURE OPTIONS(MAIN);
   DECLARE(RAIN,LOW,HIGH,POLLUTION)FLOAT;
   DECLARE(DAY,MONTH_LENGTH)FIXED;
   GET LIST(MONTH_LENGTH);
   DAY=0;
   RAIN=0;
   DO WHILE(RAIN=0&DAY<MONTH_LENGTH);
      GET LIST(RAIN,LOW,HIGH,POLLUTION);
      DAY=DAY+1;
      END;
   IF RAIN>0 THEN
      PUT LIST('DAY',DAY,'WAS RAINY');
   ELSE
      PUT LIST('NO RAINY DAYS');
   END;
```

2. See if the data cards for the days of the month are
reasonable. Verify that the rainfall does not exceed 100 and is
not negative. Verify that the temperature lies between -100 and
200 and that the high is at least as large as the low. Verify
that the pollution count is neither above 25 nor below zero.

(The following program validates the month's data and is a solution for this exercise.)

```
VERIFY:PROCEDURE OPTIONS(MAIN);
   DECLARE(RAIN,LOW,HIGH,POLLUTION)FLOAT;
   DECLARE(DAY,MONTH_LENGTH)FIXED;
   GET LIST(MONTH_LENGTH);
   DO DAY=1 TO MONTH_LENGTH;
      GET LIST(RAIN,LOW,HIGH,POLLUTION);
      IF RAIN<0|RAIN>100 THEN
         PUT SKIP LIST('DAY',DAY,'HAS WRONG RAIN:',RAIN);
      IF LOW<-100|LOW>HIGH|HIGH>200 THEN
         PUT SKIP LIST('DAY',DAY,
            'HAS WRONG TEMPERATURES:',LOW,HIGH);
      IF POLLUTION<0|POLLUTION>25 THEN
         PUT SKIP LIST('DAY',DAY,
            'HAS WRONG POLLUTION:',POLLUTION);
      END;
   END;
```

3. What was the warmest day of the month, based on the high?

4. What was the first rainy day having a high temperature above 38?

5. What were the days of the month with more than a 5-degree difference between the high and low temperatures?

6. What were the two warmest days of the month?

7. Did the pollution count ever exceed 5 on a day when the temperature stayed above 35?

8. What three consecutive days had the most total rainfall?

9. Was it true that every rainless day following a rainy day had a lower pollution count than the rainy day?

10. Using the first 10 days' data, "predict" the weather for the 11th day. Compare (either by hand or within the program) the prediction with the data for the 11th day.

CHAPTER 7

SP/4: ALPHABETIC INFORMATION HANDLING

We have said that computers can handle alphabetic information as well as perform numerical calculations. But most of the emphasis so far, except for labeling our tables of numerical output, has had very little to do with alphabetic data handling. It is true that we have been dealing with words, like identifiers, but these have been in the PL/1 programs rather than being handled by them as data. We have, in fact, never had anything but numbers, either float or fixed, on the data cards following the $DATA control card. In this chapter we will learn how to read in alphabetic data from data cards, how to move it from one place to another in the memory of the computer, how to join different pieces of information together, and how to separate out a part of a large piece of information.

CHARACTER STRINGS

The term "alphabetic information" that we used in the last section is really not general enough to describe what we will learn to handle in this subset of PL/1. It is true that we will be able to handle what you normally mean by alphabetic information, things like people's names

JENNIFER JOHNSTON

but we also want to handle things like street addresses. For example, an address like

2156 CYPRESS AVENUE

includes digits as well as letters of the alphabet. This kind of information we call alphanumeric or alphameric for short. But that is not all; we want to handle any kind of English text with words, numbers, and punctuation marks, like commas, semicolons, and question marks.

THIS TEXT CONTAINS 7 WORDS; DOESN'T IT?

We have defined a word as being a string of one or more characters preceded and followed by a blank or a punctuation mark, other than an apostrophe. This definition makes 7 a word.

The information we want to handle is any string of characters that may be letters, digits, punctuations marks or blanks. We tend to think of a blank as being not a character, but a string of blanks is quite different from a string with no characters at all. We call the special string with no characters at all a null string. We often write b for the blank character so that you can count how many blank characters are in a string.

HEREbISbAbCHARACTERbSTRINGbSHOWINGbTHEbBLANKSbEXPLICITLY.

In Chapter 3 we introduced the characters in the PL/1 language. In that listing there are more than we have referred to so far in this chapter. The list of special characters includes symbols we need for arithmetic operations +, -, /, *, as well as for making comparisons in logical conditions >, <, ¬, =, or for combining logical conditions into compound conditions &, |. Then often we used parentheses, not to mention the characters like $, #, ∂, classified as letters in PL/1, or % and _, the break character.

One reason we want to be able to handle strings of any of these characters is to be able to work with PL/1 programs themselves as data. This is the kind of job a compiler must do, and a programming language like PL/1 should be suitable for writing a compiler program.

CHARACTER STRING VARIABLES

Just as we had to set aside space in the computer memory for storing fixed or float numbers, we must have space for storing strings of characters. Character strings are much more changeable than numbers in that they can contain values with different lengths. For example, some people's names have many characters; others' have few.

We might declare a character string variable named TEXT by the declaration

DECLARE(TEXT)CHARACTER(50)VARYING;

We know it is a character string variable because of the keyword CHARACTER. The amount of memory reserved for the variable TEXT is enough for a maximum of 50 character spaces. This will be a number of machine words as each character requires about 6 bits

to represent it. The word <u>VARYING</u> in the declaration indicates
that the character string stored in the variable might not be as
long as 50 characters. The length of the string will vary
between zero characters, for the null string, and 50 characters,
which is the maximum available space for this string.

READING AND PRINTING STRINGS

We learned in the first subset how to print a string of
characters that was in the form of a literal such as 'COST=', and
we have been using this for printing labels on our numeric
output. We just put the literal, which is a string of characters
enclosed in single quotes, in the list of a PUT LIST statement.
The string would be printed, left-justified in the field and with
the quotation marks removed. If the length of the string exceeds
the field size it spills over into the next field.

Now that we can have character string variables we can read
information into them from cards and print them out. For
example, this program reads and prints character strings.

```
$JOB ID='STEVE POZGAJ'
 IN_OUT:PROCEDURE OPTIONS(MAIN);
    DECLARE(TEXT)CHARACTER(78)VARYING;
    GET LIST(TEXT);
    PUT LIST(TEXT);
    END;
$DATA
 'HERE IS A SAMPLE TEXT'
```

The output printing would be

```
HERE IS A SAMPLE TEXT
```

Notice that the input data must have quotes around the character
string and that these quotes are not printed since they are not
part of the string. The largest string that can be put on an 80-
column card is 78 characters, since the quotation marks take two
columns. It is best to limit variables that are input to those
that will fit on to a card. On output the size is limited by the
length of a print line. Variables that go from card to card or
line to line are difficult to manage. Some compilers limit
string variables to being at most 127 characters.

Character string variables may also be given values in an
assignment statement. In the example

```
DECLARE(NAME)CHARACTER(10)VARYING;
NAME='CORLEY PHILLIPS';
PUT LIST(NAME);
```

the character string to be assigned to NAME has more characters
than the maximum 10 that are declared. This means that the

leftmost 10 characters are stored in NAME and the rest are lost.
The output would be

    CORLEY PHI

This is a string of length 10. Remember the blank is a
character.

JOINING STRINGS TOGETHER

    Character strings may be read in, stored, and printed out.
But we can do more than that. We can perform certain operations
on them.

    The first of these operations is to join two strings together
to make one longer string. This operation is called
concatenation and the operator is two vertical lines with no
space between them ||. (The single vertical line is the one we
use for the logical or operation.) Here is an example of
concatenation:

```
DECLARE(LINE)CHARACTER(20)VARYING;
LINE='UP'||'STAIRS';
PUT LIST(LINE);
```

The output is UPSTAIRS; the two strings have been joined into
one.

    Here is a program using concatenation that has a loop in it:

```
$JOB  ID='PAUL WALSH'
 BUILD:PROCEDURE OPTIONS(MAIN);
    DECLARE(STARS)CHARACTER(25)VARYING;
    DECLARE(I)FIXED;
    STARS='';
    DO I=1 TO 25;
       STARS=STARS||'*';
       PUT SKIP LIST(STARS);
       END;
    END;
$DATA
```

The output will be

```
*
**
***
****
```
etc., until we have a line of 25 asterisks.

In the example the variable STARS is initialized to the null
string which is written as ''. Each time the loop is executed,

an asterisk is concatenated on to the string and the resulting
string printed.

SELECTING PARTS OF STRINGS

In addition to joining strings together, we can also take
them apart by selecting parts of strings. We call a part of a
string a substring. To do this operation we use what is called a
built-in function named SUBSTR, which is short for substring. To
obtain a substring of a string we write

SUBSTR (string,starting position,length of substring)

For example

SUBSTR('MILLION',2,3)

is ILL. We start at the second character and the substring is to
be 3 characters long. We have an alternate form which has only
two items in the parentheses. For example

SUBSTR('MILLION',4)

is LION. Here the third item in parentheses is missing; the
substring goes from the fourth character to the end of the
string. This can be useful when we want to remove a letter from
the beginning of a word but do not know how long the word is.

The following program will count the number of characters in
a string that precede a certain character. We will suppose that
the certain character is a blank. This is useful for reading
words in a sentence. We will input a word followed by a blank as
it would appear in a sentence and let the program count the
number of letters in it.

```
$JOB ID='K.C. SMITH'
 MEASURE:PROCEDURE OPTIONS(MAIN);
    DECLARE(WORD)CHARACTER(30)VARYING;
    DECLARE(COUNT)FIXED;
    GET LIST(WORD);
    PUT LIST(WORD);
    COUNT=1;
    DO WHILE(SUBSTR(WORD,COUNT,1)¬=' ');
       COUNT=COUNT+1;
       END;
    PUT LIST('NUMBER OF LETTERS=',COUNT-1);
    END;
$DATA
 'PHILOSOPHYb'
```

The output will be

PHILOSOPHY   NUMBER OF LETTERS=   10

In the next section we will see that there is a built-in function
for finding the length of strings.

FINDING THE LENGTH OF A STRING

We can determine how long a string is by using the built-in
function LENGTH. For example

```
DECLARE(STRING)CHARACTER(10)VARYING;
STRING='SENSATIONAL';
PUT LIST(LENGTH(STRING));
STRING='STOP';
PUT LIST(LENGTH(STRING));
END;
```

The output for this is

    10   4

Are you surprised? Notice that the string SENSATIONAL has 11
characters but when assigned to STRING it will be chopped to 10,
the last one being dropped.

The LENGTH built-in function is useful in chopping letters
off the end of words. This program will print the last letters
of a series of 4 words.

```
$JOB  ID='DON IVEY'
 ENDING:PROCEDURE OPTIONS(MAIN);
    DECLARE(WORD)CHARACTER(20)VARYING;
    DECLARE(I)FIXED;
    DO I=1 TO 4;
        GET LIST(WORD);
        PUT SKIP LIST(WORD,SUBSTR(WORD,LENGTH(WORD)));
        END;
    END;
$DATA
 'SPLASH'
 'SICK'
 'SO'
 'SLOPPY'
```

The output will be

```
SPLASH     H
SICK       K
SO         O
SLOPPY     Y
```

AN EXAMPLE PROGRAM

We will now give a program which conjugates French verbs. It cannot conjugate every French verb. The program works only for regular verbs of the so-called ER variety. But you do not need to know any French to follow this example. If the program reads the verb "parler" which means "to speak", then it prints the following.

```
JE PARLE        (I speak)
TU PARLES       (you speak)
IL PARLE        (he speaks)
NOUS PARLONS    (we speak)
VOUS PARLEZ     (you speak)
ILS PARLENT     (they speak)
```

The equivalent English is shown in parentheses at the right. Here is the complete job:

```
$JOB ID='HENRI ARNAUD'
 BONJOUR:PROCEDURE OPTIONS(MAIN);
    DECLARE(INFINITIVE,ROOT)CHARACTER(30)VARYING;
    GET LIST(INFINITIVE);
    /* THE INFINITIVE IS ASSUMED TO END IN 'ER' */
    /* THE ROOT IS THE INFINITIVE LESS THE 'ER' */
    ROOT=SUBSTR(INFINITIVE,1,LENGTH(INFINITIVE)-2);
    /* IF THE INFINITIVE IS 'PARLER' THEN THE ROOT IS 'PARL' */
    PUT SKIP LIST('JE '||ROOT||'E');
    PUT SKIP LIST('TU '||ROOT||'ES');
    PUT SKIP LIST('IL '||ROOT||'E');
    PUT SKIP LIST('NOUS '||ROOT||'ONS');
    PUT SKIP LIST('VOUS '||ROOT||'EZ');
    PUT SKIP LIST('ILS '||ROOT||'ENT');
    END;
$DATA
 'PARLER'
```

The most difficult part of this program is the determination of the root of the verb given its infinitive. The root is identical to the infinitive except that the final 'ER' of the infinitive is removed. This means that the root is the substring of the infinitive starting from the first character and continuing through the third to last character of the infinitive. Writing this in PL/1, it comes out as

```
ROOT=SUBSTR(INFINITIVE,1,LENGTH(INFINITIVE)-2);
```

Although our program cannot conjugate all French verbs, it can handle a number of common ones such as donner (to give), marcher (to walk), crier (to cry), demander (to ask), compter (to count) and rouler (to roll).

COMPARISON OF STRINGS FOR RECOGNITION

We need to be able to compare one string with another for two purposes. One purpose is for the recognition of strings. In this we are concerned with whether two strings are the same or not. String comparisons are made in logical conditions since their result is either true or false; the strings are the same or they are not. Here is a program that reads and prints words until it reaches the word STOP:

```
$JOB ID='JOHN GUTTAG'
 READING:PROCEDURE OPTIONS(MAIN);
    DECLARE(WORD)CHARACTER(10)VARYING;
    DECLARE(COUNT)FIXED;
    COUNT=0;
    GET LIST(WORD);
    DO WHILE(WORD¬='STOP');
       PUT LIST(WORD);
       GET LIST(WORD);
       COUNT=COUNT+1;
       END;
    PUT SKIP LIST(COUNT);
    END;
$DATA
 'SOUP' 'SLOW' 'SIP' 'STOP' 'SIT'
```

The output will be

```
 SOUP    SLOW    SIP
    3
```

The logical condition (WORD¬='STOP') controls the DO WHILE. It is true until the WORD read is STOP. If there were no word STOP in the program the computer would inform you of an end-of-file error, as you would just run off the end of the list of words.

SEQUENCING STRINGS

The other use of string comparisons is to sequence strings, to put them in order. Usually we speak of alphabetic order for alphabetic strings.

ABCDEFGHIJKLMNOPQRSTUVWXYZ

The alphabet and digits have the normal order among themselves: 0 comes before 9, A comes before Z. Blanks have the lowest value. The operators > and < are used to compare the strings. If the two strings being compared are of unequal lengths, blanks are added on the right of the shorter string to make them equal in length. The following comparisons are labeled as true or false:

Comparison	Value
('JOHN' > 'JIM')	true
('JOHN' < 'JOHNSTON')	true
(' A' <'A')	true because blank<A
('MCLEOD' >'MACKAY')	true
('22' >'156')	true because 2>1

The following program reads in 10 names and prints out the one
that is the last alphabetically.

```
$JOB  ID='LAURIE JOHNSTON'
 LAST:PROCEDURE OPTIONS(MAIN);
    DECLARE(NAME,FINAL)CHARACTER(15)VARYING;
    DECLARE(I)FIXED;
    FINAL='AAAAA';
    DO I=1 TO 10;
       GET LIST(NAME);
       IF(NAME>FINAL) THEN
         FINAL=NAME;
       END;
    PUT LIST(FINAL);
    END;
$DATA
 'HUME' 'HOLT' 'HULL' 'SEVCIK' 'PHILLIPS' 'WORTMAN'
 'HORNING' 'TSICHRITZIS' 'GOTLIEB' 'SWENSON'
```

This program will output

    WORTMAN

ANOTHER EXAMPLE PROGRAM

We will now give a program which uses character string
variables in producing a "personalized" fairy tale. The program
first reads in the name of a child and the name of a friend of
the child. The program then writes a story about the child and
his friend. The text of the story is provided on data cards.
The program simply reads and prints the story. Whenever the
program reads 'CHILD' it substitutes the child's name and when it
reads 'FRIEND', it substitutes the friend's name. In this
example, the fairy tale has only been started. You can supply
your own plot by providing more data.

```
$JOB ID='RIC HOLT'
 STORY:PROCEDURE OPTIONS(MAIN);
    DECLARE(NAME_OF_CHILD)CHARACTER(20)VARYING;
    DECLARE(NAME_OF_FRIEND)CHARACTER(20)VARYING;
    DECLARE(LINE,TEXT)CHARACTER(80)VARYING;
    GET LIST(NAME_OF_CHILD,NAME_OF_FRIEND);
    LINE='';
    GET LIST(TEXT);
    DO WHILE(TEXT¬='END');
       IF TEXT='CHILD' THEN
          TEXT=NAME_OF_CHILD;
       IF TEXT='FRIEND' THEN
          TEXT=NAME_OF_FRIEND;
       LINE=LINE||TEXT;
       IF LENGTH(LINE)>42 THEN
          DO;
             PUT SKIP LIST(LINE);
             LINE='';
             END;
       GET LIST(TEXT);
       END;
    PUT SKIP LIST(LINE);
    END;
$DATA
    'ADAM' 'ADRIENNE'
  'ONCE UPON A TIME THERE LIVED A GREAT '
  'FIERY DRAGON.  ' 'THIS FIERY DRAGON ' 'HAD A '
  'FRIEND NAMED ' 'CHILD' '.  AND '
  'CHILD' ' HAD A FRIEND NAMED ' 'FRIEND' '.  EARLY ONE '
  'COLD MORNING...' 'END'
```

This job will print the following:

```
    ONCE UPON A TIME THERE LIVED A GREAT FIERY DRAGON.
    THIS FIERY DRAGON HAD A FRIEND NAMED ADAM.   AND
    ADAM HAD A FRIEND NAMED ADRIENNE.   EARLY ONE
    COLD MORNING...
```

As you can see in the program, whenever at least 42 characters
are collected, a line is printed.

Our program is a very simple computer text editor. A much
fancier computer text editor was used in preparing the text you
are now reading.

                        CHAPTER 7 SUMMARY

    In this chapter we have given methods of manipulating strings
of characters. We introduced character string variables and we
explained how to put strings together, to take them apart and to
find their lengths. Using these basic string operations, we can
write programs which can modify strings in various ways,

including extending them on the left or right, or inserting or removing parts. The following important terms were presented:

Maximum length - Each character string variable has a maximum length given in its declaration which determines the longest string which can be assigned to the variable. For example, if the maximum length of character string variable S is 5, then S can have the value STICK, but not the value STICKY.

Null string - The string of length zero, that is, the string with no characters. In PL/1 programs, the null string is written as ''.

Length of a string - The number of characters in a string. A character string variable can have any length from zero, for the null string, up to the declared maximum length of the variable.

LENGTH - a built-in function which can be used to determine the length of the string. For example, LENGTH('HO') has the value 2 and LENGTH(S) gives the current length of the character string variable S.

String truncation (or chopping) - throwing away characters from the right-hand end of a character string. Suppose a character string is assigned to a character string variable S, and the length of the string exceeds the maximum length of S; then S takes the value of the string as truncated to the maximum length of S. (No error message is printed.)

Concatenation (or, simply, catenation) - means putting strings together, one after the other, to form another string. The strings 'PINE' and 'APPLE' can be concatenated to form the string 'PINEAPPLE'. In PL/1, two vertical bars (the same ones which alone mean "or") indicate concatenation. For example, 'PINE'||'APPLE' is equivalent to 'PINEAPPLE'.

Substring - means a part of a string. For example, SEW is a substring of HOUSEWIFE and ALE is a substring of SALESMAN.

SUBSTR - the built-in function for finding substrings. This built-in function is used in the form

      SUBSTR(string,starting position [,length])

The square brackets show that the length, and its preceding comma, can be omitted. The string can be any string expression, such as a string variable, a concatenation of strings, etc. The starting position is any numeric expression and gives the location of the first character of the substring. The length, if given, determines the number of characters in the substring. If the length is omitted, the substring extends to the end of the string. For example, SUBSTR('HOUSEWIFE',4,3) is 'SEW' and SUBSTR('HOUSEWIFE',6) is 'WIFE'. The starting position and length must specify a

substring that lies entirely within the string. This means
that position should be at least 1, length should be positive
or zero, and position plus length minus one should not exceed
the length of the string; otherwise there is an error.

String comparisons - used to test character strings for equality
and for ordering. Strings can be compared using the
following operators:

<   comes before (less than)
>   comes after (greater than)
<=   comes before or is equal (less than or equal)
>=   comes after or is equal(greater than or equal)
=   equal
¬=   not equal

Blank padding - extending a character string on the right with
blanks so it can be compared with a longer string. For
example, in PL/1, the comparison

'JONES'='JONES '

is true because the shorter string is temporarily extended on
the right with blanks.

CHAPTER 7 EXERCISES

1. Which of the following comparisons of strings are true?

(a) 'DAVID BARNARD'='DAVID BARNARD   '
(b) 'E. WONG'='EDMUND WONG'
(c) 'MARK FOX'='MARK FOX'
(d) 'JOHNSTON' > 'JOHNSON'
(e) '416 ELM ST' < '414 ELM STREET'
(f) 'HUME,PAT' >= 'HOLT,RIC'
(g) 'ALLEN' ¬= 'ALAN'

2. Suppose H and L have been declared to be CHARACTER(20)
VARYING and the following two statements have been executed:

    H='HOUSE';
    L='LIGHT';

What do each of the following statements print?

(a) PUT SKIP LIST(L||H);
(b) PUT SKIP LIST(L||' '||H);
(c) PUT SKIP LIST(H||' '||L);
(d) PUT SKIP LIST(SUBSTR(H,1,2));
(e) PUT SKIP LIST(SUBSTR(H,3));
(f) PUT SKIP LIST(SUBSTR(H,4,1)||L);
(g) PUT SKIP LIST(SUBSTR(L,1,1)||SUBSTR(H,2));

3. Suppose that P has been declared as CHARACTER(78)VARYING, and that P has as its value a phrase, such as

    ONE SWALLOW DOESN'T MAKE A SUMMER
or
    AN OUNCE OF PREVENTION IS WORTH A POUND OF CURE

Write statements to accomplish each of the following.

   (a) Find the first blank in P and set its location into the fixed variable L.

   (b) Set the fixed variable L to the location of the beginning of the last word in P.

   (c) Change P by adding a period to its right end.

   (d) Change P by replacing its first word by the character '1'.

   (e) Change P by extending it on the left by the phrase THEY SAY.

   (f) Set the fixed variable COUNT to the number of words in P. You can assume that each word, except the last word, is followed by a single blank.

   (g) If P contains the word POUND then replace it by the phrase 0.45 KILOGRAMS.

4. Write a program which looks up Nancy Wong's telephone number and prints it. You are given a set of data cards, each containing a name and a phone number. For example, the first card of this deck might be

    'JOHN ABEL'   '443-2162'

The last data card is the dummy card

    'ZZZ'   '000-0000'

5. You are to write a program which prints "personalized" appeals for contributions to the annual fund drive of the Loyal Order of Wallalumps, an exclusive men's club.

    Each club member is recorded on a card. Each member is to be sent a letter of the following form:

Dear XXXXXX,
    Thank you so much for your last year's
contribution of CCCCCCC dollars.
    Since your contribution last year was
PPPPPPPPPPPP
to help us meet our quota this year.
                    Yours sincerely,

Each data card contains the member's last name, his nickname if known (if not, '?' is used), his last year's contribution and his estimated salary.

The field XXXXXX should be filled in with the member's nickname, if known, but otherwise with Mr. YYYYYY, where YYYYYY is the member's last name. The phrase PPPPPPPPPPPP should be either

    so generous, we are counting on you

or

    not as large as hoped, we need you

Phrase PPPPPPPPPPPP is picked according to whether last year's contribution was more or less than .1% of the member's estimated salary.

The following is an example data card:

'LAZOWSKA' 'FUNK'   15   12000

6. Write a program that checks to see that the "I before E except after C" rule in spelling is followed. Your program should read some text which appears as a series of strings. It should search for I and E appearing next to each other. If the combination is EI and is not immediately preceded by a C, then the string should be printed together with an appropriate warning message. Similar action should be taken if C immediately precedes IE.

7. Write a program that will accept names of persons punched one to a data card in quotation marks in the form

    'LOUISA LOGAN MOLYNEUX'

and print out

    MOLYNEUX, L.L.

Make sure your program will work for any number of names before the surname and for names already abbreviated to initials. Arrange that the program will work for a number of cards on each run.

8. Write a program which reads text and determines the percentage of words having three letters. For simplicity, use text without any punctuation. The text should be a series of strings, one per data card.

CHAPTER 8

SP/5: ARRAYS

So far in our programming, each memory location for data had its own special name; each variable had a unique identifier. In this chapter we will introduce the idea that groups of data will share a common name and be differentiated from each other by numbering each one uniquely.

Suppose that we have a list of names of students. We could give the list the name STUDENT and identify the first name as STUDENT(1), the second as STUDENT(2), and so on. We call the number that is enclosed in parentheses the index of the list or array. The reason why we should use this method of identifying variables is not clear. We will have to do an example so that you can see the power of the new method. As an example, suppose you wanted to read in a list of names of 50 students and print them out in reverse order, that is, last first. We would need to read in the entire list before we could begin the printing. This means we must have a memory location for each name. We must be able to reserve this space by a declaration.

DECLARATION OF ARRAYS

For the list of names of students we would use a declaration

DECLARE(STUDENT(1:50))CHARACTER(20)VARYING;

Each name is a character string variable whose maximum length is allowed to be 20. The fact that the variable identifier STUDENT is a list is shown by having something in parentheses after it. And what is shown is the fact that it is a list numbered, or indexed, from 1 to 50. As a matter of fact we could write STUDENT(50) and get exactly the same result. It might just happen, though, that you wanted a list numbered from 51 to 100,

in which case you would declare STUDENT(51:100). Most examples
we have will just use numbering starting at 1, and so what is
shown in parentheses is the number of entries in the list.

                          HANDLING LISTS

    We are now ready for the program that reverses the order of a
list of names. Here the array index is a fixed variable I.

```
$JOB  ID='LES MEZEI'
 REVERSE:PROCEDURE OPTIONS(MAIN);
    DECLARE(STUDENT(50))CHARACTER(30)VARYING;
    DECLARE(I)FIXED;
    /* READ LIST OF NAMES */
    DO I=1 TO 50;
       GET LIST(STUDENT(I));
       END;
    /* PRINT REVERSED LIST */
    DO I=50 TO 1 BY -1;
       PUT SKIP LIST(STUDENT(I));
       END;
    END;
$DATA
 (list of 50 names, each in quotes)
```

    Now, perhaps, you can see what a powerful programming tool
the indexed variable can be. The index I that is counting the
loop can be used to refer to the different members of the list.
In the first DO loop the names are read; the first is stored in
the variable STUDENT(1), the second in STUDENT(2), and so on. In
contrast, the first iteration of the printing loop outputs
STUDENT(50), the next STUDENT(49), and so on.

    Suppose, as a second example, we had a list of 50 integers
and we wanted the sum of all the numbers. Here is the program:

```
    DECLARE(NUMBER(50),SUM,I)FIXED;
    /* READ IN NUMBERS */
    DO I=1 TO 50;
       GET LIST(NUMBER(I));
       END;
    /* ADD NUMBERS */
    SUM=0;
    DO I=1 TO 50;
       SUM=SUM+NUMBER(I);
       END;
    PUT LIST(SUM);
```

In the last example, it is not necessary to read all the numbers
and then add them up but we did it that way just to show what is
necessary for reading or summing a list. We could have written
only one loop, combining the two operations.

```
/* READ AND ADD NUMBERS */
SUM=0
DO I=1 TO 50;
   GET LIST(NUMBER(I));
   SUM=SUM+NUMBER(I);
   END;
PUT LIST(SUM);
```

Usually, there is more to be done that requires having the list
still present. For instance we could think of dividing each
member of a list by the sum and multiplying by 100. This would
express each entry as a percentage of the group. To do this we
would add these statements:

```
DO I=1 TO 50;
   NUMBER(I)=(NUMBER(I))*1E2/SUM+.5E0;
   PUT SKIP LIST(NUMBER(I));
   END;
```

In the DO loop the single statement with the index I results in
each member of the list being operated on and changed to a
percentage.

AN EXAMPLE PROGRAM

Arrays can be used in manipulating various kinds of lists.
We will now give an example in which the list is the timetable
for teachers in a high school. The timetable has been prepared
as a deck of cards. Each card has a teacher's name, a period (1
to 6) and a room number.

The cards look like the following:

```
(teacher)         (period)        (room)
'MS. WEBER'          1              216
'MRS. IRELAND'       6              214
'MISS SINOPOLI'      1              103
'MS. WEBER'          4              200
'MRS. CAIN'          2              216
...
'XXX'                0                 0(dummy card)
```

A program is needed to print out the timetable in order of
periods. First, all teachers with their classrooms for the first
period should be printed; then all teachers with their classrooms
for period 2 and so on up to period 6. The output from the
program should begin this way:

```
PERIOD              1
MS. WEBER          216
MISS SINOPOLI      103
...
```

The following program produces this output:

```
 1 PERIODS:PROCEDURE OPTIONS(MAIN);
 2    DECLARE(TEACHER(0:50))CHARACTER(20)VARYING;
 3    DECLARE(PERIOD(1:50),ROOM(1:50))FIXED;
 4    DECLARE(I,THIS_PERIOD,HOW_MANY)FIXED;
 5    /* INITIALIZE FOR READING TIME TABLE */
 6    I=0;
 7    TEACHER(I)='ANYTHING BUT XXX';
 8    /* READ THE TIMETABLE */
 9    DO WHILE(TEACHER(I)¬='XXX');
10       I=I+1;
11       GET LIST(TEACHER(I),PERIOD(I),ROOM(I));
12       END;
13    HOW_MANY=I-1;
14    /* PRINT THE TIMETABLE BY PERIODS */
15    DO THIS_PERIOD=1 TO 6;
16       PUT SKIP LIST('PERIOD',THIS_PERIOD);
17       DO I=1 TO HOW_MANY;
18          IF PERIOD(I)=THIS_PERIOD THEN
19             PUT SKIP LIST(TEACHER(I),ROOM(I));
20          END;
21       END;
22    END;
```

The first loop in this program reads in the cards representing the timetable. In lines 6 and 7, the initialization for this loop sets TEACHER(0), element zero of the TEACHER array, to 'ANYTHING BUT XXX'. This guarantees that the loop will be executed at least one time. In the declaration of the TEACHER array, we specified that its index could range from zero to 50. The only reason the bottom of the range was specified as zero rather than 1 was to simplify the initialization for this DO WHILE loop. The program would still work correctly if we specified the lower bound as 1 while replacing lines 6 and 7 by the following:

```
I=1;
GET LIST(TEACHER(I),PERIOD(I),ROOM(I));
```

Our program is able to read in a timetable consisting of at most 50 cards, including the dummy card. If there are more than 50 cards in the timetable, then line 10 will eventually set I to 51; this value of I will be used in line 11 as an index for the TEACHER, PERIOD and ROOM arrays. This would be an error, because the declarations specify that 50 is the largest allowed array index. The problem is that the index is out of bounds in line 11 when I exceeds 50. Many PL/1 processors, such as the University of Toronto's SP/k processor and Cornell University's PL/C processor, detect out-of-bounds array indexes and print appropriate error messages while the program is executing.

You should take care that array indexes in your programs stay within their declared bounds. In our example program, we can prevent bounds errors by changing line 9 to the following.

```
DO WHILE(I<50&TEACHER(I)¬='XXX');
```

Our change guarantees that no more than 50 cards will be read. Unfortunately, the modified program fails to report the situation when there were too many data cards. We can remedy this problem by inserting the following between lines 12 and 13:

```
IF TEACHER(I)¬='XXX' THEN
   PUT SKIP LIST('**ERROR:ONLY 50 CARDS WERE READ');
```

The program now supplies a more appropriate error message than the system would provide, and continues on to give a period-by-period listing of the cards it actually read.

TWO-DIMENSIONAL ARRAYS

It is possible to have arrays that correspond to entries in a table rather than just a single list. For instance, a table of distances between 4 cities might be

```
         1     2     3     4
      -------------------------
   1 |  0    20    38    56
   2 | 20     0    12    30
   3 | 38    12     0    15
   4 | 56    30    15     0
```

We could call this array DISTANCE and DISTANCE(1,4) is 56 or DISTANCE(3,4) is 15. The first number in the parentheses refers to the row in the table, the second to the column. You can see that DISTANCE(3,1) has the same value as DISTANCE(1,3); the table is symmetric in this case about the diagonal line running from top left to bottom right. All entries on this diagonal are zero; the distance from a city to itself is zero.

We must learn how to declare such a two-dimensional array. All that is necessary is to write

```
DECLARE(DISTANCE(1:4,1:4))FIXED;
```

or   `DECLARE(DISTANCE(4,4))FIXED;`

The first index is the number of rows, the second the number of columns. As an example, we will read in this table and store it in the memory. On each input data card we will punch one row of the data:

```
DECLARE(DISTANCE(4,4),I,J)FIXED;
DO I=1 TO 4;
   DO J=1 TO 4;
      GET LIST(DISTANCE(I,J));
   END;
END;
```

In this program there is one DO loop nested inside another. We
have used two indexes, I to give the row number, J to give the
column number. When I=1 the inner loop has J go from 1 to 4.
This means the elements of the array on the first card are stored
in these variables:

DISTANCE(1,1) DISTANCE(1,2) DISTANCE(1,3) DISTANCE(1,4)

These are the elements in row 1 of the table. Since our table is
symmetric it does not matter if we interchange rows and columns,
because we get exactly the same result. For most tables it does
matter, and you must be careful.

ANOTHER EXAMPLE PROGRAM

We will illustrate the use of two-dimensional arrays in terms
of a set of data collected by a consumers' group. This group has
been alarmed about the recent rapid rise in price of processed
wallalumps. They sampled grocery store prices of processed
wallalumps on a monthly basis throughout 1972, 1973 and 1974 and
observed that prices varied from 75 cents to 155 cents as the
following table shows:

Month

	1	2	3	4	5	6	7	8	9	10	11	12
1972	87	89	89	89	85	85	85	75	90	100	100	100
1973	95	95	95	95	90	90	85	90	100	110	120	110
1974	110	110	115	115	115	100	100	110	120	140	145	155

These 36 prices were made available on data cards and a program
was needed to analyze the price changes.

The following program reads in the data and determines the
average price for 1973:

```
COST:PROCEDURE OPTIONS(MAIN);
   DECLARE(PRICE(12,1972:1974))FIXED;
   DECLARE(MONTH,YEAR,TOTAL)FIXED;
   DO YEAR=1972 TO 1974;
      /* READ IN PRICES FOR ONE YEAR */
      DO MONTH=1 TO 12;
         GET LIST(PRICE(MONTH,YEAR));
         END;
      END;
   /* DETERMINE THE AVERAGE PRICE IN 1973 */
   TOTAL=0;
   DO MONTH=1 TO 12;
      TOTAL=TOTAL+PRICE(MONTH,1973);
      END;
   PUT SKIP LIST('AVERAGE 1973 PRICE:',TOTAL/12E0);
   /* ADD STATEMENTS HERE TO CALCULATE OTHER AVERAGES */
   END;
```

In this program, the array PRICE is declared so it can have a
first index which can range from 1 to 12 and a second index which
can range from 1972 to 1974. Effectively, the PRICE array is a
table in which entries can be looked up by month and year. The
first part of the program uses the data to fill up the PRICE
array. The second part of the program sums up the prices for
each month during 1973 and calculates the average 1973 price.

We could as well calculate the average price for a particular
month. For example, the following calculates the average price
in February:

```
TOTAL=0;
DO YEAR=1972 TO 1974;
   TOTAL=TOTAL+PRICE(2,YEAR);
   END;
PUT SKIP LIST('AVERAGE FEB. PRICE:',TOTAL/3E0);
```

We could calculate the average price for the entire three-year
period as follows.

```
TOTAL=0;
DO YEAR=1972 TO 1974;
   DO MONTH=1 TO 12;
      TOTAL=TOTAL+PRICE(MONTH,YEAR);
      END;
   END;
PUT SKIP LIST('OVERALL AVERAGE:',TOTAL/36E0);
```

This example has illustrated the use of two-dimensional
arrays. It is possible to use arrays with three and more
dimensions. For example, our consumers' group might want to
record prices for five grades of processed wallalumps (that makes
one dimension), each month (that makes two dimensions), for three
years (that makes three dimensions). The array declaration

```
    DECLARE(PRICE(5,12,1972:1974))FIXED;
```

would set up a table to hold all this data.

ARRAYS AS DATA STRUCTURES

We have spoken of structured programming and shown how
control flow is structured in a program. Now we can speak of the
structure of data. Giving variables identifiers that are
meaningful has been the only way we could systematize data so
far. But with arrays we find that data can be structured or
organized into one-dimensional forms called lists, or two-
dimensional forms called tables. We can use even higher-di-
mensional arrays when we need them.

When we approach a problem and want to solve it by creating a
computer program we must decide on the data structures we will
use. We must decide in particular whether or not we need to
establish arrays for any of the data, or whether single variables
will serve us well enough.

Arrays will be useful whenever we must store groups of
similar pieces of information. They are not necessary when small
amounts of information come in, are processed, and then go out.

OTHER DATA STRUCTURES

Just so that you do not think that single variables and
arrays are the only kind of data structures we can have, we will
mention a few others.

One common structure is the tree structure. The easiest way
to think of a tree is to imagine a family tree. At the risk of
being called chauvinists we will show only the male members in
the tree and talk of fathers and sons. This keeps it simple.

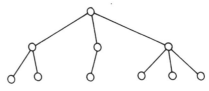

TREE STRUCTURE

The diagram is showing a man with three sons. The first son has
two sons, the second one son, the third three. The grandfather
is the root of the tree. The tree is of course growing upside
down. The lines joining the relatives are called branches; the
people themselves are nodes.

The data we might store could be the names of the people, and the tree structure would have to be stored also. The way it is done is to have <u>pointers</u> stored with the data to give the structure. Each father entry requires a pointer for each of his sons.

A list can also be arranged with elements and pointers instead of in an array. This means that some of the information stored is used to describe the data structure and some to give the data. With arrays, the structure is given by the fact that one element follows right next to the preceding element. It does not need a pointer.

Later we will be investigating other data structures in detail. Often we will use the array structures to implement structures like trees or lists with pointers from one element to another.

CHAPTER 8 SUMMARY

This chapter has introduced array variables, which are used for manipulating quantities of similar data. An array is made up of a number of elements, each of which acts as a simple, non-array variable. The following terms are used in describing arrays and their uses.

<u>Array declaration</u> - sets aside <u>memory space</u> for an array. For example, the declaration

    DECLARE(COST(4))FLOAT;

sets aside space for the array elements COST(1), COST(2), COST(3) and COST(4). Each of these elements can be used like a simple, non-array FLOAT variable.

<u>Array index</u> (sometimes called <u>array subscript</u>) - used to designate <u>a particular element of array.</u> For example, in COST(I), the variable I is an array index. An array index can be any arithmetic expression, and can even include array elements.

<u>Array bounds</u> - the <u>range</u> over which <u>array indexes may vary.</u> For example, given the declaration

    DECLARE(PRICE(12,1972:1974))FIXED;

an array element of PRICE can be specified by PRICE(M,Y), where M can range from 1 to 12 and Y can range from 1972 to 1974.

<u>Out-of-bounds index</u> - an <u>array index</u> which is <u>outside the bounds specified in the array's declaration.</u> This is an error.

Multiply-dimensioned arrays - arrays requiring more than one index, such as the PRICE array given above.

CHAPTER 8 EXERCISES

1. What does the following program print?

```
FLOWERS:PROCEDURE OPTIONS(MAIN);
   DECLARE(POEM(2))CHARACTER(6)VARYING;
   DECLARE(PART,SAY_IT_AGAIN)FIXED;
   POEM(1)='A ROSE';
   POEM(2)='IS';
   DO SAY_IT_AGAIN=1 TO 3;
      DO PART=1 TO 2;
         PUT SKIP LIST(POEM(PART));
         END;
      END;
   PUT SKIP LIST(POEM(1));
   END;
```

2. What does the following program print?

```
$JOB ID='MARK FOX'
 RUMORS:PROCEDURE OPTIONS(MAIN);
    DECLARE(HE(4),SHE(4))CHARACTER(10)VARYING;
    DECLARE(WHO)FIXED;
    PUT SKIP LIST('HERE THEY ARE');
    DO WHO=1 TO 4;
       GET LIST(HE(WHO),SHE(WHO));
       PUT SKIP LIST(' ',HE(WHO),SHE(WHO));
       END;
    PUT SKIP LIST(HE(1),'SAYS',SHE(2),'LOVES',HE(2));
    PUT SKIP LIST('HOWEVER--');
    DO WHO=2 TO 3;
       PUT SKIP LIST(SHE(WHO),'SAYS',HE(WHO+1),'SAYS');
       END;
    PUT SKIP LIST(SHE(2),'IS JUST SHOPPING AROUND');
    END;
 $DATA
  'JOHN' 'ANN' 'FRED' 'JUDY'
  'ED' 'ALICE' 'BILL' 'JANE'
```

3. What does this program print?

```
$JOB ID='DIANE KITCHEN'
 POLISH:PROCEDURE OPTIONS(MAIN);
    DECLARE(NAME(50))CHARACTER(10)VARYING;
    DECLARE(PRICE(50))FIXED;
    DECLARE(I,P,N)FIXED;
    GET LIST(N);
    DO I=1 TO N;
       GET LIST(NAME(I),PRICE(I));
       PUT SKIP LIST(NAME(I),PRICE(I));
       END;
    GET LIST(P);
    DO I=1 TO N;
       IF PRICE(I)>P THEN
          PUT SKIP LIST(NAME(I));
       END;
    END;
$DATA
   3
   'JOHNSONS'  518
   'LEMON OIL' 211
   'DOMINO'    341
   300
```

4. Write a program which reads yesterday's and today's stock-market selling prices and prints lists of rapidly rising and rapidly falling stocks. A typical data card will look like this:

    'GENERAL ELECTRIC' 93.50 81.00

The card gives you the company's name followed by yesterday's price, followed by today's price. Your program should print a list of companies whose stock declined by more than 10 per cent, and then a list of companies whose stock rose by more than 10 per cent.

5. What will the following program, called SINGOUT, print? What error would occur if the second data card was changed to

    'FLEA' 'GERM' 'ALL DONE'

Explain how this error can be avoided by changing one declaration. Add statements so that if more than six objects are read in, the program will print THANK YOU, YOU HAVE BEEN A WONDERFUL AUDIENCE, and quit.

```
$JOB ID='BRIAN CLARK'
 SINGOUT:PROCEDURE OPTIONS(MAIN);
    DECLARE(OBJECT(8))CHARACTER(10)VARYING;
    DECLARE(VERSE,V)FIXED;
    PUT SKIP LIST('SONG OF THE GREEN GRASS');
    PUT SKIP LIST('');
    VERSE=1;
    OBJECT(VERSE)='TREE';
    DO WHILE(OBJECT(VERSE)¬='ALL DONE');
       IF VERSE=1 THEN
          PUT SKIP LIST('THERE WAS A TREE');
       ELSE
          DO;
             PUT SKIP LIST('AND ON THAT '||OBJECT(VERSE-1));
             PUT SKIP LIST('THERE WAS A '||OBJECT(VERSE));
             PUT SKIP LIST('THE PRETTIEST '||OBJECT(VERSE));
             PUT SKIP LIST('THAT YOU EVER DID SEE');
             DO V=VERSE TO 2 BY -1;
                PUT SKIP LIST('AND THE '||OBJECT(V)||' WAS ON THE '
                   ||OBJECT(V-1));
                END;
             END;
       PUT SKIP LIST('AND THE TREE WAS IN THE GROUND');
       /* BELT OUT THE CHORUS */
       PUT SKIP LIST('AND THE GREEN GRASS GREW ALL AROUND, '||
          'ALL AROUND');
       PUT SKIP LIST('AND THE GREEN GRASS GREW ALL AROUND');
       PUT SKIP LIST('');
       VERSE=VERSE+1;
       GET LIST(OBJECT(VERSE));
       END;
    END;
$DATA

 'BRANCH' 'NEST' 'BIRD' 'WING' 'FEATHER'
 'FLEA' 'ALL DONE'
```

6. Do you know the song about the old lady who swallowed a fly? If so, write a program to print its words. Otherwise, if you know the song "Alouette", write a program to print its words. Otherwise, if you know the song "The Twelve Days of Christmas", write a program to print its words. Otherwise learn one of these three songs and repeat this exercise.

7. You work for the Police Department and you are to write a program to try to determine criminals' identities based on victims' descriptions of the criminals. The police have cards describing known criminals. These cards have the form

     name   height   weight   address

Here is an example:

```
'JOEY MACLUNK' 67      125      '24 MAIN ST.'
```

There is another set of cards giving descriptions of criminals participating in unsolved crimes. Here is such a deck:

```
'14 DEC: SHOP LIFTING'      72      190
' 9 NOV: PURSE SNATCHING'   66      130
' 6 NOV: BICYCLE THIEVERY'  67      135
'XXX'                        0        0
```

The two numbers give the criminal's estimated height and weight. Write a program which first reads in the deck describing the unsolved crimes. Then it reads the file cards giving the known criminals' names, descriptions and addresses. Each known criminal's height and weight should be compared with the corresponding measurements for each unsolved crime. If the height is within 2 inches and the weight is within 10 pounds, your program should print a message saying the criminal is a possible suspect for the crime. (Note: Joey MacLunk is not a real person!)

CHAPTER 9

STRUCTURING YOUR ATTACK
ON THE PROBLEM

STEP-BY-STEP REFINEMENT

Most of the examples of programming so far have been short examples. Nevertheless we have emphasized some of the aspects of good programming. These were:

1. choosing meaningful words as identifiers

2. placing comments in the program to increase the understandability

3. paragraphing the DO loops and IF...THEN...ELSE statements to reveal the structure of control flow

4. choosing appropriate data structures

5. reading programs and tracing execution by hand, to strive for correctness before machine testing.

All of these are important even in small programs, but it is only when we attempt larger programs that our good habits will really start to pay off.

And when we work on larger programs we will find that we have something else to structure, and that is our attack on the problem. To solve a problem we must move from a statement of what the problem to be solved is, to a solution, which is a well-structured program for a computer. The language of our program will be PL/1.

The original statement of a problem will be in English, with perhaps some mathematical statements. The solution will be in PL/1. What we will look at in this chapter is the way we move

from one of these to the other. We will be discussing a method
whereby we go step by step from one to the other. This
systematic method we will refer to as <u>step-by-step refinement</u>.
Sometimes we say that we are starting at the top, the English-
language statement of the problem, and moving down in steps to
the bottom level, which is the PL/1 program for the solution. We
speak of the <u>top-down approach</u> to problem solution.

TREE STRUCTURE TO PROBLEM SOLUTION

To illustrate the technique of structuring the solution to a
problem by the step-by-step refinement, or the top-down approach,
we need a problem as an example. We need a problem that is large
or difficult enough to show the technique, but not so large as to
be too long to follow. If a program is too long and involved we
will use another technique that divides the job into modules and
does one module at a time. This is called <u>modular programming</u>.
It is another form of structured programming. But it must wait
until we have learned SP/6.

The example we choose is sorting a list of names
alphabetically. We will now start the solution by trying to form
a tree which represents the structure of our attack. The root of
the tree is the statement of the problem. In the first move we
show how this is divided into three branches:

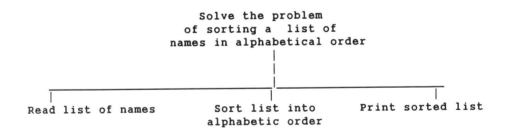

At each of the three nodes that descend from the root we have an
English statement. These statements are still "what-to-do"
statements, not "how-to-do-it." A statement of how to do
something or other is called an <u>algorithm</u> for doing it. A set of
instructions for assembling a hi-fi amplifier is an algorithm for
making a hi-fi amplifier. A cake recipe in a cookbook is an
algorithm for making a cake. The problem of making a cake is
solved by following the recipe.

We will be moving down each branch of the solution tree
replacing a statement of "what to do" by an algorithm for doing
it. The algorithms will not necessarily be in the PL/1 language.
We will use a mixture of English and PL/1 at each node until in
the nodes farthest from the tree root we have a PL/1 program.

CHOOSING DATA STRUCTURES

Before we try to add more branches to the solution tree, we should decide on some data structures for the problem of sorting the list of names. We need not make all the decisions at this stage, but we can make a start.

We will use a one-dimensional array called NAME to hold the list of names to be sorted. The length of this list we will call N and we will allow names up to 30 characters in length. What we are deciding on is really the declarations for the PL/1 program, and for now we have decided that we need

```
DECLARE(NAME(100))CHARACTER(30)VARYING;
DECLARE(N,I)FIXED;
```

In these declarations we are allowing a maximum size for the list of 100 names. The actual list will have N names, and we must read this number in as part of the input. For indexing the list we clearly will need an index I. We will assume for the moment that we will keep the sorted list in the same locations as the original list. The names will have to be rearranged, and this means some swapping will be needed. We will need a single variable TEMP with type CHARACTER (30) VARYING to do this swapping.

GROWING THE SOLUTION TREE

Having decided on at least some of the data structures, we are prepared to continue the process of structuring the solution tree. We can see how to develop the left and right branches now, even as far as transforming them into PL/1 program segments. The middle branch can be refined a little by saying that sorting will be accomplished by element swapping. Here is the tree now:

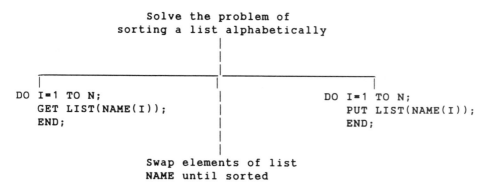

At this stage we must obviously face up to designing an algorithm for producing a sorted list by swapping.

DEVELOPING AN ALGORITHM

We want the names to be in the sorted list so that each name has a smaller value than the name ahead of it in the list.

In the sorted list

```
HOLT
HORNING
HULL
HUME
```

we see   ('HORNING'>'HOLT')
          ('HULL'>'HORNING')
          ('HUME'>'HULL')

are all true conditions.

In our solution tree one branch must be developed further; this is, "Swap elements of list NAME until sorted." We have seen from the example that a sorted list has the largest value in the last position. This is also true of the list if an element is removed from the end. The new last element is the largest one of the smaller list. So our next refinement in the solution is to arrange the list in this way. We write:

"Do with LAST varying from N to second,
    swap elements so largest is in LAST"

We must still refine the part,

"Swap elements so largest is in LAST"

but the first part of this can be written in PL/1 now as

```
DO LAST=N TO 2 BY -1;
```

We will now refine the remaining part; it becomes

"DO with I varying from first to (LAST-1),
    if element(I)>element(I+1),
    swap elements"

The first two parts of this can now become PL/1; this produces

```
DO I=1 TO LAST-1;
   IF(NAME(I)>NAME(I+1)) THEN
      swap elements;
```

We must now refine the statement "swap elements". It is

```
TEMP=NAME(I);
NAME(I)=NAME(I+1);
NAME(I+1)=TEMP;
```

Because these three statements go after a THEN, we must precede them by DO and follow them by END.

Now we can assemble the complete program.

THE COMPLETE PROGRAM

```
$JOB ID='RICK BUNT'
 SORT:PROCEDURE OPTIONS(MAIN);
    /*SORT LIST OF N NAMES ALPHABETICALLY */
    DECLARE(NAME(50),TEMP)CHARACTER(30)VARYING;
    DECLARE(I,LAST,N)FIXED;
    /*READ NAME LIST*/
    GET LIST(N);
    DO I=1 TO N;
       GET LIST(NAME(I));
       END;
    /*SWAP ELEMENTS OF LIST UNTIL SORTED*/
    /* DO WITH LAST VARYING FROM N TO SECOND */
    /* SWAP ELEMENTS SO LARGEST VALUE IS IN LAST */
    DO LAST=N TO 2 BY -1;
       /* DO WITH I VARYING FROM FIRST TO LAST-1 */
       /* IF ELEMENT(I) > ELEMENT(I+1) */
       /* SWAP THESE ELEMENTS */
       DO I=1 TO LAST-1;
          IF(NAME(I)>NAME(I+1)) THEN
             DO;
                TEMP=NAME(I);
                NAME(I)=NAME(I+1);
                NAME(I+1)=TEMP;
                END;
          END;
       END;
    /*PRINT NAME LIST*/
    DO I=1 TO N;
       PUT SKIP LIST(NAME(I));
       END;
    END;
$DATA
 5
 'ANN'
 'ALLEN'
 'AXELBLATT'
 'AYNE'
 'ATHELSTANE'
```

Notice that the English parts of the solution tree remain as comments in the final program. Comments are not added after a program is written, so that it can be understood at a later date, but are an integral part of the program construction process.

ASSESSING EFFICIENCY

In this approach to problem solution we have moved step by step to refine the statement of the problem in English into a program in a language that is acceptable to a computer, namely PL/1. In the process, as we constructed the solution tree, we gradually replaced statements of what is to be done by statements of how it is to be done; we devised an algorithm for performing the process. The algorithm was expressed in English, or a mixture of English and PL/1. Then finally we had a PL/1 program.

Nowhere during this process have we spoken about the efficiency of the method that we have chosen, that is, the efficiency of our algorithm. This is because the issue of efficiency complicates the solution. Since in structured programming we are trying to control complexity, we have in this first attempt eliminated efficiency from our considerations.

This means that to now add the refinement of a more efficient algorithm will require us to back up to an earlier point in the solution tree and redo certain portions. In the step-by-step refinement method of problem solution we do not always move from the top down in the solution tree. In that sense, then, the top-down approach is slightly different. In it you would move always in the one direction. In practice this would be impractical, as afterthoughts must always be allowed to improve a method of solution. The only reason to reject afterthoughts is that the work in incorporating them is not justified, considering the gain that would result.

In our particular example you can see that it is possible, at a certain stage, that the list might be sorted and that there is no need to keep on to the bitter end. What we should incorporate is a way of recognizing that the list is sorted so that the mechanical sorting process can stop.

A BETTER ALGORITHM

What we must do is to back up in the solution tree to the point where we had in the middle branch the words, "Swap elements of NAME until sorted." We have translated this essentially by the statement, "Swap elements of NAME in such a way that at the end of the swapping process the list is sure to be sorted."

We are going to change now to the statement, "Swap elements of NAME in such a way that at the end of the swapping process the list would be sorted, and stop either when the list is sorted or when the normal end of the swapping process is reached." You can see that we are going to have a DO loop now with two conditions. The condition of the swapping process's being finished is the same as what we have now. What we must add is the second condition

```
DO WHILE (list is not sorted);
```

But how do we know when the list is sorted? We must devise an
algorithm to test whether or not the list is sorted. You will
notice that if in any iteration of the inner DO loop there are no
names swapped, the list <u>must</u> be sorted. We should have a flag
called SORTED that can be set to 1 to indicate that the list is
sorted or 0 to indicate that the list is not sorted.

The outer DO loop would then be

```
DO WHILE(SORTED¬=1&LAST>=2);
```

We would have to initialize this loop by having these
instructions precede it.

```
SORTED=0;
LAST=N;
```

These set the flag and start the count. Inside the loop we must
perform the adjustment in the index LAST by -1; since we are now
using a DO WHILE loop instead of a counted DO loop we must do our
own counting. This would mean we need the instruction

```
LAST=LAST-1;
```

just before the END of the loop. We want SORTED to be changed to
1 if <u>no</u> swapping takes place in the inner DO loop. This can be
accomplished if we set it to 1 just before we enter the inner
loop and return it to zero if any swapping does take place. The
altered part of the program is as follows.

```
/*SWAP ELEMENTS OF LIST UNTIL */
/*EITHER SWAPPING PROCESS IS COMPLETED*/
/*OR THE LIST IS SORTED AS INDICATED*/
/*BY THE FLAG 'SORTED' BEING 1*/
SORTED=0;
LAST=N;
DO WHILE(SORTED¬=1&LAST>=2);
   SORTED=1;
   DO I=1 TO LAST-1;
      IF(NAME(I)>NAME(I+1)) THEN
         DO;
            SORTED=0;
            TEMP=NAME(I);
            NAME(I)=NAME(I+1);
            NAME(I+1)=TEMP;
            END;
      END;
   LAST=LAST-1;
   END;
/*PRINT NAME LIST*/
  (as before)
```

BETTER ALGORITHMS

In our example we could see that an improvement in the efficiency of the sorting algorithm could be achieved, and we backed up the solution tree and redid a portion to incorporate the improvement. This was an easier job than trying to think about efficiency in the first place. This is why in the step-by-step refinement method we do not consider efficiency at first. In a way we were lucky that our algorithm could be modified so readily. We might have done the swapping in an entirely different way, in which we would not be able to detect a sorted list by the absence of swapping on any iteration of the process.

To see how this might be, suppose that to sort this list each element were compared with the first element. If it were smaller, the two would be swapped. With the smallest in the first position the list would be shortened by one and the process repeated. The difficulty here is that the fact that no swapping occurs in any round only means that the smallest is already in the first position, not that the list is sorted. We have no way of seeing that the list is sorted unless we compare each list member with its next-door neighbor. And this is what we did in our sorting method.

So our method is more suited to this particular improvement than a method that involves swapping by comparison of each element with one particular element. If we had started this way we would have had to revise completely. To say that efficiency considerations are left until after a first algorithm is programmed produces disadvantages. For many standard processes like sorting, various algorithms have been explored, their efficiencies evaluated, and a best algorithm determined. The method we have developed is certainly not the best that has been devised.

This best, or optimal, algorithm often depends on the problem itself. For instance, one algorithm may be best for short lists, another for long lists. Establishing "the" best method is very difficult and depends on circumstances. Always try to pick a "good" algorithm if you are programming a standard process. At least avoid "bad" algorithms. Very often, programs are already written using good algorithms and you can use them directly in your own program. But that is something we will discuss in the subset SP/6. We can create programs from modules that are already made for us. Then one of the branches of your solution tree is filled by a <u>prefabricated</u> <u>module</u>. We need only learn how to hook it up to our own program. We can also create modules of our own. This technique is called <u>modular</u> <u>programming</u> and it is an additional way to conquer problem solving, by dividing the problem into parts.

CHAPTER 9 SUMMARY

In previous chapters we concentrated primarily on <u>learning</u> a programming language; we have covered variables, loops, character strings, arrays and so on. In this chapter, the focus has been on <u>using</u> a programming language to solve problems.

The method of problem solving which we described is based on the idea of dividing the problem into parts - the divide-and-conquer strategy. Each of these parts in turn is divided into smaller parts. This continues until eventually the solution to the problem has been broken into small parts which can be written in a programming language like PL/1. We will review this method of problem solving using the following terms:

Top-down approach to programming. When using a computer to solve a problem, you should start by understanding the problem thoroughly. You start at the "top" by figuring out what your program is supposed to do. Next you split your prospective program into parts, for example, into a reading phase, a computation phase, and a printing phase. These phases represent the next level in the design of your program. You may continue by defining the data which these phases use for passing information among themselves, and then by writing PL/1 statements for each of the phases. The PL/1 statements are the bottom level of your design; they make up a program which should solve your problem. In larger programs, there may be many intermediate levels between the top - understanding the problem completely - and the bottom - a program which solves the problem. (Beware:top-down program design does <u>not</u> mean writing PROCEDURE OPTIONS(MAIN) at the top of the page, followed by declarations, followed by statements! The top level in top-down design means gaining an understanding of the problem to be solved, rather than writing the first line of PL/1.)

Step-by-step refinement. When you are writing a program, you should start with an overall understanding of the program's purpose. You should proceed step by step toward the writing of this program. These steps should each refine the proposed program into a more detailed method of solving the problem. The last step refines the method to the level where the computer can carry out the required operations. This means that the final refinement results in a program which can be executed by the computer. As you can see, the idea behind top-down programming is step-by-step refinement leading from the problem statement to the final program.

Tree structures to problem solution. In this chapter we have illustrated top-down programming by drawing pictures of trees. The root, or base, of the tree is labelled by the statement of the problem. Once the problem has been refined into subproblems, we have our tree grow a branch for each subproblem. In turn, each subproblem can be divided, resulting in sub-branches, and so on. When you are actually solving problems, you will probably not actually draw such a tree. However, you may well use the idea behind drawing this tree, namely, step-by-step refinement leading from problem statement to problem solution.

Use of comments. One of the purposes of comments, /*...*/, in a program is to remind us of the structure of the program. This means that comments are used to remind us that a particular sequence of PL/1 statements has been written to solve one particular part of the problem.

CHAPTER 9 EXERCISES

1. You are to have the computer read a list of names, followed by the dummy name 'ZZZ', and print the names in reverse order. In your top-down approach to writing your program, you first decided your program should have the overall form:

(a) Read in all of the names;

(b) Print the names in reverse order;

Next, you decided that the names will be passed from part (a) to part (b) via an array declared by

    DECLARE(NAME(50))CHARACTER(10)VARYING;

The index of the last valid name read into this array will be passed to part (b) in a FIXED variable called HOW_MANY. Making no changes to this overall form, you must now complete the program. Include comments at the appropriate places to record the purpose of the two parts of your program. Answer the following questions about your completed program.

- Can you think of another way to write part (a) of your program without changing part (b)? How?

- Can you think of another way to write part (b) of your program without changing part (a)? How?

2. The school office wants a list of all A students and a list of all B students. There is a punched card for each student giving his grade, for example:

    'DAVE TILBROOK'   'A-'

Each grade is A,B,C,D or F, which may be followed by + or -. The names and grades are followed by the dummy card

    'ZZZ'   'NONE'

The school's programmer has designed the following three possible structures for a program to read these cards and print the two required lists.

First program structure:
(a) Read names and grades and save all of them in arrays;
(b) Print names having A grades;
(c) Print names having B grades;

Second program structure:
(a) Read names and grades and save only those with A's or B's in arrays;
(b) Print names having A grades;
(c) Print names having B grades;

Third program structure:
(a) Read names and grades, printing names with As and saving only names with Bs.
(b) Print names having Bs.

Suppose the final program will have room in arrays to save at most 100 students' names. What advantage does the second program structure have over the first one? What advantages does the third program structure have over the second one? You do not need to write a program to answer these questions.

3. A company wants to know the percentage of its sales due to each salesman. Each salesman has a card giving his name and the dollar value of his sales. The last salesman's card is followed by a card giving the dummy name 'NOBODY' and sales of zero dollars. The top-down design of a program to print the desired percentages has resulted in this program structure:

(a) Read in salesmen and sales and add up total sales;
(b) Calculate each salesman's percentage of the total sales;
(c) Print the salesmens' names and percentages.

Parts (a) and (c) have been written in PL/1. You are to write part (b) in PL/1, add declarations and complete the program. Here is part (a) written in PL/1:

```
/* READ IN SALESMEN AND SALES AND ADD UP TOTAL SALES */
TOTAL_SALES=0;
I=1;
GET LIST(SALESMAN(I),SALES(I));
DO WHILE(SALESMAN(I)¬='NOBODY');
   TOTAL_SALES=TOTAL_SALES+SALES(I);
   I=I+1;
   GET LIST(SALESMAN(I),SALES(I));
   END;
```

Here is part (c) written in PL/1:

```
/* PRINT SALESMEN'S NAMES AND PERCENTAGES */
PUT SKIP LIST('SALESMAN','PERCENT');
I=1;
DO WHILE(SALESMAN(I)¬='NOBODY');
    PUT SKIP LIST(SALESMAN(I),PERCENT(I));
    I=I+1;
    END;
```

Your are to complete the program without changing parts (a) and (c).

CHAPTER 10

THE COMPUTER CAN READ ENGLISH

In the subset SP/4 you learned how to handle character strings; you could join strings together, select parts of strings, and determine their lengths. As well, you learned how to compare strings, either for the purpose of recognizing particular strings or for putting various strings in order. In this chapter we will show how these capabilities can be used to create the illusion that the computer does things that we normally associate with people, and we might say that it is "intelligent". We say it has an artificial intelligence, since it is of course <u>not</u> human, and thinking is what humans do. The field of artificial intelligence in computer science concerns itself with getting the computer to perform acts that we think of as the province of humans. Of course, when we see how it is done, we realize it is just a mechanical process. It has to be mechanical or a machine could not do it. But if you do not know how the "trick" is performed, it does seem as if the machine can "think".

The field of artificial intelligence is involved with many different activities of man as imitated by machine, but one of the most interesting is the way that a machine is made to deal with statements made in <u>natural language</u>. We call a language, like English, a natural language because it evolved over a period of time through use. A language like PL/1 is a <u>formal language</u>. It has been defined, it is unambiguous and it is really very limited. Trying to get computers to deal with natural language is a major task. We would like to be able to write questions in natural language and have the computer provide answers to our questions from a bank of information. This is a goal in information retrieval systems.

We have not yet got very far along the way towards question-answering systems in natural language, but it is clear there are basic "skills" the computer must have to ever cope with this at all. One of these skills is the ability to read.

WORD RECOGNITION

When you first learn how to read you must learn to recognize words. To do this you must recognize what a word is. You learn the basic characters, the letters, then you learn that a word is a string of characters with a blank in front and a blank after it and no blanks in between. We are now going to write a program that will input a line of text and split it up into words. To simplify the job, we will begin our problem without any punctuation marks in the text and arrange to have exactly one blank after each word and no blanks at the beginning of the text. As an example,

                'HEREbISbAbTEXTb'

where we have used b to represent a blank. The method of dealing with problem solving by simplification is very helpful. Solve a simpler problem before you try a harder one. We will learn to cope with punctuation marks later.

Our solution tree for this problem is:

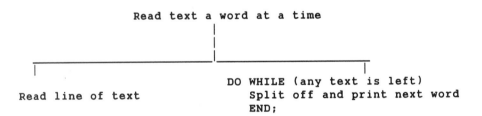

```
                    Read text a word at a time
                              |
                              |
 _____|_____
 |                           |                           |
                            DO WHILE (any text is left)
 Read line of text            Split off and print next word
                              END;
```

All the parts are straightforward except "Split off and print next word." We will refine it further:

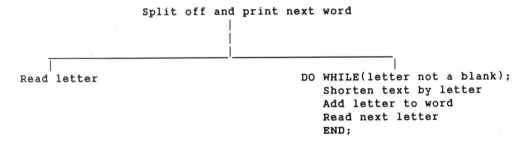

```
                    Split off and print next word
                              |
                              |
 _____|_____
 |                           |                           |
 Read letter                DO WHILE(letter not a blank);
                              Shorten text by letter
                              Add letter to word
                              Read next letter
                              END;
```

To determine the letter at the beginning of the text we use

```
      LETTER=SUBSTR(TEXT,1,1);
```

To shorten the text by removing the letter at the beginning we write

```
      TEXT=SUBSTR(TEXT,2);
```

Remember, if there is no third item in the parentheses after SUBSTR then the substring continues to the end of the string TEXT. To add a letter to WORD use

```
      WORD=WORD||LETTER;
```

We are ready now for the program:

```
$JOB ID='JULIE FISCHETTE'
 READING:PROCEDURE OPTIONS(MAIN);
    /* READ TEXT A WORD AT A TIME */
    DECLARE(TEXT,WORD)CHARACTER(78)VARYING;
    DECLARE(LETTER)CHARACTER(1)VARYING;
    GET LIST(TEXT);
    /* SPLIT OFF AND PRINT NEXT WORD */
    DO WHILE(TEXT¬=' ');
       /* INITIALIZE LOOP; SET WORD TO NULL; GET FIRST LETTER */
       WORD='';
       LETTER=SUBSTR(TEXT,1,1);
       DO WHILE(LETTER¬='b');
          /* ADD LETTER TO WORD */
          WORD=WORD||LETTER;
          /* SHORTEN TEXT BY LETTER */
          TEXT=SUBSTR(TEXT,2);
          /* READ NEXT LETTER */
          LETTER=SUBSTR(TEXT,1,1);
          END;
       PUT SKIP LIST(WORD);
       /* CHOP OFF BLANK */
       IF TEXT¬=' ' THEN
          TEXT=SUBSTR(TEXT,2);
       END;
    END;
$DATA
 'SEEbTHEbCOMPUTERbREADb'
```

Again, we see how the English entries in the solution tree become comments in the program. We have added two more comments concerning loop initialization and chopping off the blank to reach the next word.

     This program is not as efficient as it might be; by backing up the solution we might improve it. We will give another way to "Split off and print next word."

```
DO WHILE(any text is left);
   Find position of first blank in text
   Split off substring up to blank as word
   Remove word and trailing blank from text
   END;
```

This will result in a replacement of the body of the outer DO WHILE loop.

```
DO WHILE(TEXT¬=' ');
   POSITION=1;
   /* FIND POSITION OF FIRST BLANK IN TEXT */
   DO WHILE(SUBSTR(TEXT,POSITION,1)¬=' ');
      POSITION=POSITION+1;
      END;
   /* SPLIT OFF SUBSTRING UP TO BLANK AS WORD */
   PUT SKIP LIST(SUBSTR(TEXT,1,POSITION-1));
   /* TEXT IS SUBSTRING FOLLOWING BLANK */
   IF POSITION<LENGTH(TEXT)
      TEXT=SUBSTR(TEXT,POSITION+1);
   END;
```

We have to declare POSITION as FIXED. This algorithm is more efficient because in the inner DO WHILE loop there is only one use of the built-in function SUBSTR. In the first algorithm there are two uses of SUBSTR and a concatenation. Outside the inner loop, the second method has one use of SUBSTR; the first method has two uses. This latter difference is not as important, as it happens only once for every word; the efficiency of the inner loop is more important because it is executed once for every letter.

WORDS WITH PUNCTUATION

We want now to modify the previous program to do the same thing when there are punctuation marks present, that is, find the words in a text and print them out one by one. We usually try to build on the previous work so that we do not need to do everything from scratch. If we could reduce the text with the punctuation marks to one without such marks, we could then use the old program. The solution tree would be:

```
              Read a text with
              punctuation marks
                      |
  _____|_____
  |                  |                    |
  Eliminate                        Read a text without
  punctuation marks                punctuation marks
```

Our problem is to eliminate punctuation marks from text. This is accomplished in this program segment:

```
DO WHILE(there are more letters);
   Read a letter
   IF letter is a punctuation mark THEN
      Remove letter from text
   END;
```

The program for this will be:

```
GET LIST(TEXT);
POSITION=1;
DO WHILE(POSITION<LENGTH(TEXT));
   /* READ A LETTER */
   LETTER=SUBSTR(TEXT,POSITION,1);
   /* IF PUNCTUATION MARK, REMOVE FROM TEXT */
   IF LETTER=','|LETTER='.'
      |LETTER='?'|LETTER=':'
      |LETTER=';'|LETTER=')'
      |LETTER='(' THEN
        TEXT=SUBSTR(TEXT,1,POSITION-1)||SUBSTR(TEXT,POSITION+1);
   ELSE
      POSITION=POSITION+1;
   END;
```

After this has been executed, TEXT can be separated into words by the previous program since all the punctuation marks have been removed. We are assuming there is only one blank between words and that the text does not end with a special character.

NAME RECOGNITION

You often want to sort names alphabetically, and this is a problem if the names are written out in full with the surname last. For a name like FRANCES CORLEY PHILLIPS the sorting must be on PHILLIPS. We are not certain in general how many names precede the surname. Some people have one, some two, some even three or four. We would like to write a program that takes a full name and rewrites it with the surname first then initials like

PHILLIPS, F. C.

Since in a sorting process blanks have a lower value than any character, it is important that the position and number of the blanks be consistent from one person's name to another, so we will have one blank after the comma and one after each period.

We have assumed in our word-recognition program that our text had one blank after each word and no more. This book is set by a computer so that the words in any line are both left- and right-justified; there is one non-blank character in the leftmost and one in the rightmost position of each line of text. This is accomplished by inserting extra blanks between words so that some have two or three blanks instead of one. It is a job that used to require a skilled linotype operator. You will notice that the computer never hyphenates words, and this may mean that some lines have rather a lot of blanks. This happens when the first word of the next line is a long one. We will speak more of text editors a little later, but now we are working on reading a person's name and bringing it to a standard form. We want the standard form so that a list of names can be sequenced alphabetically. As we read the full name initially we should not count on there being only one blank between names.

We now have two different ways of handling this problem. One is to start at the end of the string and read the surname backwards until a blank is reached; after finding the surname, the process of extracting the initials from the first names can proceed using a loop. Another method would be to read each name into an array location, keeping count of the number of names in the full name. Then the complete name could be reassembled. We will use this method.

We will use the single variable FULL_NAME for the name as input, the array NAME(I) to store each part of the name in turn, and STD_NAME for the form with initials following surname. We will assume that FULL_NAME contains a surname and one to seven first names. On input an extra blank is added to FULL_NAME so that the last letter of the name can be read. Inside the DO loop which is collecting names and storing them in NAME(I) there are two other loops, one for eliminating blanks in front of the name and one for collecting the letters in the name. We will not concern ourselves with program efficiency right now.

```
$JOB ID='GLENN MACEWEN'
 NAMES:PROCEDURE OPTIONS(MAIN);
    /* CHANGE FORM OF EACH NAME TO SURNAME    */
    /*   FOLLOWED BY INITIALS                 */
    DECLARE(FULL_NAME,STD_NAME)CHARACTER(80)VARYING,
       (NAME(8))CHARACTER(20)VARYING,
       (NEXT_CHAR)CHARACTER(1)VARYING,
       (I,NAME_COUNT)FIXED;
    GET LIST(FULL_NAME);
    DO WHILE(FULL_NAME¬='ZZZ');
       /* ADD EXTRA BLANK TO FULL_NAME */
       FULL_NAME=FULL_NAME||   ;
       NEXT_CHAR=SUBSTR(FULL_NAME,1,1);
       I=1;
       DO WHILE(LENGTH(FULL_NAME)>1);
          /* TRIM OFF LEADING BLANKS */
          DO WHILE(NEXT_CHAR=    LENGTH(FULL_NAME)>1);
             FULL_NAME=SUBSTR(FULL_NAME,2);
             NEXT_CHAR=SUBSTR(FULL_NAME,1,1);
             END;
          NAME(I)='';
          /* ASSEMBLE LETTERS IN NAME */
          DO WHILE(NEXT_CHAR¬=    LENGTH(FULL_NAME)>1);
             NAME(I)=NAME(I)||NEXT_CHAR;
             FULL_NAME=SUBSTR(FULL_NAME,2);
             NEXT_CHAR=SUBSTR(FULL_NAME,1,1);
             END;
          I=I+1;
          END;
       /* PREPARE FULL NAME IN STANDARD FORM */
       NAME_COUNT=I-1;
       /* CORRECT COUNT FOR CASE OF TRAILING BLANKS */
       IF(NAME(NAME_COUNT)='')
          THEN NAME_COUNT=NAME_COUNT-1;
       /* SELECT SURNAME */
       STD_NAME=NAME(NAME_COUNT)||   ;
       /* ADD INITIALS */
       DO I=1 TO(NAME_COUNT-1);
          STD_NAME=STD_NAME||SUBSTR(NAME(I),1,1)||   ;
          END;
       PUT SKIP LIST(STD_NAME);
       GET LIST(FULL_NAME);
       END;
    END;
$DATA
 'RICHARD CRAIG HOLT'
 'JAMES NAIRN PATTERSON HUME'
 'ZZZ'
```

The output for this program is

```
    HOLT, R. C.
    HUME, J. N. P.
```

Now we will give an improved program from the viewpoint of efficiency.

```
$JOB ID='WES GRAHAM'
 NAMES:PROCEDURE OPTIONS(MAIN);
    /* CHANGE FORM OF EACH NAME TO SURNAME      */
    /*   FOLLOWED BY INITIALS                   */
    DECLARE(FULL_NAME,STD_NAME)CHARACTER(80)VARYING,
      (NAME(8))CHARACTER(20)VARYING,
      (I,FULL_NAME_LENGTH,NAME_COUNT,NAME_START,POSITION,SIZE)FIXED;
    GET LIST(FULL_NAME);
    DO WHILE(FULL_NAME¬='ZZZ');
       /* ADD EXTRA BLANK TO FULL_NAME */
       FULL_NAME=FULL_NAME||' ';
       I=1;
       FULL_NAME_LENGTH=LENGTH(FULL_NAME);
       POSITION=1;
       DO WHILE(POSITION<FULL_NAME_LENGTH);
          DO WHILE(SUBSTR(FULL_NAME,POSITION,1)=' ' &
                POSITION<FULL_NAME_LENGTH);
             POSITION=POSITION+1;
             END;
          NAME_START=POSITION;
          DO WHILE(SUBSTR(FULL_NAME,POSITION,1)¬=' ');
             POSITION=POSITION+1;
             END;
          SIZE=POSITION-NAME_START;
          NAME(I)=SUBSTR(FULL_NAME,NAME_START,SIZE);
          I=I+1;
          END;
       /* PREPARE FULL NAME IN STANDARD FORM */
       NAME_COUNT=I-1;
       /* CORRECT COUNT FOR CASE OF TRAILING BLANKS */
       IF(NAME(NAME_COUNT)='')
          THEN NAME_COUNT=NAME_COUNT-1;
       /* SELECT SURNAME */
       STD_NAME=NAME(NAME_COUNT)||    ;
       /* ADD INITIALS */
       DO I=1 TO(NAME_COUNT-1);
          STD_NAME=STD_NAME||SUBSTR(NAME(I),1,1)||    ;
          END;
       PUT SKIP LIST(STD_NAME);
       GET LIST(FULL_NAME);
       END;
    END;
$DATA
(same data as before)
```

This is a more efficient program because the two inner DO WHILE loops that are scanning for letters or blanks require only one use of SUBSTR; the first method used SUBSTR twice for each character. Another saving is that the function LENGTH(FULL_NAME) is evaluated only once and assigned to FULL_NAME_LENGTH, where in the first method it is evaluated for every character. Note that if SIZE=0 then the value of NAME(I) will be the null string.

WORD STATISTICS

We have learned to read words of a text, recognize certain words such as STOP, replace words and to treat words in a list in different ways as we did with the list of names. Another important use of a computer in dealing with words involves keeping statistics about the lengths of words. Different authors have different patterns of use of words and this shows up in the frequency with which they use words of different lengths. Some authors use a lot of long words; others rarely do.

In this section we will read a text and from it prepare a frequency distribution of word lengths. To add a little extra interest to this problem, we will display the results in graphic form. For instance, we will have a display like this for output:

```
LENGTH OF WORD         FREQUENCY
      1                ***
      2                ******
      3                ********
      4                *****
```

This display, called a histogram, represents the result of analyzing the frequency of different word lengths in a text. It shows that there were 3 one-letter words, 6 two-letter words, 8 three-letter words, and 5 four-letter words.

We will use what we have learned so far about reading words, but instead of forming the words we will just count the number of letters, then after each word concatenate an asterisk on to a string stored in an array location corresponding to the letter count. We will use the array FREQUENCY to store the strings of asterisks; FREQUENCY(4) will store a string of asterisks corresponding to the number of four-letter words. We will assume a maximum of 20 letters in a word and that there are no punctuation marks. Here is our program:

```
$JOB ID='PHYLLIS GOTLIEB'
 DISPLAY:PROCEDURE OPTIONS(MAIN);
    /* DETERMINE WORD FREQENCIES (UP TO 20)
    DECLARE(TEXT,FREQUENCY(20))CHARACTER(80)VARYING,
      (I,COUNT,TEXT_LENGTH,POSITION,WORD_START)FIXED;
    DO I=1 TO 20;
       FREQUENCY(I)='';
       END;
    GET LIST(TEXT);
    DO WHILE(TEXT¬='ZZZ');
       TEXT=TEXT||'b';
       TEXT_LENGTH=LENGTH(TEXT);
       POSITION=1;
       DO WHILE(POSITION<TEXT_LENGTH);
          DO WHILE(SUBSTR(TEXT,POSITION,1)=' ' &
             POSITION<TEXT_LENGTH);
             POSITION=POSITION+1;
             END;
          WORD_START=POSITION;
          DO WHILE(SUBSTR(TEXT,POSITION,1)¬=' ');
             POSITION=POSITION+1;
             END;
          COUNT=POSITION-WORD_START;
          IF COUNT<=20 & COUNT>=1 THEN
             FREQUENCY(COUNT)=FREQUENCY(COUNT)||'*';
          END;
       GET LIST(TEXT);
       END;
    PUT SKIP LIST('LENGTH OF WORD','FREQUENCY');
    DO I=1 TO 20;
       PUT SKIP LIST(I,FREQUENCY(I));
       END;
    END;
$DATA
 'ROSES ARE RED'
 'VIOLETS ARE BLUE'
 'HONEY IS SWEET'
 'AND SO ARE YOU'
 'ZZZ'
```

Handwritten annotations: loop to initialize frequencies; marker for end of file; loop to determine 1st non-blank in text; loop to determine length of word

The output for this is

LENGTH OF WORD	FREQUENCY
1	
2	**
3	******
4	*
5	***
6	
7	*
...	
20	

You can see how similar the program is to the more efficient one for reading names. It would be handy to have some more built-in functions for dealing with strings. In PL/1 there are a number of these built-in functions, but in SP/6 we will learn how to create our own functions.

READING PL/1

We have been reading English text and performing operations on it, or as the result of it. All these operations, we see, are absolutely mechanical but give you the impression that the computer is capable of doing things we think of as "intelligent work". One of the fields of artificial intelligence that has been explored is the translation from one language to another. The translation of one natural language into another, such as English to French, has had only qualified success. It works, but not well when the text is ambiguous or difficult. The translations are not good literature, to say the least.

But computers are being used for language translation every day, for the translation of programming languages into machine languages. The reason this is possible is that programming languages are well defined and quite limited.

Your PL/1 programs are translated by the compiler program into machine language programs before execution. We want to look a little at how this can be done. The different parts of the program are separated by semicolons, which appear after each statement. Right after each semicolon there is a keyword with one exception, and that is if the statement is an assignment statement. These keywords are limited to a very small list; they include GET, PUT, DO, IF, DECLARE, END. We can thus decide whether or not a statement is an assignment statement by reading the first word after the semicolon. If it is not one of the keywords it is an assignment statement.

We will look later at the problem of actually preparing a translation for the various types of statements, but at this stage you can at least see how the keywords can be used in the translation process.

CHAPTER 10 SUMMARY

In this chapter we have shown how the computer can, in a sense, understand English. The computer can recognize words by scanning for their beginnings and endings. Typically, words in English are surrounded by blanks or special characters; programs can be written which separate out words by searching for these characters. Due to the great speed of computers, they sometimes have the appearance of being intelligent, in spite of the fact that their basic mode of operation is very simplistic, such as

seeing if a given character is a blank. PL/1 compilers, such as
the SP/k compiler and the PL/C compiler, have been developed to
read text which looks somewhat like English; the text which they
have been designed to read is PL/1 programs.

CHAPTER 10 EXERCISES

1.A <u>palindrome</u> is a word or phrase which is spelled the same
backwards and forwards.   The following are examples of word
palindromes: "I",   "mom",   "deed" and "level".   Blanks and
punctuation are ignored in phrase palindromes, for example,
"Madam, in Eden I'm Adam" and "A man, a plan, a canal, Panama".
Write a program which reads a string and determines if it is a
palindrome.

2. You are to write a program which will help in reviewing a
script to determine its suitability for television screening.
Your program is to give a list of the frequency of use of the
following unacceptable words:

    'PHOOEY' 'SHUCKS' 'JEEPERS' 'GOLLY'

Make up a few lines of script to test out your program.

3. You are employed by an English teacher who insists that "and"
should not be preceded by a comma. Hence, "Crosby, Stills, Nash
and Young" is acceptable, but "Merril, Fynch, and Lynn" is not.
Write a program which reads lines of text, searches   for
unacceptable commas, removes them, and makes stern remarks such
as the English teacher would make about errors.

4. Write a program which reads text and then prints it so that
its left and right margins are vertical. First the program is to
read the number of characters to print per line. Whenever enough
words for one line have been collected, blanks are inserted
between words to expand the line to the desired width. Then the
expanded line is printed.

CHAPTER 11

SP/6: PROCEDURES

In this subset we will be introducing the idea of procedures
other than the MAIN procedure that has constituted all programs
so far. The purpose of having subsidiary procedures or
subprocedures is so that a larger program can be divided into
parts. In this way we "divide and conquer" a complicated
problem. Sometimes a part of the solution of one problem can be
used in many different problems, and making it into a procedure
creates a module or building block which can be used in many
programs.

DEFINITION OF A PROCEDURE

We have seen in Chapter 10 that the process of obtaining the
next word from a text is a very common one, and that if we had a
procedure for doing this we might use it frequently. The
procedure must take in certain information, namely the text whose
next word is to be found. It must then give out information,
namely the next word and the text with that word removed from it.
We say that the procedure has one input parameter, TEXT, and two
output parameters, NEXT_WORD and TEXT, which has had the word
chopped off it. To define a procedure that will do this we must
give it a name, say WORD, and begin the <u>procedure</u> <u>definition</u> in
this way:

    WORD:PROCEDURE(TEXT,NEXT_WORD);

This gives the keyword PROCEDURE preceded by a colon and the name
of the procedure. In parentheses is a list of the procedure
parameters. Some of these are input to the procedure; some are
output from the procedure. In this case TEXT is both an input
and an output parameter. Each procedure must contain
declarations for all its parameters. The declarations <u>must</u> show

the attribute, but need not show the maximum length for character
or array parameters. These are just written with an asterisk
where the maximum size would normally be. For instance, we could
write for our example

    DECLARE(TEXT,NEXT_WORD)CHARACTER(*)VARYING;

The reason that the actual size is not necessary is that when the
procedure is used in another program there must be declarations
there that give this information. What is established inside the
procedure definition itself is that the parameter is of type
character.

   Here is the complete definition for this procedure.

```
WORD:PROCEDURE(TEXT,NEXT_WORD);
   DECLARE(TEXT,NEXT_WORD)CHARACTER(*)VARYING;
   DECLARE(L,POSITION,WORD_START,WORD_LENGTH)FIXED;
   /* ADD BLANK TO END OF TEXT */
   TEXT=TEXT||' ';
   L=LENGTH(TEXT);
   POSITION=1;
   /* REMOVE LEADING BLANKS */
   DO WHILE(SUBSTR(TEXT,POSITION,1)=' ' & POSITION<L);
      POSITION=POSITION+1;
      END;
   WORD_START=POSITION;
   DO WHILE(SUBSTR(TEXT,POSITION,1)¬=' ');
      POSITION=POSITION+1;
      END;
   WORD_LENGTH=POSITION-WORD_START;
   NEXT_WORD=SUBSTR(TEXT,WORD_START,WORD_LENGTH);
   /* NOTE: IF WORD_LENGTH IS ZERO NEXT_WORD IS NULL */
   /* REMOVE WORD AND BLANK ADDED TO END OF TEXT */
   TEXT=SUBSTR(TEXT,POSITION,L-POSITION);
   END;
```

   You will notice that, after the declaration of the procedure
parameters, several variables are declared. These are L,
POSITION, WORD_START, and WORD_LENGTH. These variables are said
to be local to the procedure WORD. At the time a procedure is
used, space reservations are made for local variables. When
control returns from a procedure to the program that is using it,
the space reserved for the local variables is given back and the
local variables disappear. This is one way in which memory space
can be conserved. If it is intended that the values of variables
be preserved on leaving a procedure then those variables must be
declared in the program that uses the procedure and not inside
the procedure definition. We say that variables used by a
procedure that are not parameters or declared locally are global
variables.

   In SP/k, procedure definitions can be placed after the
declarations of the MAIN procedure. This means that in PL/1
terms they are what are called internal procedures.

USING PROCEDURES

We have just constructed a procedure for reading words. (We have again made the simplification that there are no punctuation marks in the text.) Now we must learn how to use this procedure. We will use it in our program to change names of people into the standard form of surname followed by initials.

To use this procedure we put this statement in the main procedure

```
CALL WORD(FULL_NAME,NAME(I));
```

which will take the character variable FULL_NAME and pick off the first word and store it in NAME(I). Here is the program using the procedure:

```
$JOB ID='DAVE SCOTT'
 NAMES:PROCEDURE OPTIONS(MAIN);
    /* CHANGE FORM OF EACH NAME TO SURNAME    */
    /*   FOLLOWED BY INITIALS                 */
    DECLARE(FULL_NAME,STD_NAME)CHARACTER(80)VARYING,
       (NAME(8))CHARACTER(20)VARYING,
       (I,NAME_COUNT)FIXED;

    /* INCLUDE DEFINITION OF PROCEDURE 'WORD' */
    WORD:PROCEDURE(TEXT,NEXT_WORD);
       DECLARE(TEXT,NEXT_WORD)CHARACTER(*)VARYING;
       (etc. exactly as shown for body of procedure)
       END;

    GET LIST(FULL_NAME);
    DO WHILE(FULL_NAME¬='ZZZ');
       I=1;
       DO WHILE(LENGTH(FULL_NAME)>0);
          CALL WORD(FULL_NAME,NAME(I));
          I=I+1;
          END;
       /* PREPARE FULL NAME IN STANDARD FORM */
       NAME_COUNT=I-1;
       /* CORRECT COUNT FOR CASE OF TRAILING BLANKS */
       IF(NAME(NAME_COUNT)='')
          THEN NAME_COUNT=NAME_COUNT-1;
       /* SELECT SURNAME */
       STD_NAME=NAME(NAME_COUNT)||',b';
       /* ADD INITIALS */
       DO I=1 TO(NAME_COUNT-1);
          STD_NAME=STD_NAME||SUBSTR(NAME(I),1,1)||'.b';
          END;
       PUT SKIP LIST(STD_NAME);
       GET LIST(FULL_NAME);
       END;
    END;
$DATA
```

You can see that what has happened is that a piece of the former program has been placed into the procedure WORD; then the one CALL WORD statement invokes the action of the whole procedure WORD.

Notice that the identifiers in parentheses following CALL WORD are not the same as those used as parameters in the definition of WORD. The items in the CALL statement parentheses are called <u>arguments</u>.

ARGUMENTS AND PARAMETERS

We have introduced two words in connection with procedures, the words "arguments" and "parameters". The parameters are the identifiers used in the definition of a procedure for information that is to be fed into a procedure or to be given out. Arguments are the expressions (often variables) in the <u>calling procedure</u> that are to be put into correspondence with the procedure parameters. And <u>there must be a one-to-one correspondence between the number and type attributes of the arguments and the</u> parameters.

You may have guessed that there is something different about parameters; when a character parameter is declared we must give its maximum length as an asterisk. The fact is that no space reservations are made for the parameters because the space needed is already reserved in the calling procedure for the arguments. All references to parameters in a procedure actually refer to the corresponding argument. This is done by means of pointers to the locations that hold the arguments.

These pointers are set automatically at the time the procedure is called. When the procedure is executing, each time the value of a parameter is changed the corresponding argument is immediately altered. In our example, the argument FULL_NAME is in correspondence with the parameter TEXT and the argument NAME(I) with the parameter NEXT_WORD. When the statement

    TEXT=TEXT||' ';

of the procedure is executed, it is equivalent to the statement

    FULL_NAME=FULL_NAME||' ';

being executed.

Here is a diagram to show the association between parameters and arguments, and the variables local to the procedure WORD.

```
FULL_NAME<-----TEXT
NAME(I)<-------NEXT_WORD
               L
               POSITION
               WORD_START
               WORD_LENGTH
```

Because the parameters of a procedure are associated with arguments at the time the procedure is called, it means that a procedure may be used in the same program with a different set of arguments in another CALL statement. Notice that L, POSITION, WORD_START and WORD_LENGTH, the local variables, are ordinary variables in the procedure and do not refer to any variables in the calling procedure. These local variables cannot be referenced outside the procedure. Each time the procedure is called, these variables must be given values before being used, because their values from any previous calls are discarded.

CONSTANTS AS ARGUMENTS

We will do another simple example to show how constants can be used as arguments. Suppose we write a procedure that will add the elements of an integer array, ARRAY, of N elements and call the total SUM. Let us call the procedure TOTAL.

```
/* ADD THE N ELEMENTS OF ARRAY */
TOTAL:PROCEDURE(ARRAY,N,SUM);
    DECLARE(ARRAY(*),N,SUM)FIXED;
    DECLARE(I)FIXED;
    SUM=0;
    DO I=1 TO N;
       SUM=SUM+ARRAY(I);
       END;
    END;
```

Now let us write a calling procedure for this:

```
$JOB ID='LARRY LAFAVE'
 BILL:PROCEDURE OPTIONS(MAIN);
    DECLARE(INVOICE(5),I,GROSS)FIXED;
    (include definition of TOTAL procedure here)
    DO I=1 TO 5;
       GET LIST(INVOICE(I));
       END;
    CALL TOTAL(INVOICE,5,GROSS);
    PUT LIST('GROSS=',GROSS);
    END;
$DATA
 25   36   21   7   2
```

The output will be

```
GROSS=      91
```

In this example, notice that the argument INVOICE is in correspondence with the parameter ARRAY. The declaration of ARRAY is indirect and its maximum size is given by an asterisk. References in the procedure to ARRAY(1) will point at INVOICE(1). There is no location in the memory identified by ARRAY(1), but there is for INVOICE(1), and ARRAY(1) simply points to INVOICE(1).

In this example, we have a constant 5 as the argument in correspondence with the parameter N. In this case a dummy argument is set up, the value 5 stored in it, and the parameter N set to point to this dummy argument. If an arithmetic expression other than a constant or a single variable is used as an argument it is first evaluated, its value stored in a dummy argument and, after that, references to it in the procedure are to the dummy argument.

Notice that the same variable identifier I is used in the main procedure BILL and also as a local variable in the procedure TOTAL. These are treated as absolutely separate variables. There is no need to worry about accidental coincidences between names of local and global variables. Inside the procedure, the local one is used exclusively. Outside the procedure, the one local to the procedure is not visible.

GLOBAL AND LOCAL VARIABLES

The statements inside a subprocedure can use variables declared in the surrounding procedure. We have not done this in any example so far, because our purpose in having procedures was to separate the parts of the program completely; the only communication has been through the list of parameters. Sometimes, if a great deal of information is to be passed, and if the procedure is being custom-made exclusively for your own program, it is appropriate for the subprocedure to reference variables that are declared only in the main procedure. Remember we call such variables global to the procedure since they are declared in a surrounding procedure. Variables that are declared in the inner procedure are said to be local to that procedure.

FUNCTIONS

There are really two kinds of procedures. The ones we have described so far are called subroutine procedures or subroutines for short. We will now describe a quite different kind of procedure called a function procedure or function for short.

Function procedures may have any number of arguments but give as a result a single value. Perhaps the easiest way to

understand this is to look at a function that we have already
been using, the substring function SUBSTR. To use the function
we write:

    SUBSTR(string,starting position,length of substring)

We get a substring of "string" beginning at the "starting
position" and having a length the "length of substring". There
are three arguments provided to this function and the function
itself provides the result, namely the required substring.

    To program a function procedure ourselves we do exactly what
we did for a subroutine procedure, but we add two things. After
the list of the procedure parameters we write RETURNS, followed
in parentheses by the attribute of the value of the function that
is returned as a result. Then, just before the END that
terminates the body of the procedure, we write RETURN followed in
parentheses by an expression whose value is what is to be
returned as a result. The attribute of this expression matches
the attribute stated after RETURNS.

    For example, if we were preparing a function procedure for
the function SUBSTR, it would be of the form

```
 SUBSTR:PROCEDURE(string,starting position,length)
     RETURNS  (CHARACTER (MAXLENGTH) VARYING);
     (declarations)
     (body of procedure)
     RETURN(required substring);
     END;
```

This would be the function procedure definition and would be
included after the declarations of the MAIN procedure. SUBSTR is
a built-in function; it is already stored in the computer with
the particular PL/1 compiler that you are using. Another built-
in function dealing with strings is the LENGTH function.

    When it is used in the form

    LENGTH(string)

it returns a value whose attribute is FIXED. It has just one
argument. We would have the function procedure defined in this
form:

```
 LENGTH:PROCEDURE(string)RETURNS(FIXED);
     (declarations)
     (body of procedure)
     RETURN(fixed expression that gives length of string);
     END;
```

As it happens, it is not possible to program a function procedure
for SUBSTR; that is why we have it as a built-in function. This
is true also of LENGTH. Although we can program a function to
find the length of a string provided one character, such as a

blank, is not allowed in the string, we cannot do it for any string in general.

Many PL/1 compilers provide a built-in function named INDEX. The INDEX function is called by

INDEX(string,form)

The two arguments, "string" and "form" must be character strings. The INDEX function searches "string" for the leftmost occurrence of "form" and returns the position of the occurrence. For example, INDEX('MISSISSIPPI','IS') returns 2. If "form" is the null string or does not occur in "string" the value 0 is returned. Since SP/k does not provide such a built-in function we will have to construct one if we want it. We will not call it INDEX in case you want to test our function and are using another compiler, say PL/C. We will call it PATTERN. Here is the definition of PATTERN:

```
PATTERN:PROCEDURE(STRING,FORM)RETURNS(FIXED);
   /* FIND LOCATION OF FORM IN STRING */
   DECLARE(STRING,FORM)CHARACTER(*)VARYING;
   DECLARE(FORM_LENGTH,LOCATION,LAST_LOCATION,I)FIXED;
   FORM_LENGTH=LENGTH(FORM);
   LOCATION=0;
   LAST_LOCATION=LENGTH(STRING)-FORM_LENGTH+1;
   I=1;
   IF FORM_LENGTH>=1 THEN
      DO WHILE(I<=LAST_LOCATION);
         IF FORM=SUBSTR(STRING,I,FORM_LENGTH) THEN
            DO;
               LOCATION=I;
               I=LAST_LOCATION+1;
               END;
         ELSE
            I=I+1;
         END;
   RETURN(LOCATION);
   END;
```

As an illustration of the use of this function procedure, we will write a program to eliminate all the punctuation marks in a text.

```
$JOB ID='DEREK CORNEIL'
 /* REMOVE PUNCTUATION MARKS FROM TEXT */
 NOMARKS:PROCEDURE OPTIONS(MAIN);
    DECLARE(NEXT_CHAR)CHARACTER(1)VARYING;
    DECLARE(TEXT)CHARACTER(80)VARYING;
    DECLARE(SPECIAL_CHARS)CHARACTER(7)VARYING;
    DECLARE(TEXT_LENGTH,I)FIXED;
    (definition of the procedure PATTERN)
    GET LIST(TEXT);
    TEXT_LENGTH=LENGTH(TEXT);
    SPECIAL_CHARS= ',.?:;()';
    I=1;
    DO WHILE(I<=TEXT_LENGTH);
       NEXT_CHAR=SUBSTR(TEXT,I,1);
       /* SEE IF NEXT_CHAR IS A SPECIAL CHARACTER. */
       IF(PATTERN(SPECIAL_CHARS,NEXT_CHAR)¬=0) THEN
          DO;
             IF I<TEXT_LENGTH THEN
                TEXT=SUBSTR(TEXT,1,I-1)||SUBSTR(TEXT,I+1);
             ELSE
                TEXT=SUBSTR(TEXT,1,I-1);
             TEXT_LENGTH=TEXT_LENGTH-1;
             END;
       ELSE
          I=I+1;
       END;
    PUT LIST(TEXT);
    END;
$DATA
 'ARE THE PERIODS, COMMAS, AND QUESTION MARKS GONE?'
```

The output for this program should be

    ARE THE PERIODS COMMAS AND QUESTION MARKS GONE

If your compiler has the INDEX function built in you can try
using it. The reason the INDEX function is not built into some
compilers is that you can write it for yourself.

EXAMPLES OF SUBROUTINES AND FUNCTIONS

There are two kinds of procedures in PL/1: subroutines and
functions. Essentially, subroutines allow you to invent new PL/1
statements, while functions allow you to invent new operations.
We will give examples of these two possibilities.

Suppose we wish to determine the larger of two FIXED numbers.
We could write a subroutine to find the larger one; this is done
in the following program:

```
$JOB ID='STEWART LEE'
 BIG_ONE:PROCEDURE OPTIONS(MAIN);
    DECLARE(DATA1,DATA2,MAXIMUM)FIXED;
    LARGER:PROCEDURE(FIRST,SECOND,RESULT);
       DECLARE(FIRST,SECOND,RESULT)FIXED;
       IF FIRST>SECOND THEN
          RESULT=FIRST;
       ELSE
          RESULT=SECOND;
       END;
    GET LIST(DATA1,DATA2);
    CALL LARGER(DATA1,DATA2,MAXIMUM);
    PUT SKIP LIST('THE LARGER IS',MAXIMUM);
    END;
$DATA
 5   31
```

When the LARGER procedure is called, via the statement

```
    CALL LARGER(DATA1,DATA2,MAXIMUM);
```

the parameter FIRST becomes another name for DATA1, SECOND becomes another name for DATA2 and RESULT becomes another name for MAXIMUM. The LARGER procedure is entered and RESULT, which is really MAXIMUM, is set to the larger of FIRST and SECOND, which are really DATA1 and DATA2. When the end of the LARGER procedure is reached, execution returns to the statement just beyond the CALL statement, which is the PUT SKIP LIST statement. Given the data values 5 and 31, the program will print

```
    THE LARGER IS     31
```

Conceptually, our subroutine provides us with a new PL/1 statement which we can use whenever we want to find the larger of two numbers.

This has been a very simple example; if you were writing such a simple program as this one you would not bother to use a procedure. We could have found the larger number by writing a function rather than a subroutine. A function named BIGGER is used in the following version of the program.

```
$JOB ID='RON BAECKER'
 BIG_ONE:PROCEDURE OPTIONS(MAIN);
    DECLARE(DATA1,DATA2,MAXIMUM)FIXED;
    BIGGER:PROCEDURE(FIRST,SECOND)RETURNS(FIXED);
       DECLARE(FIRST,SECOND)FIXED;
       DECLARE(ANSWER)FIXED;
       IF FIRST>SECOND THEN
          ANSWER=FIRST;
       ELSE
          ANSWER=SECOND;
       RETURN(ANSWER);
       END;
    GET LIST(DATA1,DATA2);
    MAXIMUM=BIGGER(DATA1,DATA2);
    PUT SKIP LIST('THE LARGER IS',MAXIMUM);
    END;
$DATA
 5   31
```

This job will print the same as the previous job, namely:

      THE LARGER IS   31

The BIGGER procedure is a function because it contains the clause
RETURNS (attribute) in its definition. Since it is a function,
it must explicitly return a value. This is done by the
statement,

      RETURN(ANSWER);

The BIGGER procedure is entered as a result of the fact that its
name appears in the assignment statement:

      MAXIMUM=BIGGER(DATA1,DATA2);

When the BIGGER procedure is entered, the parameter FIRST is
taken as another name for DATA1 and SECOND as another name for
DATA2. The variable named ANSWER is declared for use inside the
BIGGER procedure. ANSWER is given the value of the larger of
FIRST and SECOND. Since ANSWER is declared inside BIGGER,
assignment of a value to ANSWER inside BIGGER has no effect
outside the BIGGER function. The statement,

      RETURN(ANSWER);

both terminates the BIGGER function and returns the value of
ANSWER so it can be assigned to MAXIMUM. Conceptually, our
function provides us with a new arithmetic operation which we can
use in arithmetic expressions. We could have replaced the
assignment to MAXIMUM and then immediately following PUT SKIP
LIST statement by the statement

      PUT SKIP LIST('THE LARGER IS',BIGGER(DATA1,DATA2));

This change would not affect the printed answer.

Our example procedures LARGER and BIGGER illustrate the following differences between subroutines and functions. The definition of a function must include the clause RETURNS(attribute), but the definition of a subroutine must not have this clause. A subroutine can end by simply reaching its final

```
    END;
```

A function must first explicitly return a value via the statement,

```
    RETURN(returned value);
```

The "returned value" must match the attribute in the RETURNS clause. For example, in the function called BIGGER, the returned value ANSWER matches the FIXED attribute of the RETURNS clause. A subroutine is entered when it is invoked via the CALL statement. A function is entered when its name appears in an expression, such as the right side of an assignment statement.

                          NESTED PROCEDURES

Once a subroutine has been defined, it can be used, via the CALL statement, just like any other PL/1 statement. It is even possible to use CALL statements inside procedures. We will give simple examples to show the use of nested procedures. The following job prints the largest of its three data values.

```
$JOB ID='SCOTT GRAHAM'
 BIG_ONE:PROCEDURE OPTIONS(MAIN);
    DECLARE(DATA1,DATA2,DATA3,MAXIMUM)FIXED;
    LARGER:PROCEDURE(FIRST,SECOND,RESULT);
       (exactly as previous version of LARGER procedure)
       END;
    LARGEST:PROCEDURE(FIRST,SECOND,THIRD,RESULT);
       DECLARE(FIRST,SECOND,THIRD,RESULT)FIXED;
       DECLARE(GREATER)FIXED;
       CALL LARGER(FIRST,SECOND,GREATER);
       CALL LARGER(GREATER,THIRD,RESULT);
       END;
    GET LIST(DATA1,DATA2,DATA3);
    CALL LARGEST(DATA1,DATA2,DATA3,MAXIMUM);
    PUT SKIP LIST('THE LARGEST IS',MAXIMUM);
    END;
$DATA
 5  31  27
```

This job will print:

```
    THE LARGEST IS      31
```

The procedure named LARGEST determines which of its first three parameters is largest and assigns the largest value to its fourth parameter, named RESULT. It accomplishes this by first using LARGER to assign the larger of the first two parameters to the variable GREATER, and by using LARGER again to assign the larger of GREATER and the third parameter to RESULT.

The procedures LARGER and LARGEST both have parameters named FIRST and SECOND. This causes no trouble because the parameters of LARGER are hidden from LARGEST and vice versa. As a rule it is good programming practice to avoid duplicate names, as they may confuse people reading a program. However, in some cases, such as this example, it seems natural to repeat names in separate procedures. Since duplicate names in separate procedures are kept separate in PL/1, this causes no difficulty.

We will now show an example of nesting calls to our BIGGER function. We will use it in the following job to print the largest of three numbers.

```
$JOB ID='HUGH DEMPSTER'
 BIG_ONE:PROCEDURE OPTIONS(MAIN);
    DECLARE(DATA1,DATA2,DATA3)FIXED;
    BIGGER:PROCEDURE(FIRST,SECOND)RETURNS(FIXED);
       (Exactly as previous version of BIGGER procedure)
       END;
    GET LIST(DATA1,DATA2,DATA3);
    PUT SKIP LIST('LARGEST IS',BIGGER(BIGGER(DATA1,DATA2),DATA3));
    END;
$DATA
 5   31   27
```

This job finds the larger of the first two data items using the BIGGER function, and uses the BIGGER function again to compare that value to the third data value. In the PUT SKIP LIST statement, the first argument to the BIGGER function is actually another call to the BIGGER function. This causes no trouble, because the inner call to BIGGER first returns 31, which is the larger of 5 and 31. Then the outer call to BIGGER compares 31 to 27 and returns the value of 31. Using a call to BIGGER inside a call to BIGGER is actually no more complicated than, say,

```
   ((5+31)+27)
```

This expression means add 5 and 31 and add 27 to the result. By comparison,

```
   BIGGER(BIGGER(5,31),27)
```

means find the larger of 5 and 31 and then find the larger of this and 27.

We will now show another kind of procedure nesting. If the procedure named LARGER is to be used only inside the procedure

named LARGEST, we can give the definition of LARGER inside
LARGEST. This is done in the following job:

```
$JOB ID='LARRY LIN'
 BIG_ONE:PROCEDURE OPTIONS(MAIN);
    DECLARE(DATA1,DATA2,DATA3,MAXIMUM)FIXED;
    LARGEST:PROCEDURE(FIRST,SECOND,THIRD,RESULT);
       DECLARE(FIRST,SECOND,THIRD,RESULT)FIXED;
       DECLARE(GREATER)FIXED;
       LARGER:PROCEDURE(FIRST,SECOND,RESULT);
          (Exactly as previous version of LARGER procedure)
          END;
       CALL LARGER(FIRST,SECOND,GREATER);
       CALL LARGER(GREATER,THIRD,RESULT);
       END;
    GET LIST(DATA1,DATA2,DATA3);
    CALL LARGEST(DATA1,DATA2,DATA3,MAXIMUM);
    PUT SKIP LIST('THE LARGEST IS',MAXIMUM);
    END;
$DATA
 5  31  27
```

The job works just like the previous job which contains a
procedure named LARGEST. The only difference is that since
LARGER has been hidden inside LARGEST, the LARGER procedure is no
longer available for use in the main procedure. The fact that
LARGER and LARGEST have parameters with the same names does not
cause trouble; each procedure will use its own local meanings for
the names FIRST, SECOND and RESULT. This example has shown how a
procedure definition can be nested inside another procedure
definition.

CHAPTER 11 SUMMARY

In this chapter we have introduced procedures. Procedures
allow us to build up programs out of modules. The reasons for
using procedures in programs include the following:

1. Dividing the program into parts which can be written by
    different people.

2. Dividing a program into parts which can be written over a
    period of time.

3. Making a large program easier to understand by building it up
    out of conceptually simple parts.

4. Factoring out common parts of a program so they need not be
    written many times within a program.

5. Factoring out commonly-used logic so that it can be used in a
    number of different programs.

6. Separating parts of a program so they can be individually tested.

There are two kinds of procedures in PL/1: subroutines and functions. Essentially, a subroutine provides a new kind of PL/1 statement and a function provides a new kind of operation. The following important terms were discussed in this chapter.

Procedure definition - means giving the meaning of a procedure to the computer. Procedure definitions in SP/k must come after declarations. Subroutine procedures can be defined using the following form:

```
name:PROCEDURE(parameters);
    declarations for parameters
    declarations for variables for this procedure
    ...
    END;
```

Function procedures can be defined using the following form:

```
name:PROCEDURE(parameters)RETURNS(attribute);
    declarations for parameters
    declarations for variables for this procedure
    ...
    RETURN(returned value);
    END;
```

If a procedure has no parameters, the parameters and their enclosing parentheses are omitted.

Procedure name - follows the rules for variable identifiers. Some compilers such as PL/C limit the MAIN procedure name to 7 characters; other names are not so limited.

Calling a procedure (invoking a procedure) - causing a procedure to be executed. A subroutine procedure is called by a statement of the form

```
CALL procedure name(arguments);
```

If the subroutine has no parameters, then the arguments with their enclosing parentheses are omitted. A function procedure is called by using its name, followed by a parenthesized list of arguments if required, in an expression.

Returning from a procedure - terminating the execution of a procedure and passing control back to the calling place. When the end of a subroutine procedure is reached, there is a return to the statement just beyond the calling statement. A function procedure must be returned from via the statement

```
RETURN(returned value);
```

This statement terminates the function and causes the
returned value to be used in the expression containing the
function call.

Arguments - A call to a procedure can pass it arguments. For
      example, in the statement

            S=SUBSTR(T,1,L+1);

      the arguments are T, 1 and L+1.

Parameters - Inside a procedure, the arguments for each call are
      referred to via parameters. In the following procedure, the
      parameters are SEQUENCE and SIZE.

```
            TOTAL:PROCEDURE(SEQUENCE,SIZE)RETURNS(FIXED);
               DECLARE(SEQUENCE(*),SIZE)FIXED;
               DECLARE(SUBTOTAL,I)FIXED;
               SUBTOTAL=0;
               DO I=1 TO SIZE;
                  SUBTOTAL=SUBTOTAL+SEQUENCE(I);
                  END;
               RETURN(SUBTOTAL);
               END;
```

      All parameters must be declared in a procedure. Since
      SEQUENCE is an array, it is declared with a range of *,
      meaning that its range is to be taken from its corresponding
      argument array.

Dummy arguments - For any given call to a procedure, its
      parameters act like new names for the arguments of the call.
      When a value is assigned to a parameter, the value is
      actually assigned to the corresponding argument. There is a
      difficulty, in that it is not possible to assign values to
      some arguments. For example, for the following CALL
      statement,

            CALL SWITCH(A,B+C*14,211);

      it is possible to assign a value to the variable A but not to
      B+C*14 or 211. To handle this difficulty, in PL/1 when an
      argument cannot be assigned a value, a dummy argument is
      created for the sole purpose of receiving values assigned to
      the corresponding parameters. Each dummy argument is
      essentially a nameless variable which is created
      automatically to handle a particular argument of a procedure
      call.

CHAPTER 11 EXERCISES

1. What does the following program print? What are the parameters
and arguments in this program?

```
NUMBERS:PROCEDURE OPTIONS(MAIN);
    DECLARE(I,OUTPUT)FIXED;
    ABSOLUTE:PROCEDURE(K,L);
        DECLARE(K,L)FIXED;
        IF K>=0 THEN
            L=K;
        ELSE
            L=-K;
        END;
    DO I=-2 TO 2;
        CALL ABSOLUTE(I,OUTPUT);
        PUT LIST(OUTPUT);
        END;
    END;
```

2. What does the following program print? What are the parameters
and arguments in this program?

```
$JOB ID='TOM HULL'
 WEATHER:PROCEDURE OPTIONS(MAIN);
    DECLARE(TEMPERATURE(31),RAIN(31))FLOAT;
    DECLARE(DAY,TIME)FIXED;
    AVERAGE:PROCEDURE(ARRAY,HOW_MANY);
        DECLARE(ARRAY(*))FLOAT,
            (HOW_MANY,I)FIXED;
        DECLARE(TOTAL)FLOAT;
        TOTAL=0;
        DO I=1 TO HOW_MANY;
            TOTAL=TOTAL+ARRAY(I);
            END;
        PUT LIST(TOTAL/HOW_MANY);
        END;
    GET LIST(TIME);
    DO DAY=1 TO TIME;
        GET LIST(TEMPERATURE(DAY),RAIN(DAY));
        END;
    PUT SKIP LIST('AVERAGE TEMPERATURE:');
    CALL AVERAGE(TEMPERATURE,TIME);
    PUT SKIP LIST('AVERAGE RAINFALL:');
    CALL AVERAGE(RAIN,TIME);
    END;
$DATA
 5  45.0  0  47.2  0  48.0  .3  47.5  2.1  48.0  0
```

3. Write a procedure which sorts an array of names into alphabetic order. For example, your procedure could be used in the following program:

```
ORDER:PROCEDURE OPTIONS(MAIN);
   DECLARE(WORKERS(100))CHARACTER(20)VARYING;
   DECLARE(I)FIXED;
   SORT:PROCEDURE(NAMES,LENGTH);
      DECLARE(NAMES(*))CHARACTER(*)VARYING,
         (LENGTH)FIXED;
      (You write this part)
      END;
   DO I=1 TO 100;
      GET LIST(WORKERS(I));
      END;
   CALL SORT(WORKERS,100);
   DO I=1 TO 100;
      PUT SKIP LIST(WORKERS(I));
      END;
   END;
```

4. What does the following program print?

```
$JOB ID='RUDY SCHILD'
 DITTY:PROCEDURE OPTIONS(MAIN);
   DECLARE(ANIMAL,NOISE)CHARACTER(20)VARYING;
   MACDONALD:PROCEDURE;
      PUT SKIP LIST('OLD MACDONALD HAD A FARM');
      PUT SKIP LIST('E I E I O');
      END;
   GET LIST(ANIMAL,NOISE);
   DO WHILE(ANIMAL¬='PLEASE STOP');
      CALL MACDONALD;
      PUT SKIP LIST('AND ON THAT FARM HE HAD A '||ANIMAL);
      PUT SKIP LIST('E I E I O');
      PUT SKIP LIST('WITH A '||NOISE||NOISE||'HERE, A '||
         NOISE||NOISE||'THERE');
      PUT SKIP LIST('HERE A '||NOISE||'THERE A '||NOISE||
         'EVERYWHERE A '||NOISE||NOISE);
      CALL MACDONALD;
      PUT SKIP LIST(' ');
      GET LIST(ANIMAL,NOISE);
      END;
   END;
$DATA
 'DUCK' 'QUACK ' 'COW' 'MOO ' 'PLEASE STOP' 'SILENCE'
```

5. What does the following program print? How would you change this program so each printed line ends with a period?

```
$JOB ID='JOHN MYLOPOULOS'
 ENCORE:PROCEDURE OPTIONS(MAIN);
    DECLARE(ANIMAL,NOISE)CHARACTER(20)VARYING;
    SING_LINE:PROCEDURE(LEFT,MIDDLE,REPEATS,RIGHT);
       DECLARE(LEFT,MIDDLE,RIGHT)CHARACTER(*)VARYING;
       DECLARE(REPEATS)FIXED;
       DECLARE(LINE)CHARACTER(60)VARYING;
       DECLARE(I)FIXED;
       LINE=LEFT;
       DO I=1 TO REPEATS;
          LINE=LINE||MIDDLE;
          END;
       PUT SKIP LIST(LINE||RIGHT);
       END;
    MACDONALD:PROCEDURE;
       CALL SING_LINE('OLD MACDONALD ','HAD ',1,'A FARM');
       CALL SING_LINE('','E I ',2,'O');
       END;
    GET LIST(ANIMAL,NOISE);
    DO WHILE(ANIMAL¬='PLEASE STOP');
       CALL MACDONALD;
       CALL SING_LINE('AND ON THAT ','FARM HE HAD A ',1,ANIMAL);
       CALL SING_LINE('','E I ',2,'O');
       CALL SING_LINE('WITH A ',NOISE,2,'HERE');
       CALL SING_LINE('A ',NOISE,2,'THERE');
       CALL SING_LINE('HERE A ',NOISE,1,'');
       CALL SING_LINE('THERE A ',NOISE,1,'');
       CALL SING_LINE('EVERYWHERE A ',NOISE,2,'');
       CALL MACDONALD;
       PUT SKIP LIST(' ');
       GET LIST(ANIMAL,NOISE);
       END;
    END;
$DATA
 'DUCK' 'QUACK ' 'COW' 'MOO ' 'PLEASE STOP' 'SILENCE'
```

6. What does the following procedure do? Write a small program which uses this procedure.

```
 METRIC:PROCEDURE(LENGTH);
    DECLARE(LENGTH)FLOAT;
    LENGTH=2.54E0*LENGTH;
    END;
```

7. What does the following procedure do? Write a small program which uses this procedure.

```
 CONVERT:PROCEDURE(INCHES)RETURNS(FLOAT);
    DECLARE(INCHES)FLOAT;
    RETURN(2.54E0*INCHES);
    END;
```

8. Write a function which returns the position of the first blank in a string. For example, your procedure could be used in the following program:

```
$JOB ID='GABE KALMAR'
 SURNAME:PROCEDURE OPTIONS(MAIN);
    DECLARE(NAME)CHARACTER(30)VARYING;
    DECLARE(P)FIXED;
    BLANK_POSITION:PROCEDURE(STRING)RETURNS(FIXED);
       DECLARE(STRING)CHARACTER(*)VARYING;
       /* ASSUME STRING CONTAINS AT LEAST ONE BLANK */
       (You write this part)
       END;
    GET LIST(NAME);
    PUT SKIP LIST('FIRST BLANK IS AT',BLANK_POSITION(NAME));
    END;
$DATA
'TOM WILCOX'
```

CHAPTER 12

MODULAR PROGRAMMING

In the last chapter we learned how to use procedures in the PL/1 language. One of the important purposes of procedures in programming languages is to divide programs into parts - parts that are convenient to use and easy to understand. This idea of dividing a program into parts is called modular programming. In this chapter we will show how a program can be divided into convenient modules; each of these modules will be a procedure.

A PROBLEM IN BUSINESS DATA PROCESSING

We will illustrate modular programming by solving a problem which might arise in a small business. Suppose that Acme Automotive Supplies uses a computer to help keep track of its customers' accounts. For each customer, there is an account card, giving the customer's account number, name, credit limit and balance owing to Acme.

For example, Cooks Garage has account number 14 and presently owes $28.32 to Acme. Cooks Garage is allowed a credit limit of $200.00; this means that if Cooks Garage is less than $200.00 behind in paying its bills to Acme, Acme will not press for payment. This information is recorded on a punched card as follows:

    14   'COOKS GARAGE'   20000   2832

To avoid the use of decimal points, a dollar amount such as $200.00 is given in cents as 20000.

The payments to Acme from its customers are recorded on transaction cards. Each transaction card gives a customer's account number and the amount of a payment by the customer. For example, the card

    14   2832

records the fact that $28.32 was received from the customer with account number 14. Since Cooks Garage corresponds to the account number 14, this means that Cooks Garage has paid $28.32 to Acme.

    The account manager for Acme needs a program to read the account cards and the month's transaction cards and print the accounts as they stand after the payments. For example, suppose that corresponding to the account card

    14   'COOKS GARAGE'   20000   2832

there is only the one transaction card

    14   2832

The account manager would like the program to print the fact that account number 14, for Cooks Garage, has a credit limit of 20000 and a current balance owing of 0. The program is supposed to read data such as:

    14   'COOKS GARAGE'   20000   2832
    6   'JONES REPAIR'   5000   8240
    ...   (more account cards)
    -1   'XXX'   0   0   (dummy account card)
    6   1000
    14   2832
    6   1000
    ...   (more transaction cards)
    -1   0   (dummy transaction card)

The program is to print the updated accounts; a report such as the following should be printed.

                    ACME AUTOMOTIVE SUPPLIES
                        ACCOUNTING REPORT

    ACCOUNT NO.   CUSTOMER   CREDIT LIMIT   BALANCE

        14   COOKS GARAGE   20000   0
        6   JONES REPAIR   5000   6240
        ...

The account manager says that Acme has accounts for 16 customers. He has told us that each customer has one account card and that an account number can be any number from 1 to 999. The transaction records are not in any particular order, and the number of payments by a particular customer each month varies widely - from no payment to quite a number of payments.

DIVIDING THE PROGRAM INTO PARTS

We need a program which reads the accounts, updates them using the month's transactions and prints the updated accounts. We start designing our program by dividing it into the three parts:

```
Read accounts;
Update accounts;
Print accounts;
```

Since PL/1 does not provide a statement, "Read accounts," we will write a PL/1 procedure called READ_ACCOUNTS. Our procedure will have the following form:

```
READ_ACCOUNTS:PROCEDURE;
    (declarations local to READ_ACCOUNTS)
    (statements)
    END;
```

Similarly, we will write PL/1 procedures called UPDATE_ACCOUNTS and PRINT_ACCOUNTS. Assuming these three procedures are available, then we can write:

```
CALL READ_ACCOUNTS;
CALL UPDATE_ACCOUNTS;
CALL PRINT_ACCOUNTS;
```

If our three procedures are written correctly, then this sequence of three CALL statements will solve our business data processing problem.

We have divided our program into three parts, or modules. Now we need to provide data so the parts can communicate.

COMMUNICATION AMONG MODULES

The procedure READ_ACCOUNTS must have a place to store the information from the account cards, so this information can be used by the procedure UPDATE_ACCOUNTS. Similarly, the UPDATE_ACCOUNTS procedure must store the updated account information, so it can be printed by the PRINT_ACCOUNTS procedure.

To meet these communication needs, we can declare arrays for the account numbers, customer names, credit limits and balances. The following declaration creates the desired arrays:

```
DECLARE(ACCOUNT_NUMBER(20))FIXED,
    (CUSTOMER(20))CHARACTER(13)VARYING,
    (CREDIT_LIMIT(20))FIXED,
    (BALANCE(20))FIXED;
```

For possible future growth, we have allowed for more accounts than Acme's present 16 accounts. The upper limit of 20 for the arrays provides room for 19 accounts plus a dummy account. We checked with the account manager to verify that 13 characters are enough to record each customer's name.

We will place this declaration in the main procedure, making the arrays global. This allows the procedures READ_ACCOUNTS, UPDATE_ACCOUNTS and PRINT_ACCOUNTS to access the arrays. The overall program organization is:

```
/* READ, UPDATE AND PRINT ACCOUNTS FOR ACME */
/*     AUTOMOTIVE SUPPLIES.                  */
ACCOUNT:PROCEDURE OPTIONS(MAIN);
    (declarations for variables, such as the ACCOUNT_NUMBER array,
        used for communication among procedures)
    READ_ACCOUNTS:PROCEDURE;
        (declarations local to READ_ACCOUNTS)
        (statements)
        END;
    (definition for the UPDATE_ACCOUNTS procedure)
    (definition for the PRINT_ACCOUNTS procedure)
    CALL READ_ACCOUNTS;
    CALL UPDATE_ACCOUNTS;
    CALL PRINT_ACCOUNTS;
    END;
```

The procedure READ_ACCOUNTS will finish by reading the dummy account card into the arrays. The procedures UPDATE_ACCOUNTS and PRINT_ACCOUNTS will recognize the end of the list of accounts when they encounter the dummy account number -1.

The three procedures communicate by changing and inspecting the arrays.

First, the READ_ACCOUNTS procedure reads the information on the account cards into the four arrays. Next, the UPDATE_ACCOUNTS procedure reads the transaction cards and updates the account information accordingly. This updating will modify the BALANCE array, but does not change the other three arrays. Finally, the PRINT_ACCOUNTS procedure prints the updated accounts. Note that this procedure does not change any of the four arrays.

WRITING THE MODULES

We are now ready to write the procedures because we have designed the overall program structure and the data to be used for communication among the three procedures.

We will start the READ_ACCOUNTS procedure by writing a comment to explain its purpose:

```
/* READ ACCOUNT CARDS INTO THE ARRAYS ACCOUNT_NUMBER, */
/*      CUSTOMER, CREDIT_LIMIT AND BALANCE.           */
```

Immediately following this comment will come the line:

```
READ_ACCOUNTS:PROCEDURE;
```

Next will come the declarations for variables that are local to the READ_ACCOUNTS procedure. We are not ready to write these declarations, because we have not yet designed the body of the procedure.

The procedure requires a loop such as the following, which repeatedly reads account cards.

```
Loop initialization;
DO WHILE(There are more account cards);
   Read another card;
   END;
```

We can fill up the arrays starting with item 1, then item 2 and so on. We will declare a variable called ITEM to keep track of the number of the item. The body of the loop, "Read another card," will use a GET LIST statement to read account cards. But the loop body must also get ready for the reading of the next card, and it must provide information to be tested to see if "There are more account cards." This can be accomplished by writing the loop body this way:

```
GET LIST(ACCOUNT_NUMBER(ITEM),CUSTOMER(ITEM),
   CREDIT_LIMIT(ITEM),BALANCE(ITEM));
ACCOUNT=ACCOUNT_NUMBER(ITEM);
ITEM=ITEM+1;
```

We will declare ACCOUNT to be a fixed variable; the loop is terminated when ACCOUNT becomes -1. We now write "Loop initialization" so that the loop is started correctly, and we have:

```
ITEM=1;
/* SET ACCOUNT SO LOOP WILL START PROPERLY */
ACCOUNT=0;
DO WHILE(ACCOUNT¬=-1);
   GET LIST(ACCOUNT_NUMBER(ITEM),CUSTOMER(ITEM),
     CREDIT_LIMIT(ITEM),BALANCE(ITEM));
   ACCOUNT=ACCOUNT_NUMBER(ITEM);
   ITEM=ITEM+1;
   END;
```

This sequence of PL/1 statements has the meaning:

Read in the account cards together with the dummy
    account card;

The variable ITEM is left having as its value one more than the
number of accounts.

This completes the writing of the READ_ACCOUNTS procedure.
Putting the pieces together, it looks like this:

```
/* READ ACCOUNT CARDS INTO THE ARRAYS ACCOUNT_NUMBER, */
/*    CUSTOMER, CREDIT_LIMIT AND BALANCE.             */
READ_ACCOUNTS:PROCEDURE;
   DECLARE(ITEM,ACCOUNT)FIXED;
   ITEM=1;
   /* SET ACCOUNT SO LOOP WILL START PROPERLY */
   ACCOUNT=0;
   DO WHILE(ACCOUNT¬=-1);
      GET LIST(ACCOUNT_NUMBER(ITEM),CUSTOMER(ITEM),
         CREDIT_LIMIT(ITEM),BALANCE(ITEM));
      ACCOUNT=ACCOUNT_NUMBER(ITEM);
      ITEM=ITEM+1;
      END;
   END;
```

We have written the READ_ACCOUNTS procedure using step-by-
step refinement. We started by deciding the purpose of the
procedure. Then we divided the procedure into pieces. Finally,
we wrote the pieces in PL/1.

We will not give detailed descriptions of the writing of the
UPDATE_ACCOUNTS and PRINT_ACCOUNTS procedures. Similar methods
can be used in writing those two procedures.

THE COMPLETE PROGRAM

Assuming the other two procedures have been written, we can
put the pieces together to make the program given on the next
page.

```
/* READ, UPDATE AND PRINT ACCOUNTS FOR ACME */
/*     AUTOMOTIVE SUPPLIES */
ACCOUNT:PROCEDURE OPTIONS(MAIN);
   DECLARE(ACCOUNT_NUMBER(20))FIXED,
      (CUSTOMER(20))CHARACTER(13)VARYING,
      (CREDIT_LIMIT(20))FIXED,
      (BALANCE(20))FIXED;

   /*READ ACCOUNT CARDS INTO THE ARRAYS ACCOUNT_NUMBER, */
   /*  CUSTOMER, CREDIT_LIMIT AND BALANCE */
   READ_ACCOUNTS:PROCEDURE;
      (exactly as given previously)
      END;

   /*READ TRANSACTION CARDS AND UPDATE THE ACCOUNTS */
   UPDATE_ACCOUNTS:PROCEDURE;
      DECLARE(ITEM,ACCOUNT,PAYMENT)FIXED;
      GET LIST(ACCOUNT,PAYMENT);
      DO WHILE(ACCOUNT¬=-1);
         ITEM=1;
         DO WHILE(ACCOUNT_NUMBER(ITEM)¬=ACCOUNT &
               ACCOUNT_NUMBER(ITEM)¬=-1);
            ITEM=ITEM+1;
            END;
         IF ACCOUNT_NUMBER(ITEM)=ACCOUNT THEN
            BALANCE(ITEM)=BALANCE(ITEM)-PAYMENT;
         ELSE
            PUT SKIP LIST('ERRONEOUS TRANSACTION ACCOUNT:',
               ACCOUNT);
         GET LIST(ACCOUNT,PAYMENT);
         END;
      END;

   /* PRINT THE ACCOUNTS */
   PRINT_ACCOUNTS:PROCEDURE;
      DECLARE(ITEM)FIXED;
      PUT PAGE LIST(' ','ACME AUTOMOTIVE SUPPLIES');
      PUT SKIP LIST(' ','   ACCOUNTING REPORT');
      PUT SKIP LIST(' ');
      PUT SKIP LIST('ACCOUNT NO.','CUSTOMER','CREDIT LIMIT',
         'BALANCE');
      PUT SKIP LIST(' ');
      ITEM=1;
      DO WHILE(ACCOUNT_NUMBER(ITEM)¬=-1);
         PUT SKIP LIST(ACCOUNT_NUMBER(ITEM),CUSTOMER(ITEM),
            CREDIT_LIMIT(ITEM),BALANCE(ITEM));
         ITEM=ITEM+1;
         END;
      END;

   /* MAIN PROCEDURE:READ, UPDATE AND PRINT ACCOUNTS */
   CALL READ_ACCOUNTS;
   CALL UPDATE_ACCOUNTS;
   CALL PRINT_ACCOUNTS;
   END;
```

In this program we used local and global variables to our advantage. The arrays are declared in the main procedure so they are available to the READ_ACCOUNTS, UPDATE_ACCOUNTS and PRINT_ACCOUNTS procedures. We made some variables, such as PAYMENT, local to the procedures using them. Although we declared three variables named ITEM, they are kept separate by PL/1 because they were declared in different procedures.

USING MODULES

In our example, we divided our program into three modules, namely, the READ_ACCOUNTS, UPDATE_ACCOUNTS and PRINT_ACCOUNTS procedures.

```
/* MAIN PROCEDURE: READ, UPDATE AND PRINT ACCOUNTS. */
CALL READ_ACCOUNTS;
CALL UPDATE_ACCOUNTS;
CALL PRINT_ACCOUNTS;
```

This main procedure is very easy to understand because it specifies the order of using the modules, without giving internal details about the modules. These details are important, but are best understood separately, in the definitions of the modules. Many of these details can be changed inside a particular module without changing either the main procedure or our understanding of the program's overall structure.

Programs that process business data typically have an organization similar to that of our example. In particular, they are often based on a set of modules which are called by a main procedure. For larger and more complex programs, individual modules may be composed of sub-modules, the sub-modules may be composed of sub-sub-modules, and so on.

Our example is not a large program. Even though it is relatively small, we have been able to make it simple by dividing it into distinct parts. It is almost impossible for programmers to write, understand or modify a large, complex program unless the program is divided into distinct parts, each having a relatively simple purpose.

MODIFYING A PROGRAM

It is common for programs to be changed during their lifetime. Sometimes a change is required to fix errors in the program. Sometimes a change is required because the purpose of the program is changed. For example, the account manager for Acme Automotive Supplies may discover that in addition to the printing of all updated accounts, he needs a separate list of customers whose credit limits have been exceeded. This is an example of exception reporting; such reporting helps managers by listing only those items that require action.

When a useful program is modified, we call this <u>program maintenance</u>. We do not <u>maintain</u> a program because it wears out! Instead, we maintain a program when there are new requirements for the program or there are errors in the program.

As an example of a program modification, we will take the situation in which a <u>credit exception report</u> is required by the Acme account manager. The program must list those customers whose balance owing is greater than their credit limit. We already have modules which read accounts, update them and print them. Given the updated accounts, we need a module which prints the names of customers with exceeded credit. The main procedure is changed to make the calls:

```
CALL READ_ACCOUNTS;
CALL UPDATE_ACCOUNTS;
CALL PRINT_ACCOUNTS;
CALL PRINT_CREDIT_EXCEPTIONS;
```

Using our old program, we add a new procedure named PRINT_CREDIT_EXCEPTIONS and a call to this procedure.

We are able to produce a program to print credit exceptions very easily. This is because our old program is easy to understand and thus easy to modify.

Since our program is modular, we can use the pieces - the modules - to build new programs. Suppose the Acme account manager decides he needs a list of accounts both before and after the update. We can easily modify our program to meet this requirement by changing the calls to:

```
CALL READ_ACCOUNTS;
CALL PRINT_ACCOUNTS;
CALL UPDATE_ACCOUNTS;
CALL PRINT_ACCOUNTS;
(more calls to procedures)
```

We simply call the PRINT_ACCOUNTS procedure twice - before and after calling UPDATE_ACCOUNTS. No modules need to be added or changed.

CHAPTER 12 SUMMARY

In this chapter we showed how modular programming can be used in solving a simple problem in data processing. We developed a program containing three modules to solve the problem. Each of these modules was a PL/1 procedure.

The overall structure of our program was designed using step-by-step refinement. Once we had stated the data processing problem to be solved, we refined the idea "solve the problem" into the three steps:

```
Read accounts;
Update accounts;
Print accounts;
```

We wrote three modules to carry out these steps.

Modules should be designed to perform conceptually simple activities, and they should use their parameters and any shared variables in a straightforward manner. When a program has been carefully divided into good modules, it can be easily understood and maintained.

CHAPTER 12 EXERCISES

All the exercises for this chapter are based on the program which reads, updates and prints accounts for Acme Automotive Supplies. Each exercise asks you to modify the program; you may need to add new modules, change or improve old modules or change the main procedure. When making these changes, be sure that old comments are appropriately modified and new comments are added as needed.

1. Add a new procedure named PRINT_CREDIT_EXCEPTIONS that prints each account having a balance greater than its credit limit. Write the main procedure so that the accounts are read and updated, then the credit exceptions are printed and then all of the accounts are printed. Test the modified program.

2. Make modifications so that the number of accounts and the number of transactions are printed before the listing of accounts. Test the modified program.

3. Make the program less vulnerable to data errors by having it check for and report the following problems:

   (a) More accounts than can be stored in the arrays.

   (b) Negative credit limits.

   (c) Unlikely payments - negative or more than $999.99.

Test the modified program.

4. Modify the program so that it prints the total of the balances of the accounts. Test the modified program.

CHAPTER 13

SP/7: CONTROLLING INPUT
AND OUTPUT

So far we have had one statement for input, the GET LIST statement, and one statement for output, the PUT LIST statement. These allowed us to read data from cards, or write data on the printer. Often we would like to arrange the format of output in a way that is different from the standard format provided by the PUT LIST statement. Input has been more flexible; we have been able to accept FLOAT numbers either in the form with just a decimal point, such as 25.32, or the form with an exponent, such as 2.532E1. As well, we could arrange the input numbers in any columns of the card that we wanted, as long as each pair of numbers was separated by at least one blank; there were no standard <u>fields</u> on the card as there were on the printed page.

In this chapter we will show how the output format can be varied more flexibly. And we will describe how to have even greater control over input. For example, we might want to read only certain data items from cards, skipping over others.

SKIPPING LINES

Our first new option involves the use of the word SKIP in the PUT LIST instruction. Up until now we have seen that

    PUT SKIP LIST(X,Y,Z);

is a statement that will cause the printing of the value of the variables X,Y, and Z in the first three fields of the printed page. Without the SKIP these values would be printed in the next three fields following along from the printing caused by the previous PUT LIST instruction.

If we follow the word SKIP by an integer n enclosed in parentheses we will not only start the output in the first field

of a new printed line but will leave (n-1) blank lines. For
example the output instructions

```
PUT SKIP LIST('1','2','3');
PUT SKIP(2)LIST('4','5','6');
PUT SKIP(1)LIST('7','8','9');
```

will cause the output

1	2	3
4	5	6
7	8	9

With a 2 in parentheses you get one blank line. With a 1 you get
exactly the result you got with nothing after the SKIP; it starts
a new line, but no blank line is inserted. An instruction for
skipping lines without printing anything is

```
PUT SKIP(n);
```

As before, the printer is positioned at the beginning of the line
and depending on whether the next output instruction is PUT LIST
or PUT SKIP LIST there will be (n-1) or n blank lines,
respectively. The use of SKIP will also apply to the new
instruction PUT EDIT that we will introduce now.

FORMAT DESCRIPTION

To have more flexible control over the input and output we
will use a new pair of statements, the GET EDIT and the PUT EDIT
statements. One difference between these and the GET LIST and
PUT LIST is that in addition to being followed in parentheses by
a list of data items to be read or written there is, as well, a
second list of format items in parentheses. There must be a
format item to describe the format of each data item. For
example,

PUT EDIT (data item1, data item2)(format item1, format item2);

the format item1 applies to data item1 and format item2 to data
item2. The data items are expressions in the PL/1 language, that
is, constants, literals, variables, arithmetic expressions, or
string expressions.

Basically, the format items describe the location of the data
item on the card or printed line, the size of the field that is
to be allotted to it, and the form that it is to take if
alternate forms are possible. Alternate forms are possible for
FLOAT numbers; as you already know, on input we can use either
the exponent form, or the form with a decimal point and no
exponent.

PRINTING FLOAT NUMBERS

As the first example of a format item we will look at the one that will let you avoid printing exponents with floating numbers. As well, it allows control over the number of digits printed to the right of the decimal point. For example,

    PUT EDIT (4/3EO, 2/3EO) (F(10,4), F(6, 3));

will output

    bbbb1.3333b0.667

We have used "b" to represent a blank. The first number in parentheses after the F in each format item gives the total width of the field in which the data is to appear. The second number, after the comma, is the number of digits to be printed to the right of the decimal point. The fractional parts are rounded off. Note that the numbers are right-justified in their fields and that the decimal point takes up one character position. If a minus sign occurs it also takes a position.

Printing FLOAT numbers in this way requires more thought on your part because you must be sure to leave enough room to the left of the decimal point. In the LIST form with the exponent there is always first one digit to the left of the decimal point and a fixed number of digits to the right.

For example, suppose the dimensions of a box in centimeters are expressed to the nearest hundredth of a centimeter and punched on a card as

    10.31   4.25   6.35

and you want the volume to the nearest hundredth of a cubic centimeter. Here is the program for doing this.

```
$JOB ID='CATHY TAFLER'
 BOX:PROCEDURE OPTIONS(MAIN);
    DECLARE(LENGTH,WIDTH,HEIGHT,VOLUME)FLOAT;
    GET LIST(LENGTH,WIDTH,HEIGHT);
    VOLUME=LENGTH*WIDTH*HEIGHT;
    PUT EDIT(VOLUME)(F(14,2));
    END;
$DATA
 10.31  4.25  6.35
```

The output will be

    bbbbbbbb278.24

We have one format item F(14,2), as there is only one data item.

The printing of FLOAT numbers can also be controlled in the exponent form. The PUT LIST instruction always prints the same

number of digits to the right of the decimal point; compilers
usually print five. This represents about the maximum number of
digits that are meaningful or significant. Since numbers are
stored in memory locations that have a fixed size, only a limited
precision is possible in representing them. You might, however,
want to print fewer than five digits to the right of the decimal.
Also, you might want to allow fewer total print positions for the
entire number. With a format item E(12,3) you would be allowing
a total of 12 character positions for the printing and 3 digits
to the right of the decimal in the fractional part. For example,

        PUT EDIT(-12.3665E1)(E(12,3));

would produce an output

        bb-1.237E+02

Notice that the number being printed is rounded off. The minimum
field width must be 7 plus the number of digits to the right of
the decimal; this allows for the sign, the one digit to the left
of the point, the decimal point itself, and the four spaces for
the exponent. The number is right-justified in the field allowed
to it.

                    PRINTING CHARACTER STRINGS

        In the example with the volume of the box we did not include
our usual labeling of the results with VOLUME=. This was because
we have not yet said how to describe the format for a character
string. We do this by the format item A(w) where w is the width
of the field to be allotted to the string. The string will be
left-justified in the field. So for our box volume program, if
we had used the output statement

        PUT EDIT('VOLUME IS',VOLUME,' CUBIC CM')(A(9),F(7,2),A(9));

the output would have been

        VOLUME IS 278.24 CUBIC CM

Here we have reduced the size of the field used for printing the
numerical value and allowed character string fields of just the
right size to hold the strings that are printed. This permits
much greater flexibility for making attractive output. We can
use the format item A alone if we want a field exactly the size
of a character string. We could have had

        PUT EDIT('VOLUME IS',VOLUME,' CUBIC CM')(A,F(7,2),A);

and got exactly the same output.

PRINTING FIXED NUMBERS

Using the PUT EDIT instruction requires the specification of the field width for all numbers, whether FIXED or FLOAT. The format item used to specify this width for a FIXED number is F(w) where w is the number of character positions allotted to the number. The integer will be right-justified in this field. For example,

    PUT EDIT(235,26,5261)(F(4),F(3),F(6));

will produce the output

    b235b26bb5261

PRINTING DOLLARS AND CENTS

The format item we will describe now is used for printing a FIXED value, that represents cents, as a value in dollars. This is the P format item. The P stands for picture because following the P we have a string of characters in quotes that gives a picture of the actual output. (Some compilers such as PL/C do not allow P format items.) In the picture, each element of the string stands for a particular character such as a $ sign, or a type of character such as a digit.

element	use
.	decimal point
,	comma
$	floating dollar sign
Z	digit position, suppress zero
9	digit position
CR	credit symbol, if negative
DB	debit symbol, if negative

Suppose that the FIXED variable COST contains the value 15672, which is the amount in cents required to buy a ten-speed bicycle. We could print out the cost in dollars by this output statement.

    PUT EDIT('COST=',COST)(A,P'$Z,ZZ9.99');

The output will be

    COST=$bb156.72

If the value of COST had been 22, meaning 22 cents, the output would have been

    COST=$bbbb0.22

The digits that correspond to Zs in the picture are suppressed until a non-zero digit is found; then all digits are printed. The comma is also suppressed if there are no digits printed to the left of it. The zero just to the left of the decimal point is not suppressed, because it corresponds to a 9 in the picture. We have said that the $ in the picture specification is a floating $ sign and, as yet, it has not moved. Allowing the $ sign to float is accomplished by having several $ signs in the picture. In our example the picture specification

    P'$$$,$$9.99'

used on the two values of COST would give

    COST=bbb$156.72
    COST=bbbbb$0.22

In accounting you often want also to indicate, say in preparing invoices, that a negative amount owing means a credit. This is accomplished by putting the letters CR at the end of the picture specification string. For example,

    PUT EDIT('AMOUNT DUE IS ',-312)(A,P'$,$$9.99CR');

would give an output of

    AMOUNT DUE IS bbb$3.12CR

Similarly in bank balances you might want to mark negative balances as debits. You could write

    PUT EDIT('BALANCE IS ',-1255)(A,P'$,$$9.99DB');

and get for output

    BALANCE IS bb$12.55DB

READING NUMBERS

There is considerable flexibility in the input of FIXED or FLOAT numbers provided by the GET LIST instruction since the numbers need not occupy any specific fields on the card; FLOAT numbers can be presented in either the exponent form or with a decimal point. There are reasons why you might want to use the GET EDIT instruction for numbers. One of these is to insert a decimal point into an integer. This can be done by using an F(w,d) format item. The number of card columns allotted to the integer is w. It is punched right-justified in this card field. It would be read into a FLOAT variable as if there were a decimal point punched so as to give d of its digits to the right of the point. As an example, suppose that measurements are given in centimeters and we want, on reading, to store the values in meters. We could use

```
GET EDIT(WIDTH)(F(5,2));
```

If the integer 416 was right-justified in the first five columns of the card, it would be read as a floating number whose value was 4.16, or 4.16E0, into the FLOAT variable WIDTH.

READING CHARACTER STRINGS

One awkward feature of using the GET LIST instruction is that character strings must be surrounded by quotes. We may have available punched cards with data such as names and addresses already punched on them, and there are no quotes punched. Provided they are punched consistently in definite fields of the card they can be read using GET EDIT, with an A(w) format item where w indicates the field width. For instance, if names are left-justified in the first 30 card columns, addresses in the next 42 columns and an integer code number in the next 7 columns, the following input statement would be appropriate:

```
GET SKIP EDIT(NAME,ADDRESS,CODE)(A(30),A(42),F(7));
```

The SKIP included in the statement indicates that the reading should begin in column 1 of the card.

Sometimes, if a standard format has not been used, an entire card is read as a unit and then the resulting character string can be dissected by the program. A statement for reading the card would be

```
GET SKIP EDIT(CARD)(A(80));
```

The various parts could be separated by detection of blanks or punctuation as we showed in Chapter 10.

SKIPPING POSITIONS

Some format items do not correspond to any data items but have the effect of either skipping card columns on input or leaving blank positions on output. This is accomplished by writing a format item X(n) where n is the number of positions to be skipped. For example, the statement

```
PUT SKIP EDIT('COST','VALUE','SALES')(X(5),A,X(6),A,X(5),A);
```

would give a printed line suitable for heading columns. It would be

```
bbbbbCOSTbbbbbbVALUEbbbbbSALES
```

In this way you can space headings without having to include all the blanks in the literal itself. Notice that the X format items do not cause a data item to be read or printed.

An alternative way to skip positions is to use the format item COLUMN(n) which provides skipping up to column number n of the card or the printed page. This would allow you to line up the headings beginning in certain column positions. For example,

PUT SKIP EDIT('COST','VALUE')(COLUMN(5),A,COLUMN(15),A);

would give

bbbbCOSTbbbbbbVALUE

If the specified column is beyond the current column, the printer automatically skips to the specified column in the next line. The COLUMN format item also applies to card columns on input.

INPUT AND OUTPUT OF LOGICAL DATA

In Chapter 5 we mentioned logical variables. These variables must be declared as BIT(1) or simply BIT. These were variables that can only have two different values, corresponding to true or false. Within a program or with a GET LIST or PUT LIST instruction we write these two values as '1'B and '0'B to distinguish them from the ordinary decimal integers.

When we use the GET EDIT or PUT EDIT instruction, these data items are punched or printed as simply 0 and 1 and have a format item B(w) to characterize them as logical variables in a field of width w. The value takes only one character position in the field. On input the character may be anywhere within the field specified; on output it would be printed left-justified and padded on the right with blanks.

MIXING LIST AND EDIT INPUT-OUTPUT

It is possible to use both LIST and EDIT input-output statements in a PL/1 program. Since these two types of input-output are quite different, using them together can cause confusion. You can avoid this confusion by following this advice:

Do not switch between GET LIST and GET EDIT statements during the reading of any single card. Similarly, do not switch between PUT LIST and PUT EDIT statements during the printing of any single line.

If the input-output statement that switches from LIST to EDIT - or vice versa - contains the SKIP keyword, then no confusion arises.

CHAPTER 13 SUMMARY

In this chapter we introduced ways to control details about reading and printing. We can control the use of lines and pages by statements such as:

```
PUT PAGE;       (starts a new page)
PUT SKIP;       (starts a new line)
PUT SKIP(2);    (skips a line, then starts a new line)
```

The parenthesized number following SKIP can be used in both PUT and GET statements and can be used with both LIST and EDIT statements. In a PUT statement, if the parenthesized number is zero or negative, this causes overprinting of the previously printed line.

The PUT EDIT and GET EDIT statements require format items to give details about how to perform the input-output. The following format items are available in SP/k.

Format Item	Example	Explanation
X(width)	X(3)	Skips next "width" columns.
COLUMN(position)	COLUMN(21)	Skips to column number "position".
F(width)	F(5)	Prints or reads an integer in a field of "width" columns.
F(width,fractional digits)	F(6,2)	Prints or reads a number as a non-integer fixed quantity, e.g., 216.53, using a field of "width" columns. The number of digits to the right of the decimal point is given by "fractional digits". This format item is usually used to print FLOAT numbers.
E(width, fractional digits)	E(11,4)	Prints or reads a number as a float quantity, e.g., 2.1653E+02, using a field of "width" columns. The number of fractional digits to the right of the decimal point is given by "fractional digits".
A(width)	A(5)	Prints or reads "width" characters.
A	A	Prints the characters of the output item. The field width is determined by the length of the character string.

B(width)   B(1)   Prints or reads a BIT value as
                                        1 or 0, using a field of "width"
                                        columns.

P specification   P'$$9.99'   Prints a FIXED number as dollars
                                        and cents.

    The following restrictions and details should be noted.   The
A format item with "width" omitted can be used for printing, but
not for reading.   The picture format item can be used only to
print FIXED numbers. The F format item can be used to   read and
print either FIXED or FLOAT numbers; when used to print a FLOAT
number, the printed value is rounded. Numbers printed using the
F and E format items are right-justified in their specified
fields.

    Usually, the "width" of a format item is given by an integer
constant, as in X(3).   It is possible to give the   "width" as a
numeric expression.   In the following example, "width" is given
by I.

    DO I=1 TO 3;
       PUT SKIP EDIT('*','*')(A,X(I),A);
       END;

This loop prints

    b
    bb
    bbb

    A numeric expression can also be given for "position" and
"fractional digits" and for the parenthesized value following
SKIP.   If the numeric expression has a float value, it is
truncated before being used.

    Each output item in a PUT EDIT statement must have a
corresponding format item; the corresponding format item must be
an F, E, A, B or P item. The same applies to input items in a
GET EDIT statement. The X and COLUMN format items can precede or
be intermixed with the F, E, A, B and P items, but must not be
last in a list of format items.

    In a P format item, the "picture specification" is a string
made up of the seven elements

    $,   Z   9   .   DB   CR

These elements must appear in this order:

    First, zero or more dollar signs with optional commas and
        decimal points.

    Next, zero or more Zs with optional commas and decimal
        points.

Next, one or more 9s with optional commas and decimal points.

Finally, an optional DB or CR; this is printed for negative
numbers.

Any leading zeros in the printed number are suppressed unless
they correspond to a 9 element. The comma and period elements
are printed only when preceded by at least one digit that is
actually printed. If dollar signs are used, one dollar sign is
printed; it will precede the first printed digit or else will
take the position of the rightmost dollar sign in the
specification.

Here are example statements illustrating uses of PUT and GET
EDIT statements:

```
PUT SKIP EDIT(24,5)(F(2),X(3),F(2));          (prints 24bbbb5)
PUT SKIP EDIT(24,5)(F(2),COLUMN(6),F(2));     (prints 24bbbb5)
PUT SKIP EDIT(61.248E+00)(F(7,2));            (prints bb61.25)
GET EDIT(CARD)(A(80));                        (reads 80 characters)
PUT EDIT(2516)     (P'$$,$$9.99DB');          (prints bbb$25.16bb)
PUT EDIT(252971)   (P'$$,$$9.99DB');          (prints $2,529.71bb)
PUT EDIT(5)        (P'$$,$$9.99DB');          (prints bbbb$0.05bb)
PUT EDIT(-481)     (P'$$,$$9.99DB');          (prints bbbb$4.81DB)
PUT EDIT(2516)     (P'ZZ,ZZ9.99DB');          (prints bbbb25.16bb)
```

CHAPTER 13 EXERCISES

1. What do the following statements print? Assume J is FIXED, Y
is FLOAT and C is CHARACTER(30) VARYING.

```
    J=29;
    Y=5.427E0;
    C='TRY FORMATTING';
    PUT SKIP EDIT(J,Y)(X(1),F(3),F(6,2));
    PUT EDIT(C)(X(2),A(14));
    PUT SKIP EDIT(C,Y)(A,F(6,1));
    PUT SKIP;
    PUT EDIT(J,Y)(COLUMN(2),F(3),COLUMN(6),F(5,2));
    PUT SKIP(2);
    PUT EDIT(C)(A);
    PUT SKIP(0)EDIT('___  _____')(A);
```

2. What do the following statements print? Assume BALANCE is a
FIXED variable.

```
    BALANCE=2154;
    PUT SKIP EDIT('OCTOBER BALANCE: ',BALANCE)(A,P'$$9.99');
    BALANCE=BALANCE-10000;
    PUT SKIP EDIT('AS UPDATED: ',BALANCE)(A,X(5),P'$$9.99DB');
    PUT SKIP(2)EDIT('YOU WIN ',100000000)(A,P'$$,$$$,$$9.99');
    PUT SKIP(3)EDIT(10000)(COLUMN(7),P'Z,ZZ9.99DB');
    PUT SKIP EDIT(BALANCE)(COLUMN(7),P'Z,ZZ9.99DB');
    PUT SKIP EDIT('_____')(COLUMN(7),A);
```

```
     PUT SKIP(2)EDIT('TOTAL',2154)(A,X(1),P'$,$$9.99DB');
```

3. Write a program that reads all the characters on a card and prints them all. Use the A format item so that quotes are not required on the card.

4. The first five columns of a particular card contain five digits. Give a GET EDIT statement that reads those five digits into FIXED variables A, B, C, D and E.

5. The stock ordering cards for P & A Groceries have this layout:

columns	contents
1-5	stock number
6-12	supplier's name
13-14	month first ordered
15-16	year first ordered
17-27	product name

Give a GET EDIT statement that reads the stock number and the product name into variables declared by

```
     DECLARE(STOCK_NUMBER)FIXED,
        (PRODUCT_NAME)CHARACTER(11)VARYING;
```

The GET EDIT statement should skip over columns 6-16.

6. Write a program that prints out a calendar. The program should read the day of the week for January 1 and the year. The program can determine whether it is a leap year via the IF statement:

```
     IF MOD(YEAR,4)=0 THEN
        FEBRUARY_LENGTH=29;
     ELSE
        FEBRUARY_LENGTH=28;
```

As used here the built-in function MOD will return a value of zero for years that can be exactly divided by 4. If your program prints the calendar for the entire year, it will produce 12 pages of output, one page for each month. You should use less paper and make your program read the number of a month and print the calendar only for that one month.

7. You are to write a program for the First Gibraltar Bank to print monthly statements for checking accounts. Here is a sample monthly statement:

                    FIRST GIBRALTAR BANK

                    MS. MARIE BEYER
                    2116 OAK BLVD.
                    CLINTONVILLE

FOR PERIOD ENDED   ACCOUNT NO.   DATE FWD.   BALANCE FWD.
DEC 14, 1980   8881-605223   NOV 16   1,141.42

CHECKS   DEPOSITS   DATE   BALANCE
20.00   NOV 21   1,121.42
15.00   NOV 22   1,106.42
16.85   NOV 25   1,089.57
                     841.46   NOV 28   1,931.03
154.49   DEC 08   1,776.54
60.12   DEC 14   1,716.42
                                                   (FINAL BALANCE)

        DEPOSITS   1   841.46
        CHECKS   5   266.46

This statement was printed as a result of reading the following
cards:

DEC 14, 1980
MS. MARIE BEYER
2116 OAK BLVD.
CLINTONVILLE
8881-605223
NOV 16 114142
NOV 21   2000
NOV 22   1500
NOV 25   1685
NOV 28   84146CR
DEC 08   15449
DEC 14   6012
XXX 00   0

Your program should read a set of cards, such as the above, and
print a monthly statement.

CHAPTER 14

SEARCHING AND SORTING

When a large amount of information is stored in a computer, it must be organized so that you are able to get at the information to make use of it. This problem of data retrieval is at the heart of all business operations. Records are kept of employees, customers, suppliers, inventory, in-process goods, and so on. These records are usually grouped in some way into what are called files. We might have, for example, a file of employee records, a file of customer records, an inventory file, and so on. Each file must be kept up to date.

A file that we all have access to is printed in the telephone book. It consists of a series of records of names, addresses, and telephone numbers. We say that there are three fields in each of these records: the name field, the address field, and the phone-number field. The file is in the alphabetic order of one of the three fields, the name field. We say that the name field is the key to the ordering of the file. The file is in alphabetic order on this field because that is how it can be most useful to us for data retrieval. We know someone's name and we want his phone number. We might also want his address and that too is available. The telephone company also has the same set of records, ordered using the phone-number field as the key.

In this chapter we will be investigating how a computer can search for information in a file and how records can be sorted.

LINEAR SEARCH

One way to look for data in a file is to start at the beginning and examine each record until you find the one you are looking for. This is the method people use who do not have large files. But for more than about 12 records it is not a good filing system. It will serve as an example to introduce us to the idea of searching mechanically and give us a bad method to compare our better methods to. We will create a file which consists of names and telephone numbers but the file will not be ordered by either name or number.

We will keep the file in two one-dimensional arrays, one called NAME and one called PHONE_NUMBER. PHONE_NUMBER(I) will be the correct telephone number for NAME(I). We will read this file, then read a list of names of people whose phone numbers are wanted. Here is the program to do this job. We are assuming that our file of names and phone numbers is punched without quotes around the names, so that we must use the GET EDIT statement.

```
$JOB ID='DON MCQUARRIE'
 PHONES:PROCEDURE OPTIONS(MAIN);
    DECLARE(NAME(50),FRIEND)CHARACTER(20)VARYING;
    DECLARE(PHONE_NUMBER(50))CHARACTER(8)VARYING;
    DECLARE(I,FILE_SIZE)FIXED;
    /* READ FILE OF NAMES AND NUMBERS */
    I=1;
    GET EDIT(NAME(I),PHONE_NUMBER(I))(A(20),A(8));
    DO WHILE(NAME(I)¬='ZZZ');
       I=I+1;
       GET SKIP EDIT(NAME(I),PHONE_NUMBER(I))(A(20),A(8));
       END;
    FILE_SIZE=I-1;
    GET SKIP EDIT(FRIEND)(A(20));
    DO WHILE(FRIEND¬='ZZZ');
       /* LOOK UP FRIEND'S NUMBER */
       I=1;
       DO WHILE(FRIEND¬=NAME(I) & I<=FILE_SIZE);
          I=I+1;
          END;
       IF FRIEND=NAME(I) THEN
          PUT SKIP EDIT(FRIEND,PHONE_NUMBER(I))(A(20),A(8));
       ELSE
          PUT SKIP EDIT(FRIEND,'UNLISTED')(A(20),A(8));
       GET SKIP EDIT(FRIEND)(A(20));
       END;
    END;
$DATA
PERRAULT,R.        483-4865
SCHUSTER,S.        769-5662
BORODIN,A.         782-8928
COOK,S.A.          763-3900
ENRIGHT,W.H.       266-1234
ZZZ
BORODIN,A.
BERNSTEIN,P.
ZZZ
```

The output will be

```
BORODIN,A.         782-8928
BERNSTEIN,P.       UNLISTED
```

We have stored the phone number as a character string because of the dash between the first three and the last four digits.

TIME TAKEN FOR SEARCH

In the last section we developed a program for a linear search. The searching process consists of comparing the friend's name, FRIEND, with each name in the file of names NAME(1), NAME(2), NAME(3), and so on until either the name is found or the end of the file is reached. For a small file, a linear search like this one may be fast enough, but it can be time-consuming if there is a lengthy file.

If there are N records in the file and the name is actually in the file, then on the average there will be N/2 comparisons. The largest number of comparisons would be N if the name were last in the file, the least number would be 1 if the name were first. A file of 1000 names would require 500 comparisons on the average. This gets to look rather formidable. It is for this reason that we do something to cut down on the effort. What we do is to sort the file into alphabetic order and then use a method of searching called <u>binary searching</u>. We will look at sorting later, but first we will see how much faster binary searching can be.

BINARY SEARCH

The telephone book is sorted alphabetically and the technique most of us use for looking up numbers is similar to the technique known as binary searching. We start by opening the book near where we think we will find the name we are looking for. We look at the page that is open and compare any name on it with the name being sought. If the listed name is alphabetically greater we know we must look only between the page we are at and the beginning of the book. We have eliminated the second part of the book from the search. This process is repeated in the part that might contain the name until we narrow the search down to one page.

In binary searching, instead of looking where we think we might find the name, we begin by looking at the name in the middle of the file and discard the half in which it cannot lie. This process cuts the possible number of names to be searched in half at each comparison.

A file of 16 names would require a maximum of 4 comparisons: one to cut the list to 8, another to 4, another to 2, and another to 1. Of course, we might find it earlier, but this is the <u>most</u> work we have to do. It is the maximum number of comparisons. With a linear search of 16 records we might have to make 16 comparisons, although 8 is the average. If we have a file of 1024 records, the binary search takes a maximum of 10

comparisons. This can be calculated by seeing how many times you
must divide by 2 to get down to 1 record . Put mathematically,
1024 is equal to

    2*2*2*2*2*2*2*2*2*2

Just one more comparison, making 11 altogether, will let you
search a list of 2048 entries. Then 4096 can be done with 12
comparisons. You can see how much more efficient binary
searching can be when the file is a long one.

A PROCEDURE FOR BINARY SEARCH

    We will now design a program for doing a binary search and
write it so that it can be called as a procedure. When we write

    CALL SEARCH(BASIC_FILE,KEY,SIZE,LOCATION)

we are asking for the value of LOCATION for which
BASIC_FILE(LOCATION)=KEY, where BASIC_FILE is an array of SIZE
items declared as CHARACTER. If the KEY is not in the file,
LOCATION will be set to zero.

    We will develop the algorithm for the binary search in two
stages as an illustration of step-by-step refinement. We will
write out our proposed solution in a linear form, in a mixture
of English and PL/1.

```
    Set LOCATION to zero in case KEY is not in BASIC_FILE;
    DO WHILE(there is more of the file to search);
        Find middle of file;
        IF middle value matches KEY THEN
            DO;
                Set LOCATION to middle;
                Discard remainder of file;
                END;
        ELSE
            IF middle value comes after KEY THEN
                Discard last half of remainder of file;
            ELSE
                Discard first half of remainder of file;
        END;
```

    It will be important to know the FIRST and LAST of the
remainder of the file at any time in order to establish the
MIDDLE and to discard the appropriate half. We initially set
FIRST to 1 and LAST to SIZE. Then to find the middle we use

    MIDDLE=(LAST+FIRST)/2E0;

It will not matter that this division is truncated as the process
of finding the middle is approximate when the number of entries
in the file is an even number. Refining the expression, "Discard
last half of remainder of file," becomes

```
    LAST=MIDDLE-1;
```

and, "Discard first half of remainder of file," becomes

```
    FIRST=MIDDLE+1;
```

Notice that we are discarding BASIC_FILE(MIDDLE) as well in each
case. The procedure can now be written:

```
 /* LOCATE KEY USING BINARY SEARCH */
 SEARCH:PROCEDURE(BASIC_FILE,KEY,SIZE,LOCATION);
    DECLARE(BASIC_FILE(*),KEY)CHARACTER(*)VARYING;
    DECLARE(SIZE,LOCATION)FIXED;
    DECLARE(FIRST,LAST,MIDDLE)FIXED;
    /* SET LOCATION TO ZERO FOR CASE OF KEY NOT IN FILE */
    LOCATION=0;
    /* INITIALIZE THE SEARCH LOOP */
    FIRST=1;
    LAST=SIZE;
    /* SEARCH UNTIL FILE IS EXHAUSTED */
    DO WHILE(FIRST<=LAST);
       MIDDLE=(FIRST+LAST)/2E0;
       IF BASIC_FILE(MIDDLE)=KEY THEN
           DO;
               LOCATION=MIDDLE;
               /* DISCARD ALL OF FILE */
               FIRST=LAST+1;
               END;
       ELSE
           IF BASIC_FILE(MIDDLE)>KEY THEN
               /* DISCARD LAST HALF */
               LAST=MIDDLE-1;
           ELSE
               /* DISCARD FIRST HALF */
               FIRST=MIDDLE+1;
       END;
    END;
```

A program that uses this procedure can now be written.

    We will use it to find the telephone numbers, and so replace
the five lines of our PHONES program following /* LOOK UP
FRIEND'S NUMBER */ by these two lines:

```
    CALL SEARCH(NAME,FRIEND,FILE_SIZE,I); IF I¬=0 THEN
```

We   are   assuming   now that the file of names is sorted
alphabetically. The procedure SEARCH would be included right
after the declarations of the main procedure.

    You will notice that the binary search program has more
instructions than the linear search that it is replacing.   Each
step is more complicated, but the whole process is much faster
for a large file because fewer steps are executed.

SEARCHING BY ADDRESS CALCULATION

We have seen that the efficiency of the searching process is very much improved by having a file sorted. The next method of searching uses data organized in a way so there is "a place for everything, and everything in its place".

Suppose you had a file of N records numbered from 1 to N. If you knew the number of the record, you would immediately know the location. The number would be the index of the array that holds the file entries. Each entry would have a location where it belonged. The trouble usually is to find the location of a record when what you know is some other piece of information such as a person's name.

Files are sometimes arranged so that they are organized on serial numbers that can be calculated from some other information in the record. For example, we could take a person's name and, by transforming it in a certain definite way, change it into a serial number. This transformation often seems bizarre and meaningless, and we say the name is hash-coded into a number. When the number has been determined the location is then definite and you can go to it without any problem.

Usually with hash coding it happens that several records have the same hash code. This means that, instead of the code providing the address of the exact record you want, what you get is the address of a location capable of containing several different records. We call such a location a bucket or bin. We then must look at the records in the bin to find the exact one we are interested in. Since the number is small they need not be sorted. A linear search is reasonable when the file is small.

If fixed-size bins are used to store the file, it is important to get a hash coding algorithm that will divide the original file so that roughly the same number of records is in each bin.

As an example of a hash-coding algorithm, suppose that we had 1000 bins and wanted to divide a file of 10,000 records into the bins. The file might already have associated with each record an identifying number. For example, it might be a Social Insurance number or a student number. These numbers might range from 1 to 1,000,000. One way to divide the records into bins would be to choose the last three digits of the identifying number as the hash code. Another hash code might be formed by choosing the third, fifth, and seventh digit. The purpose is to try to get a technique that gives about the same number of records in each bin. More complicated hashing algorithms may be necessary.

SORTING

We have already developed a sorting program as an example of step-by-step refinement in Chapter 9. The method we used is called a <u>bubble</u> <u>sort</u>. Each pair of neighboring elements in a file is compared and exchanged, to put the element with the larger key in the array location with the higher index. On each exchange pass, the element with the largest key gets moved into the last position. The next pass can then exclude the last position because it is already in order.

We have shown that the binary search technique is much more efficient for a large file than a linear search. In the same way, although a bubble sort is a reasonable method for a small file, it is not efficient for a large file. What we usually do to sort a large file is to divide it into a number of smaller files. Each small file is sorted by a technique such as the bubble sort, then the sorted smaller files are merged together into larger files.

We will look at an example in which two sorted files are merged into a single larger sorted file.

SORTING BY MERGING

We will develop a procedure called MERGE to merge FILE1, which has SIZE1 records ordered on the field KEY_FILE1, with FILE2, which has SIZE2 records ordered on the field KEY_FILE2, and store it in FILE3. We will invoke this procedure with the statement

    CALL MERGE(KEY_FILE1,SIZE1,KEY_FILE2,SIZE2,KEY_FILE3);

Here is the MERGE procedure:

```
/* MERGE TWO SORTED FILES */
MERGE:PROCEDURE(KEY_FILE1,SIZE1,KEY_FILE2,SIZE2,KEY_FILE3);
    DECLARE(KEY_FILE1(*),KEY_FILE2(*),
        KEY_FILE3(*))CHARACTER(*)VARYING;
    DECLARE(SIZE1,SIZE2)FIXED;
    DECLARE(I1,I2,I3,J)FIXED;
    I1=1;
    I2=1;
    I3=1;
    /* MERGE UNTIL ALL OF ONE FILE IS USED */
    DO WHILE(I1<=SIZE1 & I2<=SIZE2);
        IF KEY_FILE1(I1)<KEY_FILE2(I2)THEN
            DO;
                KEY_FILE3(I3)=KEY_FILE1(I1);
                I1=I1+1;
                END;
        ELSE
            DO;
                KEY_FILE3(I3)=KEY_FILE2(I2);
                I2=I2+1;
                END;
        I3=I3+1;
        END;
    /* ADD REMAINING ITEMS TO END OF NEW FILE */
    IF I2<=SIZE2 THEN
        DO J=0 TO(SIZE1+SIZE2-I3);
            KEY_FILE3(I3+J)=KEY_FILE2(I2+J);
            END;
    ELSE
        DO J=0 TO(SIZE1+SIZE2-I3);
            KEY_FILE3(I3+J)=KEY_FILE1(I1+J);
            END;
    END;
```

EFFICIENCY OF SORTING METHODS

The number of comparisons required to merge the two
previously sorted files in our example is SIZE1+SIZE2. To sort a
file of length N by the bubble sort we can count the maximum
number of comparisons that are needed. It is

$$(N-1)+(N-2)+(N-3)+...+1$$

This series can be summed and the result is

$$N(N-1)/2 \quad \text{which is}$$

$$N^2/2 - N/2$$

When N is large, the number of comparisons is about $N^2/2$, since
this is very large compared to N/2. We say the execution time of

the algorithm varies as N^2; sorting 100 items takes 100 times the number of comparisons that sorting 10 items does. We will now make calculations to see why sorting by merging is useful for long files. To sort a file of N items, by first using a bubble sort on two files N/2 in length then merging, requires $N^2/4-N/2$ for the bubble sort and N for the merge. This makes a combination total of

$$N^2/4 + N/2 \quad \text{comparisons.}$$

Using a bubble sort on the whole file gives a result of

$$N^2/2 - N/2 \quad \text{comparisons.}$$

When N=100, the bubble sort merge method requires 2,550 comparisons, the straight bubble sort requires 4,950 comparisons. We can keep dividing files and subfiles, sorting them by merging, with further improvements. In the limit we have a <u>successive merge</u> sort that is efficient enough to be used for large files.

CHAPTER 14 SUMMARY

This chapter has presented methods of searching and sorting that are used in computer programs. These methods manipulate <u>files</u> of <u>records</u>. Each record consists of one or more <u>fields</u>.

A search is based on a <u>key</u>, such as a person's name, that appears as one field in a record of a file. A <u>linear search</u> locates the desired record by starting at the first record and inspecting one record after another until the given key is found. A linear search is slow and should not be used for large files; a faster search method, such as binary search, should be used for large files.

A binary search requires that the file be ordered according to the key field of the records. An unordered file can be ordered using one of the sorting methods given in this chapter. The binary search inspects the middle record to determine which half of the file contains the desired record. Then the middle record of the correct half is inspected, to determine which quarter of the file contains the desired record, and so on, until the record is located.

If the key is a number that is identical to the index of the desired record then no searching is required, because the key gives the location of the record. Sometimes the key can be manipulated to create a <u>hash code</u> that locates a small set of records, called a <u>bucket</u>, that includes the desired record.

A file of records can be ordered using the bubble sort. This method repeatedly passes through the file, interchanging adjacent out-of-order records until all records are in order. The bubble sort is slow and must not be used for large files; a faster sorting method, such as the successive merge sort, should be used for large files.

A file can be sorted by merging in the following manner. First the file is divided into two sub-files and each of the sub-files is sorted by some method, such as the bubble sort. Then, starting with the first records of the two sub-files, the ordered file is created by passing through the sub-files and successively picking the appropriate (smaller key or alphabetically first key) record. If the sub-files are large, they should be sorted by a fast method, such as a merge, and this process is repeated as often as required.

CHAPTER 14 EXERCISES

1. The students for a particular high-school class have their names recorded on cards, for example:

    'ABBOT, HAROLD'

These cards are arranged alphabetically. Another deck of cards contains the names of newly-entered students for the same class; these cards are also alphabetically arranged. Write a program that reads the two sets of cards and prints out all the names alphabetically. Your program should read the smaller deck first and store its names in an array. Then the alphabetized list should be printed at the same time the larger deck is read. Explain why it is better to read the smaller deck first. What is the advantage of printing the list while the second deck is being read, rather than waiting till both decks are read?

2. Do exercise 1 assuming that the large deck is alphabetized, but the small deck is not.

3. Write a program that maintains a "lost and found" service. First the program reads cards giving found objects and the finders' names and phone numbers. For example, this card

    'SIAMESE CAT' 'MISS MABEL DAVIS' '714-3261'

means Miss Mabel Davis, having phone number 714-3261, found a Siamese cat. These cards are to be read and ordered alphabetically and then a similar set of cards for losers of objects is to be processed. If a lost object matches a found object, then the program should print the name of the object as well as the finder, the loser and their telephone numbers. Assume the loser cards are not alphabetized. Process each loser card as it is read, using a binary search.

CHAPTER 15

MAKING SURE THE PROGRAM WORKS

Throughout this book, we have emphasized structured programming techniques; these include step-by-step refinement, programming without the GO TO statement, choosing good variable names and so on. These techniques make it easier to write correct programs. We have also given techniques for testing and debugging programs. In this chapter we will collect and expand upon these techniques for making sure a program works.

SOLVING THE RIGHT PROBLEM

The _specifications_ for a program tell what the program must do to solve a problem. Before starting to write a program, the programmer needs the detailed specifications for the program. Suppose the problem is to print pay checks for the employees of a company; there is a card giving each employee's name and amount of payment. The programmer needs to know the format of the data on the cards as well as the format for the pay checks. These formats are part of the specifications for the program to print pay checks.

Sometimes the program specifications are not completely agreed upon and written down. If an employee's card indicates an amount of $0.00, this may mean that the employee is on leave and is to receive no pay check. If the programmer does not know the special significance of $0.00 - because the specifications are not complete - he may write a program that prints hundreds of worthless pay checks. All too often programs fail to handle special situations such as $0.00 correctly. If the programmer is in doubt about such a situation, he should check the specifications and make sure they are complete.

DEFENSIVE PROGRAMMING

Errors are sometimes made in the preparation of data for a
program. Amounts may be mispunched on cards; more data may be
supplied than anticipated. The method of handling data errors
may be given in the program specifications, or it may be left to
the discretion of the programmer. Sometimes a programmer can
write his program so that it detects and reports bad data. This
is called defensive programming. Some programs are written to
accept absolutely any data; after reporting a bad data item, the
program ignores the item or attempts to give it a reasonable
interpretation. If a program is written assuming no data errors,
bad data items may prevent the program from doing its job. It is
the programmer's responsibility to make his program sufficiently
defensive to solve the problem at hand.

ATTITUDE AND WORK HABITS

The quality of a computer program is determined largely by
the attitudes and work habits of the programmer. Some
programmers underestimate the programming task. They write
programs too quickly, they do not test their programs
sufficiently, and they are too willing to believe that their
programs are correct.

Most programs, when first written, contain some errors. This
is not surprising when you consider the vast number of possible
programming errors and the fallibility of every programmer. The
programmer should take the attitude that a program is not correct
until it is shown to be correct.

One good method of preparing computer programs is to write
them using a soft lead pencil. This allows easy corrections and
improvements by erasing and replacing lines. If a major change
is required, an entire page should be recopied. The program
should be submitted to the computer only when the programmer
feels confident that no more changes are required. This method
of program preparation can save the programmer a lot of time.
The savings come because it is easy to change a program when it
is still on paper and fresh in the programmer's mind. Each later
change requires the programmer to relearn the program before he
can confidently make modifications. A few minutes of desk-
checking a program can save hours of debugging time. The
programmer who tries to "do it right the first time" comes out
ahead, saving his own time and writing programs with fewer
errors.

PROVING PROGRAM CORRECTNESS

The most effective way to make sure a program works correctly
is to study the program thoroughly. It should be read again and

again until the programmer is thoroughly convinced that it is right.

It helps if a second programmer reads and approves the program. Ideally, the second programmer should read the program after its author feels that it is correct, but before it is submitted to the computer. The second reader provides a new point of view and may be able to find typical errors such as incorrect loop initialization.

This process of studying programs to make sure they are correct can be called "proving program correctness". Sometimes programs are proven correct using a mathematical approach; proving that a program is correct is then similar to proving that a theorem in geometry is true. More often, programs are proven correct by a non-mathematical, common-sense approach. The program is considered to have errors until proven correct.

PROGRAMMING STYLE

A program should be easy to read and understand; otherwise the job of studying it to verify its correctness will be hopeless. The programmer should strive for a good <u>programming style</u>, remembering that other readers will be in a hurry and will be critical of sloppiness or unnecessary confusion in the program. It commonly happens that as a programmer makes a program clearer and easier to understand, he discovers ways to improve or correct the program.

It takes work to write programs that are easy to read - just as it takes work to write clear English. Good writing requires care and practice. One way of making programs readable and understandable is to give them a simple organization - so the reader can easily learn the relationship among program parts. We have previously presented step-by-step refinement and modular programming as techniques for designing programs. As well as aiding in the writing of programs, these techniques help make programs easier to read.

USE OF COMMENTS AND IDENTIFIERS

One of the rules of good programming style is this: comments and identifiers should be chosen to help make a program understandable. Comments should record the programmer's intentions for the parts of the program. It is a good idea to write comments as the program is being written.

Good programs require few comments, because the program written in PL/1 closely reflects the intentions of the programmer. Programs become more difficult to read if they are cluttered with obvious comments such as

```
/* INCREASE N BY 1 */
N=N+1;
```

Comments are usually needed to record:

- Overall purpose of a program. What problem the program is to solve. As well, comments may be used to record the program's author and its date of writing.

- Purpose of each module. Similar to the comments for an overall program.

- Purpose of a collection of statements. Such a comment might give the purpose of a loop.

- Assumptions and restrictions. At certain points in a program, certain assumptions and restrictions may apply to variables and the data. For example, one program part may assume that another program part has set NUMBER_OF_ACCOUNTS to a positive number less than 20 to indicate the number of customer accounts.

- Obscure or unusual statements. As a rule, such statements should be avoided. If they are required they should be explained. Here is an example:

```
/* ROUND CENTS TO NEAREST DOLLAR */
DOLLARS=(CENTS+50)/100E0;
CENTS=100*DOLLARS;
```

Well-chosen identifiers make a program easier to read. Each identifier should record the function of the named object. For example, an array used to save account numbers should be named ACCOUNT_NUMBER and not ARRAY. A procedure used to read accounts should be named READ_ACCOUNTS and not P1 or MARGARET.

If a variable has a very simple purpose, such as indexing through an array, a one-letter name such as I, J or N may be appropriate. This is because these letters are commonly used for indexing in mathematics. But if the index variable has some additional meaning, such as counting input data cards, a longer name may help the reader.

Avoid abbreviations, such as TBNTR for table entry. Avoid acronyms, such as SAX for sales tax. Unless abbreviations or acronyms are well known to the reader before seeing the program, they impose an extra memorization task that interferes with understanding the program.

Avoid meaningless identifiers such as A, B, C, D and TEMP1. A single-letter identifier such as D is sometimes appropriate for a simply-used variable when the name D is relevant, for example, it stands for diameter. Adding a digit such as 1 or 2 to the end of an identifier, as in TEMP1, can be confusing unless it explains the purpose of the named object.

TESTING

After the program has been written and studied to verify its correctness, it should be tested. The purpose of testing is to run the program to demonstrate that it is working properly.

The tests must be chosen with care because only a limited number of them can be run. Consider a program designed to sort any list of 100 names into alphabetic order. Certainly we could not test it exhaustively by trying every possible list of 100 names. We would be testing for years! Rather than exhaustive testing we need to design tests which try every type of situation the program is to handle.

Well-designed tests should point out any errors in the program. Ultimately, testing demonstrates errors better than it demonstrates program correctness.

When testing reveals an error, that is, a bug, in the program, the programmer is faced with a debugging task. We shall present debugging techniques later. Right now, we will give techniques for testing.

The programmer will need to study the program in order to design good tests. The tests should make each statement execute at least once - but this is not enough. Suppose the statement

    AVERAGE=TOTAL/COUNT;

is tested and computes the desired average. This does not demonstrate that all is well; it may be that in some situations COUNT can become zero. If this statement is executed with COUNT set to zero, the statement does not make sense. So, not only should every statement be executed, but it should be executed for the type of situation it is expected to handle. Care should be taken to:

   - Test end conditions. See that each loop is executed correctly the first time and last time through. See that indexes to arrays reach their smallest and largest possible values. Pay particular attention to indexes and counters which may take on the value zero.

   - Test special conditions. See that data which rarely occurs is handled properly. If the program prints error messages, see that each situation requiring such a message is tested.

Designing tests to exercise all end conditions and special conditions is not easy - but it is worthwhile in terms of program reliability.

The programmer should be able to tell from test results if the program is executing correctly. Sometimes this is easy because the program prints intermediate results as it progresses. Sometimes the programmer will need to add special printing statements so he can verify that the program is running correctly. These statements can:

<u>Print</u> <u>data</u> <u>as</u> <u>it</u> <u>is</u> <u>read</u>. If there is not too much data, it may be good to have the program print the data as it is read.

<u>Print</u> <u>messages</u> <u>to</u> <u>record</u> <u>the</u> <u>statements</u> <u>being</u> <u>executed</u>. For example, a message might say READING ACCOUNTS PROCEDURE ENTERED.

<u>Print</u> <u>values</u> <u>of</u> <u>variables</u>. This allows the programmer to verify by hand that the values are correct. The best time to print variables is when modules start and when they finish, so the programmer can verify that variables were modified correctly.

<u>Print</u> <u>warnings</u> <u>of</u> <u>violated</u> <u>assumptions</u>. Suppose a procedure is used to set WHERE to the index of the smallest number in a list of 12 numbers. The assumption that WHERE receives a value from 1 to 12 can be tested by

```
IF WHERE<1 | WHERE>12 THEN
    PUT SKIP LIST('ERROR:WHERE=',WHERE);
```

Care must be taken to design appropriate printing statements for testing. Too much printing will not be read by the programmer; too little printing will not give the programmer sufficient information about the execution of the program.

Ideally, tests should be designed before the program is submitted to the computer. With the program still fresh in his mind, the programmer can more easily invent tests that try out every statement. Sometimes a programmer discovers that parts of a program are difficult to test; a slight change in the program may overcome this difficulty. It is best to make these changes when the program is still on paper, before time has been invested in punching or mark-sensing the program and submitting it to the computer. Designing tests requires the programmer to read his program with a new point of view. It sometimes happens that this point of view uncovers errors in the program. The best time to fix these errors is when the program is still on paper.

As programs become larger, it becomes increasingly difficult to test them thoroughly. Large programs can be tested by first testing the modules individually. Then the modules are combined into larger modules and these are tested and so on. The process is called <u>bottom-up</u> <u>testing</u>. This method of testing uses specially-written test programs that call the modules with various values of parameters, shared variables and input data.

Whenever a program is modified, it should be retested. All the changed parts should be tested. In addition, it is a good idea to test the entire module containing changes, or even the entire program. The reason is that modifications often require a precise understanding of the surrounding program, and this understanding is sometimes not attained. Very commonly, program modifications introduce errors.

DEBUGGING

A program has bugs (errors) when it fails to solve the problem it is supposed to solve. When a program misbehaves we are faced with the problem of debugging - correcting the error. The program's misbehavior is a symptom of a disease and we must find a cure. Sometimes the symptom is far removed from the source of the problem; erroneous statements in one part of a program may set variables' values incorrectly and trigger a series of unpredicted actions by the program. When the symptoms appear via incorrect program output, the program may be executing in a different module. The programmer is left with a few clues: the incorrect output. He has to solve the mystery and cure the disease. Solving these debugging mysteries can take more time than writing the program.

When a program contains a bug, this means that the programmer made at least one mistake. We can categorize programmer errors as follows:

Errors in making the program machine-readable. If the program is prepared on punch cards, PROCEDURE might be mis-punched as PROCDEURE. These are keypunching errors.

Errors in using the programming language. The programmer did not understand a language construct. For example, his program may be wrong because he assumed that 'JONES' comes alphabetically before 'JONES '. (When PL/1 compares the two it concludes they are alphabetically equal.)

Errors in writing program parts. Although a particular program part was properly designed, it was not correctly written in PL/1. For example, a loop designed to read in account cards might always execute zero times because of writing the loop's terminating condition incorrectly.

Errors in program design. The program parts and their interactions might be improperly designed. The program designer might forget to provide for the initialization of variables used by some modules. He might overlook the fact that one module, say, PRINT_ACCOUNTS, should be called only after calling another module, say, READ_ACCOUNTS.

Solving the wrong problem. The programmer did not understand the nature of the problem to be solved. He may have misunderstood the program specifications. Perhaps the specifications were not correct or complete.

This list of possible errors has proceeded from the least serious to the most disastrous. The first type of errors, such as keypunching errors, can be corrected easily once detected. The last type of error, misunderstanding the purpose of the program, may require scrapping the entire program and starting over again.

Some programmers are overly optimistic and immediately conclude that any bugs in their programs are not very serious. Such a programmer is quick to make little changes in his program to try to make the symptoms of the problem disappear. The wise programmer knows that program misbehavior is an indication of sloppiness and that sloppiness leads easily to disastrous errors. He takes program misbehavior as a sign that the program is sick - he gives it a checkup by studying it.

The overly optimistic programmer is forever saying, "I just found the last bug." When the wise programmer finds a bug, he looks for five more.

Many of the least serious errors, such as misspelled keywords, are automatically pointed out by error messages, because the error results in an illegal PL/1 program. These errors are usually easy to fix. Some errors are particularly treacherous; they seem to defy attempts to correct them. Here is some advice - some of it repeated from earlier parts of this book - to help you track down treacherous bugs.

Read all error messages. In their hurry to read their program's output, some programmers fail to notice error messages. These messages may pinpoint a bug.

Beware of automatic error repair. Compilers try to make it easier to get programs working by "repairing" errors. For example, the programmer might carelessly write X=2Y; the compiler might repair this to X=2; such repairs can save time by allowing more of the program to be compiled and executed on one run. However, these repairs should not be taken as intelligent advice; remember, the compiler has no idea what problem you are trying to solve.

The first error messages may help more than later ones. This is because the first messages are closer to the source of the problem. Later messages may simply indicate that a previous error is still causing trouble.

Beware of confusion between I and 1. Some people can consistently read X=X+I; to mean increase X by one. Errors like this can be found by reading the program character by character - as a computer does! In general, the human tendency to read what we want to be there, rather what is actually there makes debugging difficult.

<u>Beware</u> <u>of</u> <u>misspellings</u>. Some words are easily misspelled. A person who is concentrating on understanding a program may overlook RECEIPT occasionally spelled as RECIEPT. In PL/C - but not in SP/k - new identifiers are automatically declared to be variables. Hence, PL/C would not warn us that RECEIPT appeared in a declaration, but that RECIEPT suspiciously did not.

<u>Beware</u> <u>of</u> <u>language</u> <u>peculiarities</u>. SP/k was designed to minimize language peculiarities, but it still has some traps for the naive programmer. Among the worst of these are:

(a) <u>Putting a semicolon after THEN</u>. The following lines of PL/1 will check to see if X is greater than 2:

```
IF X > 2 THEN;
   Y=X;
```

Whether this is true or not, Y will be set to X. The semicolon after THEN acts as a null statement, which is executed when X is greater than 2.

(b) <u>Using incorrect attributes for procedure parameters</u>. The following procedure will change the sign of a fixed variable.

```
NEGATE:PROCEDURE(I);
   DECLARE(I)FIXED;
   I=-I;
   END;
```

If this procedure is erroneously called with a float argument X, then X will be converted from float to fixed. The converted value is passed to the procedure and has its sign changed. But the value of X the float variable remains unchanged. The program will fail if it depends upon changing the sign of X. This sort of problem can occur in SP/k when a float argument is passed to a fixed parameter (or vice versa) and the parameter has a value assigned to it.

If everything else fails in the debugging effort, the programmer is forced to rerun his program to gain more information about the errors. The programmer may add statements to print variables or to trace the program's execution. These statements are designed using the same techniques used in testing to show programs work properly. If the original tests had been carefully enough designed, there is a good chance they would have pinpointed the error and eliminated later time-consuming debugging.

CHAPTER 15 SUMMARY

In this chapter we have listed techniques for making sure a program works. There are a vast number of ways a program can be wrong, so the programmer should learn to be careful at all the stages of program preparation. When a programmer is too hasty to submit his program to the computer, this results in persistent bugs and excessive time spent in debugging. The following important techniques and terminology were presented in this chapter.

Program specifications - explanation of what a program is to do. This should include the forms of the input and output data and the type of calculation or data manipulation to be performed. Essentially, program specifications explain how the computer is to be used to solve a particular problem.

Programming habits - the way a programmer goes about his work. Ideally, he should take the slow but sure approach, completing his program in pencil and thoroughly studying it before submitting it to the computer.

Proving program correctness - studying a program to verify that it satisfies its specifications.

Programming style - if the style is good, then the program can be easily read and understood.

Use of comments and identifiers - good programming style requires that comments and identifiers be chosen to make a program understandable. Comments should record the programmer's intentions; identifiers should record the function or use of the named object.

Testing - running a program to demonstrate that it is correct. Tests should be designed to try every type of situation the program is to handle. Ultimately, testing is better at demonstrating bugs than demonstrating program correctness.

Debugging - correcting errors in a program. Debugging can be the most difficult and time-consuming part of trying to make a program work. These difficulties can be minimized by using the techniques listed in this chapter.

CHAPTER 15 EXERCISES

1. In this exercise you are to use defensive programming. Modify the following program so that it will handle errors in the data gracefully. The program reads a list of names and prints

the list in reverse order. You have no control over the data, but if you wish, you can add a redundant dummy data card to the end of the data.

```
/*PRINT NAMES IN REVERSE ORDER */
REORDER:PROCEDURE OPTIONS(MAIN);
   DECLARE(NAME(10))CHARACTER(15)VARYING,
     (HOW_MANY,I)FIXED;
   GET EDIT(HOW_MANY)(F(3));
   DO I=1 TO HOW_MANY;
      GET SKIP EDIT(NAME(I))(A(15));
      END;
   DO I=HOW_MANY TO 1 BY -1;
      PUT SKIP EDIT(NAME(I))(A(15));
      END;
   END;
```

2. You are to debug the following program. It is supposed to read strings and determine if they are palindromes. A string is a palindrome if reversing it yields the same string again; for example, each of the following are palindromes: 'MOM', 'OH HO', ' ' and 'DEED'. Do not submit the corrected program to be run by the computer.

```
$JOB ID='SUE DENIM'
 /* THIS PROGRAM IS FULL OF BUGS */
 REVERSE:PROCEDURE OPTIONS(MAIN);
    DECLARE(STRING,REVERSED)CHARACTER(10)VARYING,
      (NUMBER_OF_STRINGS,I,J,HALF_LENGTH)FIXED;
    GET LIST(NUMBER_OF_STRINGS);
    PUT SKIP LIST('TEST',NUMBER_OF_STRINGS,'STRINGS');
    GET LIST(STRING);
    DO I=1 TO NUMBER_OF_STRINGS;
       HALF_LENGTH=LENGTH(STRING)/2E0;
       PUT SKIP LIST(STRING);
       I=LENGTH(STRING);
       DO WHILE(I>HALF_LENGTH);
          REVERSED=REVERSED||SUBSTR(STRING,I,1);
          I=I-1;
          END;
       IF SUBSTR(STRING,1,HALF_LENGTH)=REVERSED THEN
          PUT LIST(' IS A PALINDROME.');
       ELSE
          PUT LIST(' IS NOT A PALINDROME.');
       END;
    END;
$DATA
 5
 'DEED'
 'OH HO'
 'AHAH MADAM HAHA'
 'ROTOR'
 ' '
```

3. Try to write a program that is completely correct before you submit it to the computer. Have a friend help you by studying

your program for errors after you are convinced that it is free
of errors. Record the time you spend preparing the program and
record any programming errors you make. Your program should
perform one of the following tasks:

(a) The program should read a series of integers followed by
the dummy value 99999. Print the sum of the positive
integers and the number of negative integers.

(b) The program should read and print a list of
alphabetically ordered names. If a name is repeated in the
data, it should be printed only once.

(c) The program should read and print a list of character
strings. Replace any occurrence of 'MRS. ' or 'MISS ' by
'MS. ' and any occurrence of 'CHAIRMAN' by 'CHAIRPERSON'.

4. The following program reads employees' names, hours worked in
a week and hourly rates of pay. It computes each employee's pay
based on his rate and number of hours, with one and a half times
the rate for overtime hours (hours beyond the first 40 hours).
Make the program readable by adding appropriate comments and by
choosing meaningful variable names. No other changes to the
program are required.

```
$JOB ID='JEANNE DAIGLE'
 /* THIS PROGRAM HAS POOR IDENTIFIERS AND NEEDS COMMENTS */
 BREAD:PROCEDURE OPTIONS(MAIN);
    DECLARE(B1)CHARACTER(13)VARYING,
      (B,A,C,B2)FIXED;
    PUT SKIP LIST('EMPLOYEE','REGULAR HRS.','OVERTIME','PAYMENT');
    GET LIST(B1);
    DO WHILE(B1¬='ZZZ');
       GET LIST(A,B);
       C=0;
       IF A>40 THEN
          DO;
             C=A-40;
             A=40;
             END;
       B2=B*(A+1.5E0*C)+0.5E0;
       PUT SKIP LIST(B1,A,C,B2);
       GET LIST(B1);
       END;
    END;
$DATA
 'LEXI KOLT'  5  3
 'JOHN EVANS' 59 5
 ...
 'ZZZ'
```

CHAPTER 16

SP/8: FILES AND RECORDS

So far we have spoken about files of records and discussed the process of searching for particular records. This process was made more efficient by having the files sorted. We then looked at ways of sorting files of records. All sorting methods involve moving records around in the computer memory. In our sorting examples, we did not really deal with the situation of sorting records that consisted of more than the one field, namely the key field of the ordering. In our examples, then, moving the record meant only moving this one field. In most data processing applications, records contain a number of fields, and it is important to be able to write statements in a program to move all the fields as a single unit. We will be introducing the idea of a record structure which is a group of several fields designed to make file processing simple to program.

When large quantities of data have to be processed, it is impossible to store files of records completely within the main memory of the computer. It is usual to keep large files in secondary storage such as magnetic tape or magnetic disk storage. We must then be able to read records from such a file and write records into it. We will be looking at the statements in PL/1 that permit us to manipulate files in secondary storage.

RECORD STRUCTURES

In PL/1, a structure is a collection of several fields and is particularly suitable for records in a file. As a simple example, suppose that we want to describe each record in the telephone file by a record structure. We would identify the entire structure by the identifier CUSTOMER and the three fields as

```
CUSTOMER.NAME
CUSTOMER.ADDRESS
CUSTOMER.PHONE_NUMBER
```

Here is a diagram of the fields:

CUSTOMER

NAME	ADDRESS	PHONE NUMBER

The field identifiers are a composite of their own identifiers, NAME, ADDRESS, and PHONE_NUMBER and the whole structure's identifier, CUSTOMER. The composite is constructed by putting a dot, or period, between the structure name and the field name.

The record structure would be declared this way.

```
DECLARE 1 CUSTOMER,
          2 NAME CHARACTER(20)VARYING,
          2 ADDRESS CHARACTER(30)VARYING,
          2 PHONE_NUMBER CHARACTER(8)VARYING;
```

This record structure consists of two levels of naming. At level 1 we have the identifier of the record structure declared, namely CUSTOMER. This has no attribute associated with it. Level 2 has three fields declared. Each of these has its own attribute. So it is possible to have each field with a different attribute. Here, all the fields are of type CHARACTER, but each has a different length.

A record structure is sometimes called the layout of a record.

MOVING RECORDS

One of the reasons for having record structures is that they make it simple to program the movement of a whole record from one place to another. When a move is to take place, the location that will receive the structure must be declared to have exactly the same set of fields. It will, of course, have its own record structure identifier. We can write this declaration as

```
DECLARE 1 WORK_SPACE LIKE CUSTOMER;
```

The record structure WORK_SPACE will have all the same fields, NAME, ADDRESS and PHONE_NUMBER. They will be referred to as WORK_SPACE.NAME, WORK_SPACE.ADDRESS, and so on. We say that the record structures CUSTOMER and WORK_SPACE have the same template.

To move the record CUSTOMER into the record WORK_SPACE we need only write

        WORK_SPACE = CUSTOMER;

This is equivalent to the group of assignment statements

        WORK_SPACE.NAME=CUSTOMER.NAME;
        WORK_SPACE.ADDRESS=CUSTOMER.ADDRESS;
        WORK_SPACE.PHONE_NUMBER=CUSTOMER.PHONE_NUMBER;

An entire structure can be assigned to another by a single assignment statement only if one structure is LIKE the other.

The PL/C compiler does not support the LIKE attribute. If you are using the PL/C compiler, you can declare a structure to be "like" a previously-declared structure by copying the first structure's field declarations (level 2) into the second structure's declaration.

ARRAYS OF RECORDS

Just as groups of variables of the same type may form arrays, records may form arrays. Each member of the array of records has the same structure. To declare an array we add, in parentheses after the structure identifier, the bounds of the array. For the telephone-book records, an array of 100 such records could be declared by

    DECLARE 1 CUSTOMER(1:100),
              2 NAME CHARACTER(20)VARYING,
              2 ADDRESS CHARACTER(30)VARYING,
              2 PHONE_NUMBER CHARACTER(8)VARYING;

The bounds of the array, namely (1:100), could have been written simply as (100). An array of records can be used for grouping records for sorting purposes. A procedure for sorting a group of CUSTOMER records that have been declared in the main procedure will be given. The records are to be sorted on the key PHONE_NUMBER. The array of record structures called CUSTOMER will be global to the procedure. The only parameter that the procedure has is NUMBER_OF_RECORDS. A WORK_SPACE structure is declared as a local variable, LIKE the global structure CUSTOMER. The dimensions of CUSTOMER are <u>not</u> given to WORK_SPACE by the LIKE, just the structure of the fields, that is, their names, levels, and attributes.

```
SORT:PROCEDURE(NUMBER_OF_RECORDS);
   /* SORT RECORDS BY PHONE_NUMBER */
   DECLARE(NUMBER_OF_RECORDS)FIXED;
   DECLARE 1 WORK_SPACE LIKE CUSTOMER;
   DECLARE(I,J)FIXED;
   DO I=1 TO NUMBER_OF_RECORDS-1;
      DO J=1 TO NUMBER_OF_RECORDS-I;
         IF CUSTOMER(J).PHONE_NUMBER>CUSTOMER(J+1).PHONE_NUMBER
            THEN
            DO;
               WORK_SPACE=CUSTOMER(J);
               CUSTOMER(J)=CUSTOMER(J+1);
               CUSTOMER(J+1)=WORK_SPACE;
               END;
         END;
      END;
   END;
```

INPUT AND OUTPUT OF RECORDS

The record is a convenient form for moving the groups of fields around in the main memory of the computer. But we have not yet said how such structures may be read into or written out from the main memory. The input-output statements that we have had so far, the GET and PUT with LIST or EDIT, can be used to read or print individual fields of a structure in exactly the same way as the values of individual variables are read or printed. But you cannot read or print the record structure as a unit by these instructions. If you input records from cards, each field is read independently. Here is a program that reads a set of at most 25 customer records, sorts them and prints them:

```
$JOB ID='STEPHEN ALEXANDER'
 NUMBERS:PROCEDURE OPTIONS(MAIN);
    DECLARE 1 CUSTOMER(25),
             2 NAME CHARACTER(20)VARYING,
             2 ADDRESS CHARACTER(30)VARYING,
             2 PHONE_NUMBER CHARACTER(8)VARYING;
    DECLARE(I)FIXED;
    DECLARE(NUMBER_OF_RECORDS)FIXED;
    (copy procedure SORT here)
    GET LIST(NUMBER_OF_RECORDS);
    /* READ RECORDS INTO ARRAY */
    DO I=1 TO NUMBER_OF_RECORDS;
        GET SKIP EDIT(CUSTOMER(I).NAME,CUSTOMER(I).ADDRESS,
          CUSTOMER(I).PHONE_NUMBER)(A(20),A(30),A(8));
        END;
    /* SORT RECORDS BY PHONE_NUMBER */
    CALL SORT(NUMBER_OF_RECORDS);
    /* PRINT SORTED ARRAY OF RECORDS */
    DO I=1 TO NUMBER_OF_RECORDS;
        PUT SKIP EDIT(CUSTOMER(I).PHONE_NUMBER,CUSTOMER(I).NAME,
          CUSTOMER(I).ADDRESS)(A(8),X(2),A(20),A(30));
        END;
    END;
$DATA
 5
JOHNSTON,R.L.        53 JONSTON CRES.        491-6405
KEAST,P.            77 KREDLE HAVEN DR.      439-7216
LIPSON,J.D.         15 WEEDWOOD ROAD         787-8515
MATHON,R.A.         666 REGINA AVE.          962-8885
CRAWFORD,C.R.       39 TREATHERSON AVE.      922-7999
```

The output for this program will be

```
439-7216  KEAST,P.         77 KREDLE HAVEN DR.
491-6405  JOHNSTON,R.L.    53 JONSTON CRES.
787-8515  LIPSON,J.D.      15 WEEDWOOD ROAD
922-7999  CRAWFORD,C.R.    39 TREATHERSON AVE.
962-8885  MATHON,R.A.      666 REGINA AVE.
```

FILES IN SECONDARY MEMORY

In our discussion of files so far, we have had the files stored in the main memory. In most real file applications, the files are too large to be contained in main memory. The part of the file being processed must be brought into main memory, but the complete file is stored in secondary memory. The secondary memory may be magnetic tape or magnetic disk.

A file in secondary storage is a collection of records all of the same template. The collection is called a dataset. One record at a time may be transferred from the dataset to a structure in main memory, or from a structure in main memory to the dataset. The record that is transferred must be the <u>next</u> record in the sequence of records in the dataset. We say that the file can be read sequentially from the secondary memory to the main memory or written sequentially from the main memory to secondary memory. This type of file is called a <u>sequential file</u>. It is not possible at any moment to get access to an arbitrary record in the file; the next record in sequence is the only one that is available.

Since <u>files in secondary storage are to be accessed</u> <u>sequentially, there must be a statement in the program that will</u> <u>position the file reader at the first record of the dataset.</u> Before a file in secondary storage can be accessed, we must write a statement of the form

        OPEN FILE(file name)INPUT;

The file name is that of the whole dataset or file. It may, for example, be named OLDFILE. This identifier is declared at the beginning of the procedure by

        DECLARE(OLDFILE)RECORD FILE;

The template of the records in the dataset is determined by the written records.

        To read the next record from the file in secondary storage, we use a statement of the form

        READ FILE(file name)INTO(structure name);

If we have records of the same template as the CUSTOMER record we could read the OLDFILE using this statement.

        READ FILE(OLDFILE)INTO(CUSTOMER);

        When the reading of a file is finished, the file must be <u>closed</u>. For a magnetic tape this will result in a rewinding of the tape so that it could be removed from the tape-reading unit. The statement for closing a file is of the form

        CLOSE FILE(file name);

For the file OLDFILE we would have

        CLOSE FILE(OLDFILE);

        For files that are to be written, the statement for opening is of the form:

        OPEN FILE(file name)OUTPUT;

To write a record into such a file, we use a statement of this form

    WRITE FILE(file name)FROM(structure name);

As with input files, output file names must be declared with the attribute RECORD FILE.

A file opened as an INPUT file can only have READ or CLOSE performed on it. A file opened as an OUTPUT file can only have WRITE or CLOSE performed on it. The OPEN statement establishes the communication path between the file and the main memory; the CLOSE statement dissolves the communication path. CLOSE must be the last operation performed on any file that has been opened. After an OUTPUT file has been written, it may be closed and then opened as an INPUT file. This is in fact how INPUT files can be obtained. Within one program, all structures read from or written to a particular file must be LIKE each other.

FILE MAINTENANCE

As an example of reading and writing files we will program a simple file-maintenance operation. We will assume that there exists a file of CUSTOMER records called OLDFILE, and we want to update this file by adding new customers. The information about the new customers is punched on cards. Each card corresponds to a transaction that must be posted in the file to produce an up-to-date customer file, which we will call NEWFILE. This is an example of file maintenance. The file OLDFILE is ordered alphabetically by CUSTOMER.NAME and the transactions are arranged alphabetically. The last record of each file has a NAME with a value ZZZ. This program will be very similar to the merge-sort program of Chapter 14, except that the records of the two files being merged are not in an array.

```
$JOB ID='HARRIET LOGAN'
 UPDATE:PROCEDURE OPTIONS(MAIN);
    /* ADD NEW CUSTOMERS TO CUSTOMER FILE */
    DECLARE 1 CUSTOMER,
              2 NAME CHARACTER(20)VARYING,
              2 ADDRESS CHARACTER(30)VARYING,
              2 PHONE_NUMBER CHARACTER(8)VARYING;
    DECLARE(OLDFILE,NEWFILE)RECORD FILE;
    DECLARE 1 TRANSACTION LIKE CUSTOMER;
    OPEN FILE(NEWFILE)OUTPUT;
    OPEN FILE(OLDFILE)INPUT;
    /* READ FIRST CUSTOMER RECORD FROM FILE */
    READ FILE(OLDFILE)INTO(CUSTOMER);
    /* READ FIRST TRANSACTION FROM CARD */
    GET EDIT(TRANSACTION.NAME,TRANSACTION.ADDRESS,
        TRANSACTION.PHONE_NUMBER)(A(20),A(30),A(8));
    /* POST TRANSACTIONS TO CUSTOMER FILE */
    DO WHILE(CUSTOMER.NAME¬='ZZZ'|TRANSACTION.NAME¬='ZZZ');
        IF CUSTOMER.NAME>TRANSACTION.NAME THEN
            DO;
                WRITE FILE(NEWFILE)FROM(TRANSACTION);
                GET SKIP EDIT(TRANSACTION.NAME,TRANSACTION.ADDRESS,
                    TRANSACTION.PHONE_NUMBER)(A(20),A(30),A(8));
                END;
        ELSE
            DO;
                WRITE FILE(NEWFILE)FROM(CUSTOMER);
                READ FILE(OLDFILE)INTO(CUSTOMER);
                END;
        END;
    /* ADD DUMMY RECORD TO END OF FILE */
    WRITE FILE(NEWFILE)FROM(CUSTOMER);
    CLOSE FILE(OLDFILE);
    CLOSE FILE(NEWFILE);
    END;
$DATA
(transactions one to a card)
ZZZ            NULL                    NULL
```

The PL/C compiler and the PL/1 compilers produced by IBM
cannot READ or WRITE structures that have CHARACTER VARYING
fields.   To run the program under one of those compilers, you
must change the declaration of the CUSTOMER structure to this:

```
    DECLARE 1 CUSTOMER,
              2 NAME CHARACTER(20),
              2 ADDRESS CHARACTER(30),
              2 PHONE_NUMBER CHARACTER(8);
```

To run under PL/C, which does not support the LIKE attribute, you
need to change the declaration of TRANSACTION to this:

```
DECLARE 1 TRANSACTION,
          2 NAME CHARACTER(20),
          2 ADDRESS CHARACTER(30),
          2 PHONE_NUMBER CHARACTER(8);
```

As you can see, in these declarations the keyword VARYING has
been omitted. As a result, NAME, ADDRESS and PHONE_NUMBER become
fixed-length character strings rather than varying-length
character strings. As long as a fixed-length character string
variable is always assigned strings of its declared length, it
acts just as if it were declared using the VARYING keyword. We
will assume that only such assignments are used, and we will have
no more to say about fixed-length character strings, which are
not properly a part of the SP/k subsets of PL/1.

CHAPTER 16 SUMMARY

In this chapter we introduced programming language constructs
for manipulating records and using files in secondary memory.
The following important terms were discussed in this chapter:

Record - a collection of fields of information. For example,
    a record might be composed of a name field, an address
    field and a telephone number field.

Structure (or PL/1 structure) - the PL/1 construct for
    records. For example, this declaration establishes a
    structure called DIRECTORY_ENTRY with name, address and
    telephone-number fields.

```
        DECLARE 1 DIRECTORY_ENTRY,
                  2 NAME CHARACTER(20)VARYING,
                  2 ADDRESS CHARACTER(30)VARYING,
                  2 PHONE_NUMBER CHARACTER(8)VARYING;
```

    The type of a field can be CHARACTER, FIXED, FLOAT or
    BIT. A field can be an array.

LIKE - a structure can be declared to be LIKE a previously
    declared structure. If the structure DIRECTORY_ENTRY
    has already been declared, we could write

```
        DECLARE 1 PHONE_BOOK(50) LIKE DIRECTORY_ENTRY;
```

    This creates an array of 50 structures where each
    structure has the same fields as DIRECTORY_ENTRY.
    PHONE_BOOK(5).NAME refers to the name field of the fifth
    structure. The structure referred to by LIKE must not
    itself be declared using LIKE. If the structure
    referred to were dimensioned, for example, if (10)
    followed DIRECTORY_ENTRY, then the dimension is not
    carried over to the new declaration.

Assigning structures - if two structures are LIKE each other, or LIKE another structure, then one can be assigned to the other by a single assignment statement. For example, we can write

    PHONE_BOOK(5)=DIRECTORY_ENTRY;

to assign the three fields of DIRECTORY_ENTRY to the three fields of PHONE_BOOK(5).

GET or PUT for structures - structures can be read or printed, field by field, using GET or PUT with LIST or EDIT.

Dataset - a file of information residing on secondary storage, typically on a disk or tape.

Sequential files - files that are always accessed (read or written) in order, from first record to second record to third record and so on.

OPEN a file - means to prepare a file for use by a program. A file in SP/k can be opened for either input or output:

    OPEN FILE(file name)INPUT;
    OPEN FILE(file name)OUTPUT;

A file that is opened for input is positioned to its first record; the file can be read but not written. A file that is opened for output is positioned for writing the file's first record; the file can be written but not read.

READ - access the next (or first) record on a file. The READ statement has the form

    READ FILE(file name)INTO(structure name);

WRITE - add a record to a file. The WRITE statement has the form:

    WRITE FILE(file name)FROM(structure name);

CLOSE a file - means to release a file that is no longer being read or written. A file can be written and later read in the same job by first opening it for output, then writing it, then closing it, then opening it for input, then reading it, and finally, closing it. In a given job, all structures written to or read from a particular file must be LIKE each other.

File declaration - any file that is used in a program must be declared using the form

```
                DECLARE(file name)RECORD FILE;
```

Some compilers restrict file names to be at most seven
characters long.

File maintenance - means to keep a file up to date. This
    involves reading transactions and adding, deleting or
    modifying file records. An existing SP/k file can be
    modified or extended only by creating a new file.

CHAPTER 16 EXERCISES

The exercises for this chapter are based on a data processing
system to be used by Apex Plumbing Supplies. For each of its
customers, Apex has a card with the fields:

```
Name          (card column 1-20)
Address       (card column 21-40)
Balance       (card column 41-50)
Credit limit  (card column 51-60)
```

These records are presently on punch cards. However, they are to
be transferred to a disk file by the following job:

```
$JOB ID='M.V.YOUNG'
 /* CREATE MASTER FILE FROM PUNCH CARDS */
 CREATE:PROCEDURE OPTIONS(MAIN);
    DECLARE 1 ACCOUNT,
               2 NAME CHARACTER(20)VARYING,
               2 ADDRESS CHARACTER(20)VARYING,
               2 BALANCE FIXED,
               2 CREDIT_LIMIT FIXED;
    DECLARE(MASTER)RECORD FILE;
    DECLARE(PREVIOUS_NAME)CHARACTER(20)VARYING;
    OPEN FILE(MASTER)OUTPUT;
    ACCOUNT.NAME='AAA';
    DO WHILE(ACCOUNT.NAME¬='ZZZ');
       PREVIOUS_NAME=ACCOUNT.NAME;
       GET EDIT(ACCOUNT.NAME,ACCOUNT.ADDRESS,
          ACCOUNT.BALANCE,ACCOUNT.CREDIT_LIMIT)
          (A(20),A(20),F(10),F(10));
       /* MAKE SURE THAT RECORDS ARE IN ORDER */
       IF ACCOUNT.NAME > PREVIOUS_NAME THEN
          WRITE FILE(MASTER)FROM(ACCOUNT);
       ELSE
          PUT SKIP LIST('RECORD OUT OF ORDER:',ACCOUNT.NAME);
       END;
    PUT SKIP LIST('MASTER FILE CREATED');
    CLOSE FILE(MASTER);
    END;
$DATA
ABBOT PLUMBING          94 N.ELM              3116         50000
DURABLE FIXIT           247 FOREST HILL          0         10000
ERICO PLUMBING          54 GORMLEY            9614          5000
  ...
ZZZ                                              0             0
```

The exercises for this chapter require you to write programs for various parts of the data processing system for Apex.

1. The program given above creates a master file for Apex Plumbing Supplies. Unfortunately, the account cards have been dropped on the floor and are no longer in order. Modify the program so that it sorts the cards before creating the file. You can assume that there are at most 20 accounts.

2. Write a program that takes an existing master file for Apex and creates a new master file by deleting or adding new customer records. For example, the data cards for your program might be

```
DAVIS REPAIR            4361 MAIN             2511         10000
ERICO PLUMBING          DELETE                   0             0
  ...
ZZZ                                              0             0
```

You can assume that these cards are in alphabetic order. If the address field on the account card specifies DELETE, the account is to be deleted from the file.

3. Write a program that reads the Apex master file and prints the list of customers whose balances exceed their credit limits.

4. Write a program that reads the Apex master file and prints a bill for each customer whose balance is greater than zero. For example, for the file record

DAVIS REPAIR   4361 MAIN   2511   10000

your program should print

    TO: DAVIS REPAIR
        4361 MAIN

    DEAR SIR OR MADAM:
        PLEASE REMIT $25.11 FOR PLUMBING SUPPLIES.
                    THANK YOU,

                    JOHN APEX, PRES.
                    APEX PLUMBING SUPPLIES
                    416 COLLEGE ST.

5. Write a program that updates the master file using billing and payment transactions. A billing transaction is a card of the form

    name   (columns 1-20)
    amount   (columns 41-50)
                  (columns 51-80 are blank)

For each billing transaction, the balance of the account is to be increased by the specified amount. A payment transaction is a card of the form

    name   (columns 1-20)
    amount   (columns 41-50)
    CR   (columns 51-52)

For each payment transaction, the balance of the account is to be decreased by the specified amount. The billing and payment cards are not in order, so they should be sorted before creating the new master file.

CHAPTER 17

DATA STRUCTURES

In the last chapter we introduced the idea of record structures. By using these structures we could move a group of items of data around in the computer as a unit. Also, we can have arrays of records.

All of the classifications, variables, arrays of single variables, records, and arrays of records are examples of what we generally call <u>data structures</u>. Just as we systematize our programs by attempting to write well-structured programs, we systematize the way in which data is stored. We structure data.

In this chapter we will describe other structural forms for data and give examples of how these structures are useful to us. We will describe data structures called <u>linked lists</u> and <u>tree structures</u>. There are many kinds of lists, for example <u>stacks</u>, <u>queues</u>, <u>doubly-linked lists</u>, and so on. Tree structures can be limited to <u>binary trees</u>, or may be more general.

These new data structures are not a part of the PL/1 language as structures or arrays are, so that when we want to store data in a linked list or a tree we use an array to implement them. We must program the structure.

LINKED LISTS

Suppose that we had a file of records stored in an array called DATA. The records are arranged in sequence on some key. For simplicity, we will consider that each record consists only of a single field which is the key to the ordering. We know that if the order is ascending and no two keys are identical, then

DATA(I+1) > DATA(I)

The difficulty with this kind of data structure for a file comes when a new item is to be added to the file; it must be inserted between two items. This means we would have to move all the items with a key higher than the one to be inserted, one location on in the array. For example, you can see what happens when we insert the word DOG in this list:

	before	after inserting DOG
DATA(1)	CAT	CAT
DATA(2)	DUCK	DOG
DATA(3)	FOX	DUCK
DATA(4)	GOOSE	FOX
DATA(5)	PIG	GOOSE
DATA(6)	-	PIG

Any list that is changing with time will have additions and deletions made to it. A deletion will create a hole unless entries are moved to fill the hole.

When the list changes with time we can use the data structure called the <u>linked list</u>. In the linked list each item has two components, the data component and the linking component or <u>link</u>. We associate with each entry in the DATA array an entry in a second array called LINK. The number stored in LINK(I) is the index of the next entry in the sequence of the DATA array. This means that the actual or <u>physical sequence</u> in the DATA array is different from the <u>logical sequence</u> in the list. Here is an example showing our previous list as a linked list. The start of the list is stored in the FIXED variable FIRST.

		FIRST	3
DATA(1)	PIG	LINK(1)	0
DATA(2)	FOX	LINK(2)	4
DATA(3)	CAT	LINK(3)	5
DATA(4)	GOOSE	LINK(4)	1
DATA(5)	DUCK	LINK(5)	2
DATA(6)	-	LINK(6)	-

Here is a diagram of this:

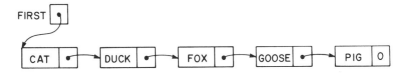

You can follow the list by beginning with the value of FIRST, which is 3. The first entry will be in DATA(3); it is CAT. By looking then at LINK(3) you find a 5 which is the index of the next list item, DATA(5), which is DUCK. You follow the list down until you reach a LINK whose value is 0; this is the signal that you have reached the end of the list. Other signals can be used, such as having a negative number.

INSERTING INTO A LINKED LIST

To see the merit of a linked list we must see how to insert
new entries. We will add DOG in its proper list position. We
will do this first by hand; afterwards we will have to program it
for the computer. We will place the entry DOG in DATA(6) since
it is an available or free location. We must now change the
values of certain of the links so that the new entry will be
inserted. We must put a value into LINK(6) and change the value
of the LINK of the entry before DOG, which is CAT, to point to
DATA(6). This means that LINK(3) must be changed to 6 and
LINK(6) must be set to 5 so that the entry after DOG is DUCK,
which is DATA(5).

The linked list then becomes

	FIRST	3		
DATA(1)	PIG		LINK(1)	0
DATA(2)	FOX		LINK(2)	4
DATA(3)	CAT		LINK(3)	6
DATA(4)	GOOSE		LINK(4)	1
DATA(5)	DUCK		LINK(5)	2
DATA(6)	DOG		LINK(6)	5

Here is a diagram:

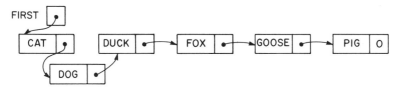

To add DOG, one LINK must be changed and one set. No
movement of the existing items in DATA is necessary. This is
surely an improvement over moving half the list, on the average,
to insert a new entry. The cost of this improved efficiency of
operation comes in having to reserve memory space for the LINK
array. This array gives the structure of the list and is stored
explicitly for a linked list. In an array, the sequence or
structure is implicit; each entry follows its neighbor. We will
see several other kinds of structures that require us to store
the structure information explicitly.

MEMORY MANAGEMENT WITH LISTS

With linked lists, some of the memory is used for structure
information and some for data. For any list, as the list grows,
we use more memory; as it shrinks, we use less. This means we
must reserve enough memory to hold the longest list that we ever
expect to have. But we should not waste memory. As we stop
using certain elements of the array by deleting entries, we must

keep track of where they are, so when additions occur we can reuse these same elements. To keep track of the available array elements we keep them together in a second linked list. The list of available array elements does not have any useful information in the DATA part, but it is structured as a list using values in the LINK part. We must keep track of the beginning of this list so we keep the index of its beginning in a FIXED variable AVAILABLE.

Here is an array of 10 elements that stores our previous data items in a different set of locations and has the available space linked up:

	FIRST	10	AVAILABLE	7
DATA(1)	GOOSE		LINK(1)	9
DATA(2)	FOX		LINK(2)	1
DATA(3)	–		LINK(3)	6
DATA(4)	DUCK		LINK(4)	2
DATA(5)	–		LINK(5)	0
DATA(6)	–		LINK(6)	5
DATA(7)	–		LINK(7)	3
DATA(8)	DOG		LINK(8)	4
DATA(9)	PIG		LINK(9)	0
DATA(10)	CAT		LINK(10)	8

In these arrays there are two linked lists, one containing the actual data, the other containing elements available for use. Each list has a pointer to its start; each has a last element with a link of 0. Every element of the array is in one list or the other.

The next problem is to write a procedure for adding a new item to the list. We will develop the algorithm for this by step-by-step refinement.

PROCEDURE FOR INSERTING INTO A LINKED LIST

The first step is to construct a solution tree. We will presume the value to be added is in the variable NEW_DATA:

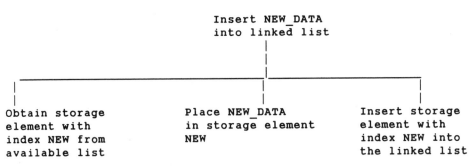

Insert NEW_DATA into linked list

Obtain storage element with index NEW from available list

Place NEW_DATA in storage element NEW

Insert storage element with index NEW into the linked list

The expansion of the left branch of the solution tree requires us to find the index NEW of the first element of the list of available elements and remove the element from the list. Here is the program segment that does this:

```
NEW=AVAILABLE;
AVAILABLE=LINK(AVAILABLE);
```

The middle branch is also simple. It is

```
DATA(NEW)=NEW_DATA;
```

We must expand the right branch still further:

```
                         Insert storage
                         element with
                         index NEW into
                         the linked list
                                |
                                |
          IF NEW_DATA goes first in list THEN
               place element at beginning of list;
          ELSE find place to insert NEW_DATA
               and adjust links to make insertion;
```

NEW_DATA will go first in the list if either the list is empty or NEW_DATA is less than the first element of the list. So we can write, "IF NEW_DATA goes first in list," in this way:

```
IF FIRST=NULL | NEW_DATA<DATA(FIRST) THEN
```

We have assumed that the variable NULL will be initialized to zero. We can write, "Place element at beginning of list," in this way:

```
DO;
    LINK(NEW)=FIRST;
    FIRST=NEW;
    END;
```

For the part of the program after the ELSE we need to examine the entries in the list and compare them with NEW_DATA. The index of the element being compared we will call NEXT. The index of the element just compared previously we will call PREVIOUS. We need to keep track of this previous element, because if

```
NEW_DATA < DATA(NEXT)
```

we must insert our element with index NEW between PREVIOUS and NEXT. Here is the program segment for this:

```
         DO;
            /* FIND PLACE TO INSERT NEW_DATA */
            PREVIOUS=FIRST;
            NEXT=LINK(FIRST);
            DO WHILE(NEXT¬=NULL & NEW_DATA>=DATA(NEXT));
               PREVIOUS=NEXT;
               NEXT=LINK(NEXT);
               END;
            /* ADJUST LINKS TO MAKE INSERTION */
            LINK(PREVIOUS)=NEW;
            LINK(NEW)=NEXT;
            END;
```

The whole procedure can now be written out. We are presuming
that DATA, LINK, FIRST, and AVAILABLE are global to this
procedure:

```
 /* INSERT NEW DATA INTO LINKED LIST */
 INSERT:PROCEDURE(NEW_DATA);
    DECLARE(NEW_DATA)CHARACTER(*)VARYING;
    DECLARE(NEW,PREVIOUS,NEXT)FIXED;
    /* OBTAIN STORAGE ELEMENT FOR NEW DATA */
    NEW=AVAILABLE;
    AVAILABLE=LINK(AVAILABLE);
    /* PLACE NEW_DATA IN STORAGE ELEMENT */
    DATA(NEW)=NEW_DATA;
    /* SEE IF NEW_DATA GOES FIRST IN LIST */
    IF FIRST=NULL | NEW_DATA<DATA(FIRST) THEN
        DO;
            LINK(NEW)=FIRST;
            FIRST=NEW;
            END;
    ELSE
        DO;
            /* FIND PLACE TO INSERT NEW DATA */
            PREVIOUS=FIRST;
            NEXT=LINK(FIRST);
            DO WHILE(NEXT¬=NULL & NEW_DATA>=DATA(NEXT));
               PREVIOUS=NEXT;
               NEXT=LINK(NEXT);
               END;
            /* ADJUST LINKS TO MAKE INSERTION */
            LINK(PREVIOUS)=NEW;
            LINK(NEW)=NEXT;
            END;
    END;
```

So far we have ignored a problem in our INSERT procedure.
The conditions for both the IF statement and the DO WHILE loop
use an element of the DATA array which may have the index
NULL (0). To avoid an out-of-bounds index, the DATA array should
be declared with a lower bound of zero, and DATA(0) should be
initialized to a large dummy value, such as 'ZZZ'.

DELETING FROM A LINKED LIST

The process of deletion is very similar. We will just record
the final procedure.

```
/* DELETE SPECIFIED DATA FROM LINKED LIST */
DELETE:PROCEDURE(OLD_DATA);
   DECLARE(OLD_DATA)CHARACTER(*)VARYING;
   DECLARE(PREVIOUS,OLD)FIXED;
   /* FIND THE ITEM TO BE DELETED */
   OLD=FIRST;
   DO WHILE(DATA(OLD)¬=OLD_DATA);
      PREVIOUS=OLD;
      OLD=LINK(OLD);
      END;
   /* REMOVE ITEM FROM LIST */
   IF FIRST=OLD THEN
      FIRST=LINK(OLD);
   ELSE
      LINK(PREVIOUS)=LINK(OLD);
   /* ADD STORAGE ELEMENT TO FREE LIST */
   LINK(OLD)=AVAILABLE;
   AVAILABLE=OLD;
   END;
```

Before using these two procedures we must set NULL to 0, set
FIRST to NULL, set AVAILABLE to 1, and LINK(I) to I+1, with the
exception of the last element which should have a NULL link.

STACKS

In the last two sections we showed how to insert and delete
items for a linked list. The insertions and deletions could be
anywhere in the list. In each case, as the list of data items
was changed, a second linked list of available storage elements
was maintained. A deletion from the list of data items resulted
in an addition to the list of available elements; an addition in
the data list produced a deletion in the available list. The
actions involving the available storage list were much simpler.
This is because the additions and deletions for it always were to
the beginning of that list. A list that is restricted to having
entries to or removals from the beginning only is called a stack.
The situation is similar to a stack of trays in a cafeteria.
When you want a tray you take it off the top of the stack; when
you are through with a tray you put it back on the top.   When a
list is used as a stack, we often call the pointer to the
beginning of the list TOP. When an entry is removed from the top
we say we have popped an entry off. TOP must then be adjusted to
point at the next entry. When we add an entry we say we have
pushed it on to the stack.

Because a stack change only occurs at one end, it is
convenient to implement a stack without using a linked list; an

ordinary array will do. In our examples, a linked list is
necessary for our stack of available storage elements because
they are scattered all over. Stacks have other uses so we will
show how a stack can be implemented using an array. We will call
the array STACK. The bottom of the stack will be in STACK(1),
the next entry in STACK(2), and so on. Sorry if our stack seems
to be upside down! Here is a stack of symbols:

```
TOP              4

STACK( 1 )       +
STACK( 2 )       -
STACK( 3 )       +
STACK( 4 )       /
```

This sort of stack is often used in PL/1 compilers for
translating arithmetic expressions into machine language.

Before using the stack we initialize it to be empty by
setting TOP to zero:

```
TOP=0;
```

To add an item to the stack we can call the procedure PUSH:

```
PUSH:PROCEDURE(SYMBOL);
   DECLARE(SYMBOL)CHARACTER(*)VARYING;
   TOP=TOP+1;
   STACK(TOP)=SYMBOL;
   END;
```

To remove the top item from the stack we can call the procedure
POP:

```
POP:PROCEDURE(SYMBOL);
   DECLARE(SYMBOL)CHARACTER(*)VARYING;
   SYMBOL=STACK(TOP);
   TOP=TOP-1;
   END;
```

The variable TOP and the array STACK must be global to the PUSH
and POP procedures. Stacks may be implemented in other ways than
shown here.

QUEUES

Another specialized type of list is a queue. For it, entries
are made at the end of the list, deletions are made from the
beginning. Rather than search for the end of the list each time
an entry is made, it is usual to have a pointer indicating the
last entry. Queues involve using things in a manner referred to
as, "First in first out" (FIFO) or, "First come first served"
(FCFS). This is the usual way for a queue waiting for tickets at

a box office to operate. By contrast, a stack is a "Last in first out" (LIFO) system.

It is not as easy to implement a queue using an array. It is always growing at one end and shrinking at the other. If an array is used, when the growth reaches the maximum limit of the array, we start it at the beginning again. Here is a queue of users of a computer waiting for service. We have a maximum of 8 elements. Five people are in the queue. The next person to be served is named MATHERS.

```
FIRST   6                LAST    2

QUEUE(1)                 GEORGE
QUEUE(2)                 JOHNSTON
QUEUE(3)                 -
QUEUE(4)                 -
QUEUE(5)                 -
QUEUE(6)                 MATHERS
QUEUE(7)                 LINNEMANN
QUEUE(8)                 LOVGREN
```

Here are procedures used to ENTER or LEAVE this queue. Before using these procedures the queue can be initialized to be empty by setting FIRST to 1 and LAST to 8.

```
ENTER:PROCEDURE(NAME);
   DECLARE(NAME)CHARACTER(*)VARYING;
   LAST=LAST+1;
   IF LAST > 8 THEN
      LAST=1;
   QUEUE(LAST)=NAME;
   END;

LEAVE:PROCEDURE(NAME);
   DECLARE(NAME)CHARACTER(*)VARYING;
   NAME=QUEUE(FIRST);
   FIRST=FIRST+1;
   IF FIRST > 8 THEN
      FIRST=1;
   END;
```

Queues can be implemented by linked lists as well as by simple arrays. Queues are used in the programs called operating systems that operate computer systems. Different jobs requiring service are placed in different queues, depending on the demands they are making on the system's resources and the priority that they possess to be given service. Also, in programs that simulate other systems such as factories, queues are maintained to determine the length of time jobs are required to wait to be served when other jobs are competing for the same production facilities.

TREES

A linked list is an efficient way of storing a list that is
changing with time, but it introduces an inefficiency in
retrieval of information from the list. In Chapter 14 we saw
that a binary search for an item in a list is much more efficient
for long lists than a linear search. Unfortunately, there is no
possibility of doing a binary search in a linked list; we must
start at the beginning and trace our way through. There is no
direct access to the middle of a linked list. It is for this
reason that a more complicated data structure called a <u>tree</u> is
used. We can get the efficiency of a binary search by having the
elements linked into a <u>binary tree structure</u>.

To show how a binary tree is formed, we will look at the
example of our list of names of animals:

```
                3-- > CAT
          2------ > DOG
                    DUCK
       1---------- > FOX
                    GOOSE
                    PIG
                    SNAKE
```

To do a binary search we should begin in the middle. We have
added SNAKE to the list so the list has a middle entry. If we
are looking for the name CAT we find that CAT < FOX, so we then
discard the middle entry and the last half of the list. The next
comparison is with the middle entry of the remaining list, namely
with DOG. Since CAT < DOG we eliminate the last half of the
smaller list. By this time, we are down to one entry, which is
the one we are looking for. It took three comparisons to get
there. A linear search for CAT would, as it happens, have taken
only 1 comparison. On the <u>average</u>, the binary search takes fewer
comparisons than a linear search. A short list is not a good
example for showing off the efficiency of binary searching, but
it is much easier to write out all the possibilities.

We will now look at the binary tree that would be used to
give the same searching technique. Here it is:

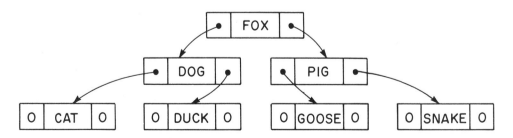

Each data element in the tree structure consists of three
parts, the DATA itself and two links that we designate as
LEFT_LINK and RIGHT_LINK. The word FOX is in a special position
in the tree, called the <u>root</u>. From FOX we have <u>branches</u> going to
the left to DOG and to the right to PIG. In a sense, DOG is in
the root position of a smaller tree, what we call the <u>left</u>
<u>subtree</u> of the main tree. PIG is at the root of the <u>right</u>
<u>subtree</u>. The words CAT, DUCK, GOOSE, and SNAKE are at the end of
branches and are called <u>leaves</u> of the tree. All the data
elements are in <u>nodes</u> of the tree; FOX is the <u>root node</u> and CAT
is a <u>leaf node</u>. To search for an entry in a binary tree, we
compare the element in the root node with the one we are seeking.
If the root is the same, we have found it. If the root is larger
we follow the LEFT_LINK to the next entry; if smaller, we follow
the RIGHT_LINK. We are then at the root of a smaller tree, a
tree with half as many entries as the original. The process is
then repeated until the looked-for data is found.

Here is our tree structure as it might be stored in three
arrays called DATA, LEFT_LINK, and RIGHT_LINK. The variable ROOT
holds the link to the root element. We have jumbled up the
sequence to show that the actual order in the DATA array makes no
difference. A zero link is used to indicate the end of a branch.

                    ROOT   4

DATA	LEFT_LINK	RIGHT_LINK
(1) GOOSE	0	0
(2) SNAKE	0	0
(3) DOG	6	7
(4) FOX	3	5
(5) PIG	1	2
(6) CAT	0	0
(7) DUCK	0	0

Starting at ROOT, we find the root is in DATA(4). LEFT_LINK(4)
leads us to DATA(3) which is DOG. RIGHT_LINK(3) leads us to
DATA(7) which is DUCK. You can see how it works.

A tree structure is a <u>hierarchical</u> <u>structure</u> for data; each
comparison takes us one <u>level</u> down in the tree.

                    ADDING TO A TREE

To add a data item to a tree structure we simply look for the
element in the tree in the usual manner, starting at the root.
If the element is not already in the tree, we will come in the
search to a link that is zero. This is where the element
belongs. In our example, if we want to add COW, we would start
at FOX, then go to DOG, then to CAT. At this point we would want
to follow the right link of CAT, but we find a zero. If we
stored the new entry in DATA(8), we would change RIGHT_LINK(6) to
8. and set

```
DATA(8)    LEFT_LINK(8)    RIGHT_LINK(8)

COW              0                0
```

As we add items to a tree, the tree becomes lopsided; it is not well balanced. Searching efficiency depends on trees being well balanced, so that in an information retrieval data bank using a tree structure, an effort should be made to keep the tree balanced. We started with a balanced tree and it became unbalanced by adding a new item. If a tree is grown from scratch using the method we have described for adding a new entry, it is unlikely to be well balanced.

DELETING FROM A TREE

Removing an entry from a tree is a more difficult operation than adding an entry. The same method is used to find the element to be deleted, but then the problem comes. It is not difficult if both links of the element to be deleted are zero, that is, if it is a leaf. We just chop it off and make the link pointing to it zero. If only one link is zero it is similar to an ordinary linked list and deletion is similar to that. We just bypass it:

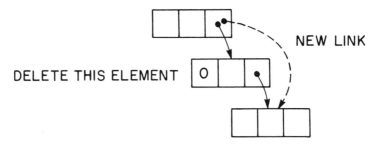

If neither link is zero in the element to be deleted, we must move another element into its position in the tree. In our original tree, if FOX is to be deleted, it must be replaced by an element that is larger then all other elements in the left subtree or smaller than all the elements in the right subtree. This means that either DUCK or GOOSE is the only possible choice. The one to be moved must be deleted in its present position before being placed in its new position.

Remember, in a linked structure, we never move a data item from its physical location in the data array; we only change the links to alter its logical position.

PRINTING A TREE IN ORDER

Trees are used where searching and updating are the main activities. Sometimes we must print out the contents of a tree. We must be systematic about it and be sure to print every node. We will show how to print it alphabetically.

An algorithm for printing a tree alphabetically can be written in this way:

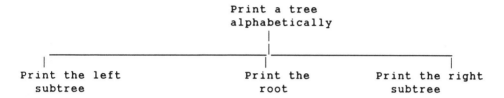

We see that we have described our algorithm in terms of three parts. The middle part, "Print the root," is easy, but the other two require us to, "Print a tree." This is exactly what our problem is, to "Print a tree." We have defined the solution to a problem in terms of the original problem. This kind of definition is called a <u>recursive</u> definition of a solution. It seems rather pointless, as if we were just going in a circle, but it really is not. The reason it is not pointless is that the tree we are attempting to print when we say, "Print the left subtree," is a smaller tree than the original tree when we said "Print a tree." When we try to print the left subtree we get this solution:

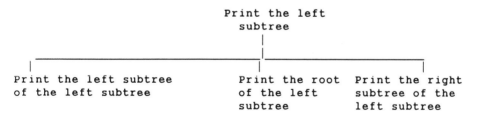

This time the left subtree of the left subtree has to be printed. It is smaller still. The algorithm is again repeated. Each application of the algorithm is on a smaller tree, until you reach a point where there is a zero link and there is <u>no</u> left subtree at all. Then the action of printing it is to do nothing: no tree, no printing. That is how recursive algorithms work. In programming terms, the algorithm calls itself over and over, each time to do a reduced task, until the task is easy to do.

In PL/1 a procedure may indeed call itself. Here is an SP/k procedure for printing a tree in alphabetic order, given that its root is ROOT and its data and links DATA, LEFT_LINK and RIGHT_LINK are global variables. Some compilers such as PL/C

allow a procedure such as ours to be recursive only if it is
labeled as such by having the keyword RECURSIVE following
PROCEDURE(ROOT).

```
PRINT_TREE:PROCEDURE(ROOT);
   DECLARE(ROOT)FIXED;
   IF LEFT_LINK(ROOT)¬=0 THEN
      CALL PRINT_TREE(LEFT_LINK(ROOT));
   PUT SKIP LIST(DATA(ROOT));
   IF RIGHT_LINK(ROOT)¬=0 THEN
      CALL PRINT_TREE(RIGHT_LINK(ROOT));
   END;
```

Each time the procedure is entered for a new subtree, a
different node is referred to by ROOT. For this job, a recursive
procedure is very easy to program. It is much more difficult to
program this job non-recursively. In a recursive algorithm, each
time a program calls itself, a record must be kept of the point
in the program where the procedure was called, so that control
can return properly. As the procedure recursively calls itself,
a list is built of these points of return. Each point of return
is added on top of the stack of other points of return. Finding
the way back involves taking return points, one after the other,
off this stack. This is all set up automatically by the
compiler.

                        CHAPTER 17 SUMMARY

     In previous chapters we have presented the data structures
provided by SP/k; these are arrays and records (PL/1 structures).
In this chapter we showed how to build up new data structures
using arrays. Some of these new data structures use links to
give the ordering of data items. The link (or links) for a given
item gives the array index of the next item.   The following
important terms were discussed:

     Linked list - a linked sequence of data items. The next item
          in the list is found by following a link from the
          present item.   The physical order of a collection of
          items, as given by their positions in an array, is
          different from their logical order, as given by the
          links.

     Inserting into a linked list - a new data item can be
          inserted by changing links, without actually moving data
          items.

     Deleting from a linked list - a data item can be deleted by
          changing links, without moving data items.

     Available list -   the collection of data elements currently
          not in use.

Stack - a data structure that allows data items to be added, or pushed, on to one end and removed, or popped, from the same end. A stack does not require the use of links. A stack handles data items in a last-in-first-out (LIFO) manner.

Queue - a data structure that allows data items to be added at one end and removed from the other. A queue handles data items in a first-in-first-out (FIFO) manner.

Binary tree - a data structure in which each item or node has two links, a left link and a right link. The left link of a node locates another node and with it a subtree. Similarly, the right link locates a subtree. There is a unique beginning node called the root. If both links of a particular node are null, meaning they do not currently locate other nodes, then the node is called a leaf.

CHAPTER 17 EXERCISES

1. The FLY-BY-NITE Airline company is computerizing its reservations system. There are four FLY-BY-NITE flights with the following capacities:

```
FLIGHT #1       5 seats
FLIGHT #2       5 seats
FLIGHT #3       8 seats
FLIGHT #4       4 seats
```

The information for passenger reservations is to be stored in a linked list. At some point during the booking period, the following diagram might represent the current passenger bookings.

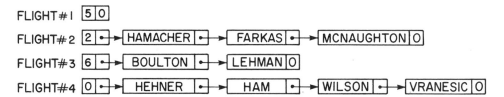

The above diagram shows the first element in each list holding the number of seats remaining. Each succeeding element holds the name of a passenger and either points to the next element or holds a 0 to indicate the end of the linked list.

    In order to set up such a linked list system you will need two arrays. The first, called FLIGHT, will contain the four "first" elements. Each of these elements holds two pieces of information, the number of seats remaining and the location of the first passenger.

The second array called PASSENGER holds all the passengers. If all seats on all flights are taken, there will be 22 passengers. Hence PASSENGER will need a maximum of 22 locations. Each element of the PASSENGER array contains two pieces of information, the passenger's name and the location of the next passenger, if any.

The PASSENGER array must be declared as a structure in order to contain two different data types:

```
DECLARE 1 PASSENGER (1:22),
          2 NAME CHARACTER(20)VARYING,
          2 LINK FIXED;
```

This will designate each element of PASSENGER(J) to contain two parts:

```
PASSENGER(J).NAME and PASSENGER(J).LINK
```

Before any events happen, the free locations must be linked together. Arrange that each PASSENGER(J).LINK contains a value J+1, except PASSENGER(22).LINK which contains a 0 as end of the list.

A variable AVAILABLE contains the location of the head of this chain of available locations. For the example given above, AVAILABLE contains 10 and PASSENGER could have these values:

```
PASSENGER(1)            PASSENGER(5)            PASSENGER(9)
   NAME   HAMACHER         NAME LEHMAN             NAME VRANESIC
   LINK   6                LINK  0                 LINK  0

PASSENGER(2)            PASSENGER(6)            PASSENGER(10)
   NAME   BOULTON          NAME FARKAS             NAME
   LINK   5                LINK  7                 LINK  11

PASSENGER(3)            PASSENGER(7)                    .
   NAME HAM                NAME   MCNAUGHTON            .
   LINK  8                 LINK   0                     .

PASSENGER(4)            PASSENGER(8)            PASSENGER(22)
   NAME   HEHNER          NAME   WILSON            NAME
   LINK   3               LINK   9                 LINK  0
```

The reservation system is to accept four types of transactions:

Type 1 is a request for a reservation. The data card contains the
    code word RES, name of the passenger, and the flight   number.

Type 2 is a request to cancel a reservation. The data card
    contains the code word CAN, name of passenger, and the flight
    number.

Type 3 is a request to print out the number of seats remaining on
    a specified flight. The data card   contains   the   code   word
    SEATS and a flight number.

Type 4 is a request to print out a passenger list for the flight indicated. The data card contains the code word LIST and a flight number.

Each type of transaction is to be handled by a procedure. PASSENGER, FLIGHT and AVAILABLE are global variables; all other variables are local to the procedure in which they are used. Here are descriptions of the procedures:

ADD(WHO,NUMBER). Adds passenger WHO to flight NUMBER. If that flight is filled, a message is printed to that effect. ADD uses a location in PASSENGER and must update AVAILABLE.

CANCEL(WHO,NUMBER). Cancels the reservation made in the name of WHO on flight NUMBER. The location in PASSENGER is returned to the free storage pool. AVAILABLE must be updated.

INFO(NUMBER). Prints out number of seats remaining on flight NUMBER.

PRINT(NUMBER). Prints a passenger list for flight NUMBER.

The data cards should simulate a real reservation system in that cards of type 1, 2, 3, 4 should be intermixed. It would seem reasonable to assume that most cancellations would be made by persons holding reservations. However, people being what they are, you should not assume too much. In order to get your system off the ground, several reservation cards should be first.

Write and test each procedure as a main procedure before putting the procedures together. Write PRINT first and call it from ADD or CANCEL to help in debugging. If you work in pairs - and this is strongly recommended for this exercise - one person should program ADD and PRINT, the other CANCEL and INFO. Turn in several runs which show the capabilities of your system. Be sure to test "odd" situations as well as the obvious ones.

2. In arithmetic and in PL/1, parentheses are used in expressions to specify the order of evaluation. For example, in the expression 9*(5+2) the parentheses specify that 5 and 2 are to be added before being multiplied by 9. When parentheses are nested, the innermost sub-expression is evaluated first. A program can be written to analyze expressions and determine the specified order of evaluation. For example, a program could read 9*(5+2) and print:

```
TO EVALUATE: 9*(5+2)
YOU SHOULD DO THE FOLLOWING.
    EVALUATE: 5+2
    EVALUATE: 9*(VALUE OF: 5+2)
```

Such a program can use a stack to keep track of the part of the expression that has been scanned, but which has not yet required evaluation. This is done in the following program:

```
$JOB ID='NANCY AUSTERE'
 /* DETERMINE ORDER OF EXPRESSION EVALUATION */
 VALUE:PROCEDURE OPTIONS(MAIN);
    DECLARE(EXPRESSION)CHARACTER(80)VARYING;
    DECLARE(NEXT_CHAR)CHARACTER(1)VARYING;
    DECLARE(STACK(0:5))CHARACTER(80)VARYING,
      (TOP)FIXED;
    GET LIST(EXPRESSION);
    PUT LIST('TO EVALUATE: ',EXPRESSION);
    PUT SKIP LIST('YOU SHOULD DO THE FOLLOWING.');
    /* EXTEND EXPRESSION WITH ')' TO FORCE FINAL PRINTING */
    EXPRESSION=EXPRESSION||') ';
    TOP=1;
    STACK(0)='';
    STACK(1)='';
    /* REPEAT UNTIL ALL OF EXPRESSION HAS ENTERED AND LEFT STACK */
    DO WHILE(TOP>=1);
       NEXT_CHAR=SUBSTR(EXPRESSION,1,1);
       EXPRESSION=SUBSTR(EXPRESSION,2);
       DO WHILE(NEXT_CHAR¬=')');
          IF NEXT_CHAR='(' THEN
             DO;
                /* GET READY TO PUT STRING ON TOP OF STACK */
                TOP=TOP+1;
                STACK(TOP)='';
                END;
          ELSE
             STACK(TOP)=STACK(TOP)||NEXT_CHAR;
          NEXT_CHAR=SUBSTR(EXPRESSION,1,1);
          EXPRESSION=SUBSTR(EXPRESSION,2);
          END;
       PUT SKIP LIST('   EVALUATE: ',STACK(TOP));
       /* REMOVE TOP OF STACK AND ADD IT TO NEXT TO TOP */
       TOP=TOP-1;
       STACK(TOP)=STACK(TOP)||'(VALUE OF: '||STACK(TOP+1)||')';
       END;
    END;
$DATA
 '9*(5+2)'
```

What does this program print when it reads each of the following?
You are to discover the answers by studying the program rather
than running it on the computer.

    a. X/(Y-3*Z)
    b. (-B+SQRT(4*A*C))/(2*A)
    c. (5/9E0)*(TEMPERATURE-32)
    d. A(I*3+2)=(A(I+5)*(B+2));

Name a computer program you have personally used many times that
uses a stack to determine the order of expression evaluation.

CHAPTER 18

SCIENTIFIC CALCULATIONS

Most of the applications that we have discussed so far in this book are connected with the use of computers in business or in the humanities. We do business applications on computers because of the large numbers of each calculation that must be done. A single payroll calculation is simple, but if a company has thousands of employees, computer processing of payroll is warranted. Computers were originally developed with scientific and engineering calculations in mind. This is because many scientific and engineering calculations are so long that it is not practical to do them by hand, even with the help of a slide rule or pocket calculator.

Often the scientific laws describing a physical situation are known in the form of equations, but these equations must be solved for the situation of interest. We may be designing a bridge or aircraft or an air-conditioning system for a building. A computer can be used to calculate the details of the particular situation.

Another important use of computers in science is to find equations that fit the data produced in experiments. These equations then serve to reduce the amount of data that must be preserved. Science as a word means knowledge. The object of scientific work is to gather information about the world and to systematize it so that it can be retrieved and used in the future. There is such a large amount of research activity now in science that we are facing an information explosion. We have talked about retrieving information from a data bank and computers will undoubtedly help us in this increasingly difficult and tedious job. But the problem of data reduction is of equal importance.

In this chapter we will try to give some of the flavor of scientific calculations, but we will not be including enough detail for those people who will need to work with them. We will give only an overview of this important use of computers.

EVALUATING FORMULAS

To solve certain scientific problems we must substitute values into formulas and calculate results. For example, we could be asked to calculate the distance traveled by a falling object after it is dropped from an airplane. A formula that gives the distance in meters traveled in time t seconds, neglecting air resistance, is

$$d = 4.9t^2$$

Here the constant 4.9 is one-half the acceleration due to gravity. Here is a program to compute the distance at the end of each second of the first 10 seconds after the drop:

```
FALL:PROCEDURE OPTIONS(MAIN);
   /* PRINT TABLE OF DISTANCE FALLEN VERSUS TIME */
   DECLARE(DISTANCE,TIME)FLOAT;
   DECLARE(I)FIXED;
   TIME=0E0;
   /* LABEL TIME-DISTANCE TABLE */
   PUT SKIP LIST('TIME','DISTANCE');
   DO I=1 TO 10;
      TIME=TIME+1E0;
      DISTANCE=4.9E0*TIME*TIME;
      PUT SKIP LIST(TIME,DISTANCE);
      END;
   END;
```


The output for this program is


```
TIME             DISTANCE
  1.00000E+00      4.90000E+00
  2.00000E+00      1.96000E+01
  3.00000E+00      4.41000E+01
  4.00000E+00      7.84000E+01
  5.00000E+00      1.22500E+02
  6.00000E+00      1.76400E+02
  7.00000E+00      2.40100E+02
  8.00000E+00      3.13600E+02
  9.00000E+00      3.96900E+02
  1.00000E+01      4.90000E+02
```


This example prints a table of values of DISTANCE for different times. Printing of tables is an interesting and historic scientific use of computers. Scientific calculations are usually done using FLOAT variables. In the output the distances and times are printed with six digits in the fraction part, one digit to the left and five to the right of the decimal point. Not all these digits are <u>significant</u>; the constant in the formula is only expressed with two digits. We must realize then that only about two digits of the distance traveled are significant.

The calculations are carried out in the computer keeping 6 digits, but this does not imply that they are meaningful. Even if the constant in the formula were entered to 6-digit precision, we would not necessarily have 6 significant digits in the answer. Because computers represent FLOAT numbers only to a limited precision, there are always what are called numerical errors. These are not mistakes you make but are inherent in the way that FLOAT numbers are represented in the computer. When two FLOAT numbers are multiplied, the product is rounded off to the same precision as the original numbers; no more digits in the product would be significant. As calculations proceed, the rounding process can erode the significance even of some of the digits that are maintained. We usually quote numerical errors by saying that a value is, for example,

19.25 ± 0.05

This means that the value could be as high as 19.30 or as low as 19.20. If the error were higher, say 0.5 instead of 0.05, then the values could range between 19.75 and 18.75. In this case the fourth digit in the value is certainly not significant, and you would say instead that the value was

19.2 ± 0.5

Or we might round it off instead of truncating the insignificant digit, and write

19.3 ± 0.5

The estimation of errors is an important job that is done by <u>numerical analysts</u>. If you are doing numerical calculations, you should be aware of the fact that answers are not exact but have errors.

BUILT-IN FUNCTIONS

Scientific calculations require mathematical functions that are not commonly used in business calculations. For many of these functions, procedures have already been written for PL/1; they are built into the compiler. For example, suppose for our falling-body calculation we wanted to compute the times when the body reached different distances. To calculate the time, given the distance, we use this form of the same formula:

$$t = \sqrt{d/4.9}$$

Now we need to be able to calculate a square root. This can be done by using the built-in function for square root, which is called SQRT. We would write in the program:

```
TIME = SQRT(DISTANCE/4.9E0);
```

Other built-in functions available to PL/1 for scientific calculations are connected with trigonometry. They include SIN and COS. These give the values of the sine and cosine, when the argument of the function is in radians. ATAN(X) gives the angle in radians whose tangent is X. The natural logarithm is obtained by using LOG, the exponential by using EXP. Other more exotic functions are available in full PL/1 but are not in SP/k.

GRAPHING A FUNCTION

Frequently a better understanding of a scientific formula can be had if you draw a graph of the function. In the first example of this chapter we evaluated a function at regular intervals. It is possible to use these values to plot a graph on the printer. We could, for instance, plot a distance-time graph for the falling object. We will show one way to plot a graph on the printer, but there are lots of other ways.

When you draw a graph of X versus Y you usually make the X-axis horizontal and have the Y-axis vertical. The values of X, which is the independent variable, increase uniformly; the corresponding values of Y are obtained by substituting X into the function $Y=f(X)$. When we plot a graph on the printer the lines of printing are uniformly spaced, so we will use the distance between lines to represent the uniform interval between the Xs. This means that the X-axis will be vertical and the Y-axis horizontal. To see the graph in the normal orientation, just rotate the page 90 degrees counterclockwise. Here is a graph for $Y=X^2-X-2$ plotted between $X=-2$ and $X=3$:

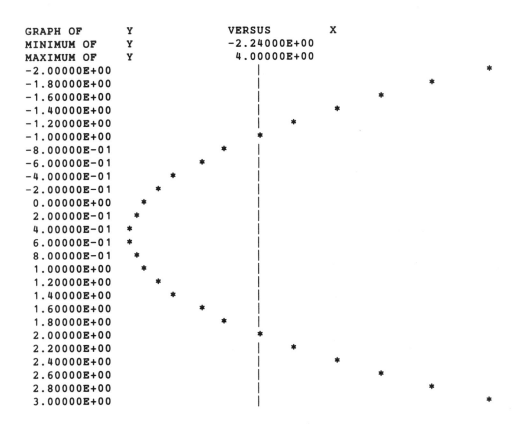

```
GRAPH OF       Y             VERSUS       X
MINIMUM OF     Y             -2.24000E+00
MAXIMUM OF     Y              4.00000E+00
-2.00000E+00                  |                                *
-1.80000E+00                  |                           *
-1.60000E+00                  |                      *
-1.40000E+00                  |                 *
-1.20000E+00                  |       *
-1.00000E+00                 *|
-8.00000E-01            *     |
-6.00000E-01         *        |
-4.00000E-01       *          |
-2.00000E-01      *           |
 0.00000E+00    *             |
 2.00000E-01    *             |
 4.00000E-01   *              |
 6.00000E-01   *              |
 8.00000E-01    *             |
 1.00000E+00    *             |
 1.20000E+00     *            |
 1.40000E+00      *           |
 1.60000E+00        *         |
 1.80000E+00         *        |
 2.00000E+00            *     |
 2.20000E+00                  | *
 2.40000E+00                  |     *
 2.60000E+00                  |          *
 2.80000E+00                  |               *
 3.00000E+00                  |                     *
```

We represent the Y-value corresponding to the X of a
particular printed line by printing an asterisk in the print
position that approximates its value. We use 51 columns to print
the range of Ys. If the lowest Y-value that we must represent is
YMINIMUM and the highest is YMAXIMUM, then the 51 print positions
must represent a range of

    YRANGE = YMAXIMUM - YMINIMUM

To find the print position for a value Y we compute a FIXED
variable YPRINT from

    YPRINT=50*(Y-YMINIMUM)/YRANGE+1.5E0;

The value 1.5E0 is added to round to the nearest integer and put
YMINIMUM in the first position. We are assuming YRANGE is not
zero so that we can divide by it. To form a string of characters
for printing, we replace the blank in the YPRINT position of a
string of blanks by an asterisk. We create a string variable
called BLANKS that holds a string of blanks. The line of
characters to be printed, which is a CHARACTER variable, we call
YLINE. It is

```
YLINE=SUBSTR(BLANKS,1,YPRINT-1))||'*'||SUBSTR(BLANKS,YPRINT+1);
```

We put an X-axis on our graph if it is in the proper range. To do this we place a vertical bar in the line of blanks and call the new variable BASIC_LINE. The axis is placed in the position where a zero value of Y would be placed. The axis does not appear at all if 0 is less than YMINIMUM or greater than YMAXIMUM. Here is the program segment for forming the BASIC_LINE.

```
IF(0>=YMINIMUM & 0<=YMAXIMUM)THEN
  DO;
    ZERO_PRINT=50*(0-YMINIMUM)/YRANGE+1.5E0;
    BASIC_LINE=SUBSTR(BLANKS,1,ZERO_PRINT-1)||
      '|'||SUBSTR(BLANKS,ZERO_PRINT+1);
    END;
ELSE
    BASIC_LINE=BLANKS;
```

Before printing the line we must place the asterisk in position in the BASIC_LINE. This is done by

```
YLINE=SUBSTR(BASIC_LINE,1,YPRINT-1)||
  '*'||SUBSTR(BASIC_LINE,YPRINT+1);
```

This takes the characters of BASIC_LINE up to the character YPRINT, concatenates an asterisk, then takes the remaining characters of BASIC_LINE from position (YPRINT+1) on to the end of the line.

We do not print a Y-axis, but we list the X-values corresponding to each line opposite the line.

A PROCEDURE FOR PLOTTING GRAPHS

Here is the complete procedure for plotting a graph from N pairs of FLOAT values of X and Y stored in arrays of those names. The values of X are uniformly spaced. The actual names of the variables to be plotted will be given as arguments XNAME and YNAME, which are character variables. The calling statement would be of the form

```
CALL GRAPH(X,Y,N,XNAME,YNAME);
```

We will call a procedure to find YMAXIMUM and YMINIMUM. It will be called MIN_MAX.

```
/* PROCEDURE TO PLOT A GRAPH */
GRAPH:PROCEDURE(X,Y,N,XNAME,YNAME);
   DECLARE(X(*),Y(*))FLOAT,
      (N)FIXED,
      (XNAME,YNAME)CHARACTER(*)VARYING;
   DECLARE(BLANKS,BASIC_LINE,YLINE)CHARACTER(52)VARYING,
      (YMINIMUM,YMAXIMUM,YRANGE)FLOAT,
      (ZERO_PRINT,YPRINT,I)FIXED;

   /* FIND SMALLEST AND LARGEST VALUES IN ARRAY */
   MIN_MAX:PROCEDURE(ARRAY,N,MINIMUM,MAXIMUM);
      DECLARE(ARRAY(*),MINIMUM,MAXIMUM)FLOAT;
      DECLARE(N)FIXED;
      DECLARE(I)FIXED;
      MINIMUM=ARRAY(1);
      MAXIMUM=ARRAY(1);
      DO I=2 TO N;
         IF ARRAY(I)<MINIMUM THEN
            MINIMUM=ARRAY(I);
         IF ARRAY(I)>MAXIMUM THEN
            MAXIMUM=ARRAY(I);
         END;
      END;

   /* FIND RANGE OF Y TO BE PLOTTED */
   CALL MIN_MAX(Y,N,YMINIMUM,YMAXIMUM);
   YRANGE=YMAXIMUM-YMINIMUM;
   /* FORM STRING OF 52 BLANKS */
   BLANKS='';
   DO I=1 TO 52;
      BLANKS=BLANKS||' ';
      END;
   /* PLACE X-AXIS MARK IN BASIC_LINE */
   IF(0>=YMINIMUM & 0<=YMAXIMUM)THEN
      DO;
         ZERO_PRINT=50*(0-YMINIMUM)/YRANGE+1.5E0;
         BASIC_LINE=SUBSTR(BLANKS,1,ZERO_PRINT-1)
            ||'|'||SUBSTR(BLANKS,ZERO_PRINT+1);
         END;
   ELSE
      BASIC_LINE=BLANKS;
   /* LABEL GRAPH */
   PUT PAGE LIST('GRAPH OF',YNAME,'VERSUS',XNAME);
   PUT SKIP LIST('MINIMUM OF',YNAME,YMINIMUM);
   PUT SKIP LIST('MAXIMUM OF',YNAME,YMAXIMUM);
   /* PREPARE AND PRINT LINES OF GRAPH */
   DO I=1 TO N;
      YPRINT=50*(Y(I)-YMINIMUM)/YRANGE+1.5E0;
      YLINE=SUBSTR(BASIC_LINE,1,YPRINT-1)||
         '*'||SUBSTR(BASIC_LINE,YPRINT+1);
      PUT SKIP LIST(X(I),YLINE);
      END;
   END;
```

USING THE GRAPH PROCEDURE

We will now give the program that was used to plot the function of x,

$$y = x^2 - x - 2$$

between the values x=-2 to x=3. We plot it at intervals of x that are 0.2 wide. There are 26 points in all. Here is the program:

```
$JOB ID='MARK NAIRN'
 /* PLOT THE FUNCTION Y=X*X-X-2 */
 CURVE:PROCEDURE OPTIONS(MAIN);
    DECLARE(X(26),Y(26))FLOAT,
       (I)FIXED;
    (copy GRAPH procedure here)
    /* COMPUTE VALUES FOR X AND Y ARRAYS */
    DO I=1 TO 26;
       X(I)=-2E0+(I-1)*.2E0;
       Y(I)=X(I)*X(I)-X(I)-2E0;
       END;
    CALL GRAPH(X,Y,26,'X','Y');
    END;
```

The output for this program was shown earlier in this chapter. You will notice that as the graph crosses the X-axis the vertical bar is replaced by an asterisk. It crosses twice, at

    x = -1.00000E+00   and at
    x = +2.00000E+00.

We say that x=-1 and x=2 are the roots of the equation

$$x^2 - x - 2 = 0$$

The function $(x^2 - x - 2)$ becomes zero at these values of x. This graphical method is one way of finding the roots of an equation. We will look later in this chapter at another way of finding roots that is numerical rather than graphical.

FITTING A CURVE TO A SET OF POINTS

In the last sections we have seen how to compute a set of points of corresponding X and Y values from a formula and then to plot a graph of these points. In some scientific experiments we measure the value of a variable Y as we change some other variable X in a systematic way. The results are displayed by plotting X and Y. If there is a theory that relates the values of X to Y in a formula or equation, then we can see how well the results fit the theoretical formula.

One way would be to compute the values of Y for each X from the formula. The measured values could be called Y(experimental) and the calculated ones Y(theoretical). The differences between corresponding values

    Y(experimental) - Y(theoretical)

are called <u>deviations</u> of experimental from theoretical values.

We have spoken so far as if it were possible to compute the proper theoretical value that corresponds to each experimental value. This is the case if the formula has no other variable in it. Frequently there are other variables in the formula that can change. For example, here is the formula for V, the velocity of an object at time T, given that its initial velocity is V_INITIAL and its acceleration is A.

    V = V_INITIAL + A*T

If we measured the velocity of an object that has a uniform acceleration we could plot a graph between V and T:

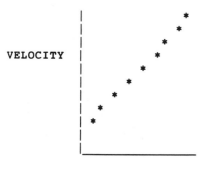

                    TIME

Theoretically, the graph should be a straight line, but the experimental points are scattered. It is possible to draw a line by eye that is placed so that the deviations of points from the line are small. Since some deviations, V(experimental)-V(theoretical), are positive and some negative their sum might be small even though individual deviations were large. To get a good fit we minimize the sum of the squares of the deviations rather than the sum of the deviations. The squares of the deviations are always positive. We choose as the best straight line the one that makes the sum of the squares of the deviations the least. This is called <u>least-squares</u> <u>fitting</u> of a curve (here a straight line) to experimental points. This process can be done very efficiently by a computer. Most computer installations provide standard procedures for least-squares fitting, so that scientists do not have to write their own.

Sometimes no theoretical curve is known. We can still fit our data to an equation. We choose an equation that has a form resembling our data. If there is no theory we say it is an empirical fit, meaning that it is an equation based on the observations.

SOLVING POLYNOMIAL EQUATIONS

The graph that we plotted as an example was of the function

$$y = x^2 - x - 2$$

This is a polynomial function of x. The places where the graph crosses the x-axis are the roots of the equation

$$x^2 - x - 2 = 0$$

This is a second-degree equation since the highest power of the unknown x is the second power. It is a quadratic equation. There are general formulas for the roots of a quadratic equation. For the equation

$$ax^2 + bx + c = 0$$

the two roots x1 and x2 are given by the formulas

$$x1 = (-b + \sqrt{b^2 - 4ac})/(2a) \quad \text{and}$$

$$x2 = (-b - \sqrt{b^2 - 4ac})/(2a)$$

Most students of mathematics know these formulas. If the quantity $(b^2 - 4ac)$ inside the square root sign is positive, all is straightforward. If it is negative, then the formula requires us to find the square root of a negative number, and we say the roots are complex. This means, in graphical terms, that the curve does not cross, or touch, the X-axis anywhere.

This procedure finds the roots of a quadratic equation. It can be improved under various circumstances to give more accurate results, for example, when B and SQRT (DISCRIMINANT) are almost equal.

```
/* FIND ROOTS OF A*X*X+B*X+C=0 */
QUADRATIC_ROOTS:PROCEDURE(A,B,C);
   DECLARE(A,B,C,DISCRIMINANT)FLOAT;
   DISCRIMINANT=B*B-4*A*C;
   IF DISCRIMINANT >=0 THEN
      PUT SKIP LIST('ROOTS ARE',(-B+SQRT(DISCRIMINANT))/(2*A),
         (-B-SQRT(DISCRIMINANT))/(2*A));
   ELSE
      PUT SKIP LIST ('ROOTS ARE COMPLEX');
   END;
```

For equations that are polynomial in x of degrees higher than two, the method for finding the roots is not as easy. For an

equation of degree 3 or 4, there is a complicated formula to find
the roots, but for higher-degree equations there are no formulas.
We must look for the roots by a <u>numerical</u> <u>method</u>.

The secret of any search is first to be sure that what you
are looking for is in the right area, then to keep narrowing down
the search area. One method of searching for roots corresponds
to the binary search we discussed in Chapter 14. First we find
two values of x for which the function has different signs. Then
we can be sure that, if it is continuous, the graph will cross
the x-axis at least once in the interval between these points.
The next step is to halve the interval and look at the middle.
If there is only one root in the interval, then in the middle the
function will either be zero, in which case it is the root, or it
will have the same sign as one of the two end points. Remember
they have opposite signs. We discard the half of the interval
that is bounded by the middle point and the end with the same
sign and repeat the process. After several steps we will have a
good <u>approximation</u> to the location of the root. We can continue
the process until we are satisfied that the error, or
uncertainty, in our root location is small enough. There is no
point in trying to locate it more accurately than the precision
with which the computer stores numbers. A numerical analyst
could determine the accuracy of the calculated answer.

SOLVING LINEAR EQUATIONS

Computers are used to solve sets of linear equations. If we
have two unknowns, we must have two equations to get a solution.
We can solve the set of equations

$$x-y=10$$
$$x+y=6$$

to get the result x=8, y=-2. To solve the equations we first
eliminate one of the unknowns. From the first equation we get

$$x=y+10$$

Substituting into the second eliminates x. It gives

$$(y+10)+y=6 \quad \text{or} \quad 2y=-4 \quad \text{or} \quad y=-2$$

Then substituting back gives

$$x=-2+10 \quad \text{or} \quad x=8$$

This process of elimination can be carried out a step at a time
for more equations in more unknowns. Each step lowers the number
of unknowns by one and the number of equations by one. A
computer program can be written to perform this job, and can be
used to solve a set of linear equations. What we must provide is
the coefficients of the unknowns and the right-hand sides of the

set of equations. A common method is called the <u>Gauss</u>
<u>elimination</u> <u>method</u>.

COMPUTING AREAS

Another numerical method that is relatively easy to
understand is the calculation of areas by the <u>trapezoidal</u> method.
Suppose we have a curve of y=f(x) and we want to find the area
between the curve and the x-axis and between lines at x=X1 and
x=X2.

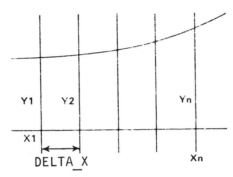

We will divide the distance between X1 and X2 into intervals of
size DELTA_X. In the drawing we have shown four intervals. The
area of the first section, thinking of it as a trapezoid, is

     (Y1+Y2)*DELTA_X/2

The total area under the curve is approximated by the sum of all
the trapezoids. The total area of the trapezoids is

    (Y1+Y2)*DELTA_X/2+(Y2+Y3)*DELTA_X/2+...(Y(n-1)+Yn)*DELTA_X/2

If we factor out DELTA_X the formula becomes

    ((Y1+Yn)/2+Y2+Y3+... +Y(n-1))*DELTA_X

This is half the sum of Y1 and Yn plus the sum of the other Ys
multiplied by the width of the trapezoids. As DELTA_X is made
smaller, the sum of the areas of the trapezoids comes closer and
closer to the area under the curve. It is a better and better
approximation. There is, however, a limit to the accuracy that
can be obtained, due to the precision of the FLOAT numbers. Here
is a program segment to compute the area if the Ys are stored in
an array:

```
SUM=(Y(1)+Y(N))/2E0;
DO I=2 TO N-1;
   SUM=SUM+Y(I);
   END;
AREA_UNDER_CURVE=SUM*DELTA_X;
```

CHAPTER 18 SUMMARY

This chapter has given an introduction to the use of computers in scientific calculations. Generally, these calculations are done using FLOAT numbers. The scientist needs to know the accuracy of the final answers. The answers may be inaccurate because of:

Measurement errors - the original data was collected by measuring physical quantities, such as length or speed. These measurements can never be perfect and an estimate of the measurement error should be made.

Round-off errors by the computer - a given computer stores FLOAT numbers with a particular precision, typically 6 decimal digits of accuracy. Calculations using FLOAT numbers will be no more accurate than the number of digits of precision provided by the computer. They could even be less accurate due to the cumulative effect of round-off. (Note: sometimes the programmer can choose between "single-precision" FLOAT, giving typically 6 digits of accuracy and "double-precision" FLOAT, giving typically 14 digits accuracy.)

Truncation errors in repeated calculations - some calculations, such as searching for the roots of a polynomial equation, produce approximations that are successively closer to the exact answer. When the repeated calculation stops, we have a truncation error, which is the difference between the final approximation and the exact answer (ignoring errors due to measurement and round-off).

The number of digits of accuracy in a particular answer is called its number of <u>significant figures</u>. The scientist needs to know that the computer produces a particular answer with enough significant figures for his purposes.

PL/1 provides built-in functions that are useful in solving scientific or mathematical problems. The function SQRT takes the square root of a non-negative number. The functions SIN, COS and ATAN (arctan) operate on or return angles in radians. LOG takes the natural logarithm of a number, and EXP raises e to a specified power.

This chapter presented the following typical scientific and mathematical uses of computers.

Evaluating formulas - a computer can produce tables of numbers, for example tables of navigational figures used on sailing boats.

Graphing functions - a computer can plot a particular function; sometimes a special <u>plotter</u> machine is attached to the computer so it can draw continuous lines as well as printing characters.

Fitting a curve to a set of points – data points from an experiment can be read by a program and used to determine an equation (a curve) that describes the data.

Solving polynomial equations – a polynomial equation such as

$$X^3 + 9X^2 + 6X - 23 = 0$$

can be solved by a program that reads the coefficients (1, 9, 6 and −23).

Solving linear equations – a set of equations such as

$$2X + 9y = 7$$
$$10X - 4y = 2$$

can be solved by a program that reads the coefficients of the unknowns (2, 9, 10 and −4) and the right sides of the equations (7 and 2).

Areas under curves – a program can find the area under a given curve by using the heights of the curve at many points. Essentially, the program slices the area into narrow strips and adds up the areas of the strips. This process is sometimes called numerical integration or quadrature.

CHAPTER 18 EXERCISES

1. One jet plane is flying 1083.7 kilometers per hour; another jet plane, chasing it from behind, is flying 1297.9 kilometers per hour. What is the relative speed of the second plane, that is, how fast is it catching up to the first plane? The speed of the first plane is known to an accuracy of ±5 km/hr and the speed of the second is known to an accuracy of ±0.5 km/hr. How accurately can we calculate the relative speed? How many significant figures are there in the first plane's speed, the second plane's speed and the relative speed?

2. Use the graphing procedure given in this chapter to plot the function SIN(X) for X varying from zero to three in steps of one tenth.

3. Use the graphing procedure given in this chapter to plot the function X*SIN(X) for X varying from 0 to 12 in steps of 0.25E0.

4. A moon rocket has an instrument that measures the rocket's acceleration every second and transmits the measurement to an on-board minicomputer. A program in the minicomputer estimates the speed of the rocket, assuming a speed of zero at launch time. Essentially, this program determines the area under the curve of

acceleration plotted against time. Using the trapezoidal method
described in this chapter, the speed at time Tn will be
approximately

    ((A1+An)/2+A2+A3+ .. + A(n-1))* DELTA_T

In this case, DELTA_T is 1 second and each acceleration is
measured in kilometers per second per second. The formula to
give the speed in kilometers per second n seconds after blast-off
is simply

    (A1+An)/2+A2+A3+...+A(n-1)

Write a program that reads in the accelerations and prints out
the speeds after each second. If you are clever you can avoid
recalculating the entire series for each acceleration reading,
and you can avoid using an array.

CHAPTER 19

ASSEMBLY LANGUAGE AND
MACHINE LANGUAGE

In this book we have presented programming in terms of the PL/1 language. PL/1 is a <u>high-level language</u>; it provides us with a convenient means for directing a computer to do work. The computer cannot execute PL/1 programs directly; it can only execute programs in machine language, a <u>low-level language</u>. Before a PL/1 program can be executed by a computer, the program must be <u>translated</u> or <u>compiled</u> to machine language. In this chapter we will explain how a computer carries out instructions. We will present features of machine languages and their associated assembly languages.

MACHINE INSTRUCTIONS

In Chapter 2 we gave a brief introduction of machine language. We explained that the instructions a computer can execute are much more basic than PL/1 statements. These <u>machine instructions</u> use a special location, called the <u>accumulator</u>, when doing arithmetic or making assignments. For example, the assignment of J to I, written as the PL/1 statement

    I=J;

could be translated to the instructions

    LOAD   J   (copy J into the accumulator)
    STORE I   (copy the accumulator into I)

As another example, the PL/1 statement

    I=J+K;

could be translated into the three instructions

```
LOAD   J   (copy J into the accumulator)
ADD    K   (add K to the accumulator)
STORE  I   (copy the accumulator into I)
```

Different kinds of computers have different machine languages. Some computers have many accumulators and some have few. Some computers have many instructions and some have few. We will introduce common features of machine languages by inventing a very simple computer. We will call our computer VS, for <u>very simple</u> computer.

The machine instructions for the VS computer are designed to be convenient for representing programs written in a subset of PL/1. The VS computer has never been built; it is just a hypothetical machine that we will use to illustrate points about computer languages.

The instructions for the VS computer have the form

    operator operand

for example,

    STORE I

The <u>operator</u> of an instruction tells the computer what to do; the <u>operand</u> tells the computer what to do it to.

After the computer executes one instruction, it continues to the next, unless the executed instruction directs the computer to jump to another instruction or to skip an instruction. We can translate the PL/1 statements

```
IF I<=K THEN
   K=I+J;
I=J;
```

into the VS computer instructions

```
    LOAD    K   (copy K into the accumulator)
    SKIP_LE I   (if I<=accumulator, skip next instruction)
    JUMP    L   (jump to instruction labeled L)
    LOAD    I   (copy I into the accumulator)
    ADD     J   (add J to the accumulator)
    STORE   K   (copy the accumulator into K)
  L:LOAD    J   (copy J into the accumulator)
    STORE   I   (copy the accumulator into I)
```

In this example, L is the <u>label</u> of an instruction; instructions are labeled so they can be jumped to. In full PL/1, but not in SP/k, there are statement labels and there is a GO TO statement that is analogous to the JUMP machine instruction. In full PL/1, the following statements are equivalent to the example we just gave:

```
    IF I>K THEN
        GO TO L;
    K=I+J;
  L:I=J;
```

GO TO statements were purposely left out of SP/k because careless use of them leads to unreadable programs. One of the reasons that low-level languages are inconvenient to use is that they do not directly provide looping constructs, such as DO WHILE ... END, and selection constructs, such as IF...THEN...ELSE. The programmer must build up these constructs using instructions like jumps and skips. When an SP/k program is translated into a low-level language, the loop and selection constructs appear as jumps and skips.

INSTRUCTIONS FOR A VERY SIMPLE COMPUTER

The VS computer has an instruction to print the value in the accumulator:

    PUT_INTEGER

This instruction needs no operand because the accumulator's value is always printed. There is an instruction to print messages:

    PUT_STRING   operand

The operand represents a string to be printed. There is an instruction that directs the machine to stop executing a program:

    HALT

The HALT instruction has no operand.

Altogether the VS computer has nine instructions; most real computers have many more instructions, typically around 100. This table lists the VS instructions.

	Operator	Operand	Action by Computer
1	LOAD	variable	Assign variable to accumulator.
2	STORE	variable	Assign accumulator to variable.
3	ADD	variable	Add variable to accumulator.
4	SUBTRACT	variable	Subtract variable from accumulator.
5	JUMP	label	Jump to labeled instruction.
6	SKIP_LE	variable	If variable<=accumulator then skip next instruction.
7	PUT_INTEGER	(none)	Print the integer in the accumulator.
8	PUT_STRING	string	Print the string.
9	HALT	(none)	Halt, the program is finished.

We have purposely kept the VS computer simple by leaving out instructions that might normally be part of the instruction set

of a computer. We have left out a whole set of skip
instructions, such as SKIP_GT (skip when greater than). We left
out instructions for doing FLOAT arithmetic and for reading from
data cards. We left out instructions for manipulating character
strings, indexing arrays, and calling and returning from
procedures. These additional instructions are important in a
real computer; if you like, you can design a "super" VS computer
that includes them.

TRANSLATION OF A PL/1 PROGRAM

If we use some care in picking our example, we can translate
an entire PL/1 program into VS instructions. This example PL/1
program requires only the types of instructions available on the
VS computer:

High-Level Language

Low-Level Language

```
T:PROCEDURE OPTIONS(MAIN);
   DECLARE(I)FIXED;
   PUT SKIP LIST('POWERS OF 2');    PUT_STRING   TITLE
   I=1;                             LOAD         ONE
                                    STORE        I
   DO WHILE(I<=8);              L1:LOAD          EIGHT
                                    SKIP_LE      I
                                    JUMP         L2
     PUT SKIP LIST(I);              LOAD         I
                                    PUT_INTEGER
     I=I+I;                         LOAD         I
                                    ADD          I
                                    STORE        I
     END;                          JUMP          L1
   END;                        L2:HALT
```

The first VS instruction in this example has as its operand
TITLE; TITLE gives the location of the string 'POWERS OF 2'.
Similarly, ONE and EIGHT give the locations of the values 1 and
8.

MNEMONIC NAMES AND MACHINE LANGUAGE

Up to this point we have written VS instructions using names
such as LOAD, STORE, I and J. These names are not present in the
machine language that a computer executes; they are replaced by
numbers. We will now show how these names can be translated into
appropriate numbers.

As you may recall from Chapter 2, the main memory of the
computer consists of a sequence of words. The words of memory
are numbered; the number that corresponds to a particular word is
called the location or address of the word. Words can be used to
represent variables. For example, the variables I, J and K could

be represented by the words with locations 59, 60 and 61.   Here
we show these three words after I, J and K have been assigned the
values 9, 0 and 14.

$$
\begin{array}{r|c|}
59 & 9 \\ \hline
60 & 0 \\ \hline
61 & 14 \\ \hline
\end{array}
$$

There is no special significance to 59, 60 and 61. We could just
as well represent I, J and K by locations 42, 3 and 87; the
important thing is to remember which location corresponds to
which variable.

    If I, J and K correspond to location 59, 60 and 61, we can
write the instructions

        LOAD   J
        ADD   K
        STORE   I

as

        LOAD 60   (copy contents of word 60 into accumulator)
        ADD   61   (add contents of word 61 to accumulator)
        STORE 59   (copy accumulator into word 59)

    The VS instruction operators, LOAD, STORE and so on, are
numbered. LOAD is operator number 1, STORE is 2, ADD is 3 and so
on.   The names LOAD, STORE and ADD as used in the VS instructions
are mnemonic names; a mnemonic name is an "easy-to-remember"
name.   We can choose the names of the operands so that they too
are easy to remember.

    Using the numbers of the operators we can write

        LOAD 60
        ADD   61
        STORE 59

as

        1   60
        3   61
        2   59

    Instructions that consist only of numbers are in machine
language. Instructions that contain mnemonic names, such as LOAD
and I, are in assembly language.

```
Assembly Language          Machine Language

    LOAD  J                   1   60
    ADD   K                   3   61
    STORE I                   2   59
```

As you can see, there is a simple translation from assembly
language to machine language. Writing programs in machine
language is even more inconvenient than writing programs in
assembly language. People almost always prefer assembly language
over machine language; they use a program called an <u>assembler</u> to
translate mnemonic names in assembly language programs to
corresponding numeric operators and operands. Although we do not
show it here, assemblers allow the programmer to reserve and
initialize memory for variables and constants. For example,
location 59 would be reserved for I, and location 98 could be
reserved for EIGHT and initialized to 8.

STORING MACHINE INSTRUCTIONS IN WORDS

The values of variables of a program are stored in words of
the computer's memory. In a similar manner, the instructions of
the program are stored in words of memory. We can use two words
to hold each VS instruction; one word for the operator and one
word for the operand. Here we show three instructions stored in
locations 18 through 23:

```
LOAD J    18 [            1 ]  19 [            60 ]

ADD K     20 [            3 ]  21 [            61 ]

STORE I   22 [            2 ]  23 [            59 ]
```

We could have saved space if the VS computer allowed us to pack
the operator and operand into a single word. For example, the
instruction

    1   59

could be packed into a single word as

    1059

with the convention that the rightmost three digits are the
operand and the other digits are the operator. Instructions for
real computers are packed into words to save space, but to keep
things simple, the VS computer uses two words for its
instructions.

A JUMP instruction has as its operand the label of an
instruction. When a JUMP instruction is written in machine
language, the label must be a number. The number used is the

location of the instruction being jumped to. Here is a
translation of assembly language into machine language; the label
L becomes 48:

JUMP L	40	5	41	48	
LOAD I	42	1	43	59	
ADD J	44	3	45	60	
STORE K	46	2	47	61	
L:LOAD J	48	1	49	60	

Just as the variables and instructions are stored in words in
memory, strings such as 'POWERS OF 2' are stored in memory. In
real computers this is done by packing several characters into
each word. Since mixing characters and numbers is confusing, we
will assume that the VS computer has a separate part of its
memory used only for strings. Each string is saved in a
different location in the special string memory. If the string
'POWERS OF 2' is in location number 1 in the special string
memory, then we translate the PL/1 statement

PUT SKIP LIST('POWERS OF 2');

to the machine instruction

8   1   (PUT_STRING TITLE)

We have now shown how to translate all VS instructions into
numbers and thus into machine language. We will return to our
program that prints powers of 2 and will translate it to machine
language.

A COMPLETE MACHINE LANGUAGE PROGRAM

We will assume that a VS computer always starts by executing
the instruction in words 0 and 1. So we will place our machine
language instructions in words 0, 1, 2, 3, ... We will continue
assuming that variable I corresponds to memory location 59. The
integer constants 1 and 8 will be represented by memory locations
91 and 98; these locations are initialized to hold the values 1
and 8 before the program is executed. We show the program as it
would appear in memory after having executed instructions in
locations 0 through 14. Up to this point the program has printed

POWERS OF 2
         1

The VS computer has an instruction pointer, presently set to 16,
that locates the next instruction to be executed. When an
instruction has no operand, we give it a dummy operand of zero;
for example, HALT becomes 9 0.

STORAGE OF PROGRAM IN COMPUTER

INSTRUCTION POINTER [16]   ACCUMULATOR [1]

MEMORY

0	8	1	(PUT_STRING TITLE)
2	1	91	(LOAD ONE)
4	2	59	(STORE I)
6	1	98	(LI: LOAD EIGHT)
8	6	59	(SKIP_LE I)
10	5	24	(JUMP L2)
12	1	59	(LOAD I)
14	7	0	(PUT_INTEGER)
16	1	59	(LOAD I)
18	3	59	(ADD I)
20	2	59	(STORE I)
22	5	6	(JUMP LI)
24	9	0	(L2: HALT)
...		...	
58		1	(59 CORRESPONDS TO I)
...		...	
90		1	(91 CORRESPONDS TO ONE)
...		...	
98	8		(98 CORRESPONDS TO EIGHT)

SPECIAL STRING MEMORY

1 ['POWERS OF 2']

2 [ ]

...

SIMULATING A COMPUTER

A VS computer has never been built and undoubtedly never will be built. It might seem that we can never have a VS machine language program executed. But we can, by making an existing computer <u>simulate</u> a VS computer. This is done by writing a program, called a <u>simulator</u>, that acts as if it is a VS computer. We will discuss later in more detail the importance of simulators in computing, but first we will develop a PL/1 procedure that is a simulator for the VS computer.

The VS computer has an accumulator, which can be simulated by a variable declared by

```
DECLARE(ACCUMULATOR)FIXED;
```

It also has a memory containing 100 words, whose addresses are 0 to 99. This can be simulated by an array:

```
DECLARE(MEMORY(0:99))FIXED;
```

There is a special string memory. Assuming that the VS computer can hold, at most, 10 strings of length at most 78, we can simulate the string memory by another array:

```
DECLARE(STRING(10))CHARACTER(78)VARYING;
```

We need an instruction pointer to keep track of which instruction is to be executed next.

```
DECLARE(INSTRUCTION_POINTER)FIXED;
```

When the VS computer is executing, the instruction pointer has a particular value, say 10, indicating that word 10 contains the operator of the next instruction to be executed. Word 11 contains the operand. If OPERATOR and OPERAND are declared as FIXED variables in the simulator, then they should be given values by:

```
OPERATOR=MEMORY(INSTRUCTION_POINTER);
OPERAND=MEMORY(INSTRUCTION_POINTER+1);
```

If the OPERATOR is 1, meaning LOAD, the simulator carries out the LOAD machine instruction by executing:

```
ACCUMULATOR=MEMORY(OPERAND);
```

If the OPERATOR is 2, meaning STORE, the simulator carries out the STORE instruction by executing:

```
MEMORY(OPERAND)=ACCUMULATOR;
```

Similarly, the simulator can carry out the other VS instructions. After each instruction is carried out, the INSTRUCTION_POINTER is incremented by 2 and OPERATOR and OPERAND are set for the next

instruction. When the instruction is a JUMP or SKIP, then
INSTRUCTION_POINTER can be modified so an instruction other than
the next sequential instruction will be selected. For example,
if the OPERATOR is 6, for SKIP_LE, the simulator executes this:

```
IF MEMORY(OPERAND)<=ACCUMULATOR THEN
    INSTRUCTION_POINTER=INSTRUCTION_POINTER+2;
```

To make the simulator more readable, we will use mnemonic
variables for each of the VS instructions:

```
DECLARE(LOAD,STORE,...,HALT)FIXED;
```

We will initialize these variables to their corresponding machine
language numeric values 1, 2, ... 9. These declarations should
be global to the simulator procedure; the variables should be
initialized before calling the simulator.

Now we give the complete simulator as a PL/1 procedure. This
procedure assumes that the MEMORY and STRING arrays have been
declared and initialized.

```
/* THIS PROCEDURE SIMULATES A VERY SIMPLE COMPUTER */
SIMULATOR:PROCEDURE;
   DECLARE(ACCUMULATOR,INSTRUCTION_POINTER)FIXED;
   DECLARE(OPERATOR,OPERAND)FIXED;
   INSTRUCTION_POINTER=0;
   OPERATOR=MEMORY(INSTRUCTION_POINTER);
   OPERAND=MEMORY(INSTRUCTION_POINTER+1);
   DO WHILE(OPERATOR¬=HALT);
      IF OPERATOR=LOAD THEN
         ACCUMULATOR=MEMORY(OPERAND);
      IF OPERATOR=STORE THEN
         MEMORY(OPERAND)=ACCUMULATOR;
      IF OPERATOR=ADD THEN
         ACCUMULATOR=ACCUMULATOR+MEMORY(OPERAND);
      IF OPERATOR=SUBTRACT THEN
         ACCUMULATOR=ACCUMULATOR-MEMORY(OPERAND);
      IF OPERATOR=JUMP THEN
         INSTRUCTION_POINTER=OPERAND-2;
      IF OPERATOR=SKIP_LE THEN
         IF MEMORY(OPERAND)<=ACCUMULATOR THEN
            INSTRUCTION_POINTER=INSTRUCTION_POINTER+2;
      IF OPERATOR=PUT_INTEGER THEN
         PUT SKIP LIST(ACCUMULATOR);
      IF OPERATOR=PUT_STRING THEN
         PUT SKIP LIST(STRING(OPERAND));
      INSTRUCTION_POINTER=INSTRUCTION_POINTER+2;
      OPERATOR=MEMORY(INSTRUCTION_POINTER);
      OPERAND=MEMORY(INSTRUCTION_POINTER+1);
      END;
   END;
```

If you want to run a VS machine language program, you can
write a main procedure to put the numbers representing the

program and constants into the MEMORY array, initialize the
STRING array and then call the SIMULATOR procedure.

USES OF SIMULATORS

We will now discuss some of the uses of simulators. Our
simulator for the VS computer can be used to execute VS machine
language programs. But it can serve another purpose, too. By
reading the SIMULATOR procedure, you can determine the actions
carried out for each VS instruction; if you did not know how a VS
computer worked, you could find out by studying its simulator.
So not only can the simulator direct one computer to act like
another, it can also show how a computer works.

Computer simulators are often used to allow programs written
for one machine to execute on another machine. For example, a
business may buy a new computer to replace an old computer.
After the old computer is removed, programs written for the old
computer can be executed by a simulator running on the new
machine.

Sometimes a hypothetical computer is designed to help solve
some particular problem. This is the case with the SP/k
compilers. A hypothetical computer was designed to allow easy
translation from SP/k programs to the hypothetical computer's
machine language. The translated SP/k programs are executed
using a simulator for the hypothetical machine. Other compilers,
such as the PL/C compiler, translate programs into the real
computer's machine language; then a simulator is not required
because the translated program is executed directly by the
computer.

CHAPTER 19 SUMMARY

In this chapter we have presented features of machine
language in terms of a very simple hypothetical computer called
VS. The VS computer has an accumulator that is used for doing
calculations. There are VS machine instructions for loading,
storing, adding to, subtracting from, and printing the
accumulator. There is a machine instruction for printing
strings. There are instructions for jumping to instructions,
skipping instructions and for halting. The nine VS machine
instructions were sufficient for the translation of the example
PL/1 program given in this chapter. Real computers typically
have many more instructions. The following important terms were
discussed in this chapter:

   Word - the computer's main memory is divided into words.
          Each word can contain a number. In real computers, a
          word can contain several characters, typically 4
          characters.

Location (or address) - the number that locates a particular word in the computer's main memory.

Operators and operands - most VS machine instructions, such as,

LOAD I

consist of an operator and an operand; these are LOAD and I in this example. Some instructions have an operator but no operand.

Mnemonic name - a name that helps programmers remember something. For example, STORE is the mnemonic name for VS machine instruction number 2.

Machine language - the purely numeric language that is directly executed by a particular type of computer. Some computer manufacturers sell families of computers, of various sizes and speeds, that all use the same machine language.

Assembly language - programs in assembly language use mnemonic names corresponding to the numeric operators of machine language. They also permit programmers to choose mnemonic names for the operands and labels.

Assembler - a program that translates programs written in assembly language to machine language.

Label - a name that gives the location of a machine instruction or a statement. The JUMP machine instruction, as written in assembly language, transfers control to a labeled instruction. The GO TO statement, as written in full PL/1, but not in SP/k, transfers control to a labeled statement.

Simulator - a program that simulates some system such as a computer. A simulator treats a sequence of numbers as a machine language program and carries out the specified operations.

CHAPTER 19 EXERCISES

1. The VS computer described in this chapter does not have an instruction for reading data. Invent an instruction named GET_INTEGER that reads the next integer in the data into the accumulator. Show how to translate a GET statement such as

GET LIST(K);

into VS machine language, as augmented by GET_INTEGER. Show how the SIMULATOR procedure given in this chapter can be modified to execute GET_INTEGER instructions.

2. Translate the following PL/1 program into VS assembly language and then into VS machine language.

```
T:PROCEDURE OPTIONS(MAIN);
   DECLARE(I,J)FIXED;
   I=1;
   J=5;
   IF I<=J THEN
      PUT SKIP LIST('I IS SMALLER');
   ELSE
      PUT SKIP LIST('J IS SMALLER');
   END;
```

3. What will the following VS assembly language program print? Translate the program to both machine language and PL/1.

```
      LOAD     ZERO
      STORE    PREVIOUS
      LOAD     ONE
      STORE    CURRENT
L1:LOAD     FIFTY
      SKIP_LE  CURRENT
      JUMP     L2
      LOAD     CURRENT
      ADD      PREVIOUS
      STORE    NEXT
      LOAD     CURRENT
      STORE    PREVIOUS
      LOAD     NEXT
      STORE    CURRENT
      PUT_INTEGER
      JUMP     L1
L2:HALT
```

4. In this chapter an example program was given that prints powers of 2. Have this program executed by the VS simulator given in this chapter. This can be done by writing a main procedure that declares MEMORY and STRING arrays, initializes these arrays to hold the machine language version of the example program, and then calls the SIMULATOR procedure.

CHAPTER 20

PROGRAMMING LANGUAGE
COMPILERS

High-level languages such as PL/1 provide a convenient tool to help us use computers. We use a <u>translator</u> or <u>compiler</u> to translate our PL/1 programs to machine language. For example, the PL/C compiler translates PL/1 programs to IBM 360 machine language. The SP/k compiler translates PL/1 to the machine language of a hypothetical machine, and then uses a simulator to execute this machine language.

In this chapter we will show how compilers bridge the gap between high-level languages, which are convenient for people, and machine languages, which can be directly executed by a computer. We will define a simple programming language called PSP/3, and then we will show how programs written in that language can be translated to the machine language for the very simple (VS) computer described in the last chapter.

We will give a compiler that reads cards containing a PSP/3 program and translates the program to VS machine language. Our compiler will be written as a PL/1 procedure that is about 200 lines long. Since our compiler is longer than any program we have given before, it provides better examples of step-by-step refinement and modular programming. Compilers are usually very large programs. For example, the SP/k compiler with its simulator is around 9,000 lines long. Even so, it is much smaller than other compilers such as PL/C.

A SIMPLE HIGH-LEVEL LANGUAGE

We will invent a simple high-level language to illustrate points about compilers and computer languages. We will call our language PSP/3, because it contains <u>part</u> of the features of SP/3.

PSP/3 does not have any of the features of SP/4 through SP/8: no character string variables, no arrays, no procedures, no EDIT input-output and no files. PSP/3 allows:

-FIXED variables named A or B or C ... or Z, but no FLOAT variables. All FIXED variables used in a program must be declared via

    DECLARE(list of variables separated by commas)FIXED;

- Addition and subtraction, but no multiplication or division, and no parentheses in expressions.

- FIXED constants 0, 1, 2,..., 9, but no multiple-digit constants such as 21, no signed constants and no FLOAT constants.

- PUT SKIP LIST statement. The SKIP is required and exactly one output item must be given. The output item can be a literal such as 'HI THERE' or a fixed expression. Literals may not contain an embedded quote, so 'DON''T' is not allowed. GET statements are not allowed.

- Assignment statements.

- DO WHILE loops. The only allowed comparison is <= (the following are not allowed: >=, =, <, >, ¬=). No logical operators (&, |, ¬) are allowed. Counted DO loops, IF statements and DO;...END; are disallowed.

- Every PSP/3 program is named T, so each program begins

    T:PROCEDURE OPTIONS(MAIN);

This list of restrictions applied to SP/3 defines the PSP/3 language.

Since PSP/3 is a subset of SP/k, a PSP/3 program can be translated by the PL/C compiler or by an SP/k compiler. PSP/3 is so limited that it is not particularly useful for solving problems; we impose these limitations so we can develop a complete PSP/3 compiler in this chapter.

Things have been arranged so that it is relatively easy to translate PSP/3 programs to machine language for the very simple (VS) computer described in the last chapter. The program from the last chapter that prints powers of 2 is an example of a PSP/3 program.

SYNTAX RULES

Each programming language has rules that a programmer must follow when writing a program. For example, in PL/1, each PUT statement must be followed by a semicolon and each DO WHILE must

be matched by a following END. Rules such as these give the
grammar or syntax of the language. By now you should know the
syntax for the SP/k subsets of PL/1 by heart; this means you
should be able to tell whether an SP/k statement is correctly
formed.

We have described the PSP/3 language by explaining how it
differs from SP/3. We will now describe PSP/3 more directly by
giving its syntax. The syntax for PSP/3 consists of nine rules.
In the syntax rules, the wiggly brackets $\{\ \}$ mean that the
enclosed item is optional or can be repeated any number of times.
Thus, the notation

    variable $\{$,variable $\}$

means a list of variables separated by commas.

1. A program is:
           T:PROCEDURE OPTIONS(MAIN);
              DECLARE(variable $\{$,variable $\}$)FIXED;
              $\{$ statement $\}$
              END;

2. A statement is one of the following:
              a. PUT SKIP LIST(output item);
              b. variable = expression;
              c. DO WHILE(expression <= expression);
                $\{$ statement $\}$
                END;

3. An output item is one of the following:
              a. expression
              b. literal

4. An expression is:
              value $\{$ operator value $\}$

5. A value is one of the following:
              a. variable
               b. integer

6. An operator is: + or –

7. A variable is: A or B or C ... or Z

8. An integer is: 0 or 1 or 2 ... or 9

9. A literal is: '$\{$ any non-quote character $\}$ '

Our syntax rules specify the allowed forms of PSP/3 programs.
Rule 2 specifies that the only allowed statements are PUT SKIP
LIST, assignment and DO WHILE ... END. Since other statements
such as GET and IF are not specified in the syntax, they are not
allowed in PSP/3. Rule 2 specifies that a DO WHILE loop contains
a list of statements; since a DO WHILE loop is itself a

statement, rule 2 implies that DO WHILE loops can be nested
inside DO WHILE loops. Rule 2 is almost a circular definition,
in that a DO WHILE loop is specified to be a "statement" and yet
a DO WHILE loop can contain "statements". We say such a
definition is <u>recursive</u>; recursive definitions provide a concise
way of stating that a particular construct, such as a DO WHILE
loop, can be nested inside a construct of the same type.

USING SYNTAX RULES TO PRODUCE A PROGRAM

A PSP/3 program is considered to be syntactically correct if
it can be <u>produced</u> or developed using the syntax rules. We start
with rule 1 and produce a "program" of the form

```
T:PROCEDURE OPTIONS(MAIN);
    DECLARE(variable {,variable} )FIXED;
    {statement}
    END;
```

The symbols written in small letters, "variable" and "statement",
will not be a part of the final program. Instead, they represent
a set of possibilities. By contrast, symbols such as "T",
"PROCEDURE", ";" and "END" are a part of the final program.
Symbols like "variable" and "statement" that do not appear in the
final program are called <u>non-terminal</u> symbols. Symbols such as
"T", "PROCEDURE", ";" and "END" are called <u>terminal</u> symbols
because they appear in the final program.

We can produce a PSP/3 program using our syntax rules by
starting with rule 1 and successively using rules to replace non-
terminal symbols, such as "statement", until we are left with
nothing but terminal symbols. In previous chapters, we have
shown how to develop programs by step-by-step refinement.
Producing programs using syntax rules is analogous to step-by-
step refinement, but serves an entirely different purpose. We
use step-by-step refinement as a method of designing programs.
By contrast, we check the syntax of a given program by trying to
produce it using the syntax rules. We will illustrate this
process by using the PSP/3 syntax rules to verify that an example
program is syntactically correct. We will use as our example the
program from the last chapter that prints powers of 2:

```
T:PROCEDURE OPTIONS(MAIN);
   DECLARE(I)FIXED;
   PUT SKIP LIST('POWERS OF 2');
   I=1;
   DO WHILE(I<=8);
      PUT SKIP LIST(I);
      I=I+I;
      END;
   END;
```

We start with rule 1 and produce

```
T:PROCEDURE OPTIONS(MAIN);
   DECLARE(variable {,variable} )FIXED;
   {statement}
   END;
```

In order to produce the desired final program we replace the parts

```
    variable {,variable}
```

and

```
    {statement}
```

by the corresponding parts

```
    variable
```

and

```
    statement
    statement
    statement
```

Our program has now become

```
 T:PROCEDURE OPTIONS(MAIN);
   DECLARE(variable)FIXED;
   statement
   statement
   statement
   END;
```

We can now use rule 7 to produce I from "variable", making the declaration become

```
    DECLARE(I)FIXED;
```

We can produce the first PUT SKIP LIST statement in our example program by applying rules 2a, 3b and 9 to the "statement" immediately following the declaration:

```
         statement
         PUT SKIP LIST(output item);    (produced using rule 2a)
         PUT SKIP LIST(literal);        (produced using rule 3b)
         PUT SKIP LIST('POWERS OF 2');  (produced using rule 9)
```

Up to now, we have used the syntax rules to produce

```
 T:PROCEDURE OPTIONS(MAIN);
    DECLARE(I)FIXED;
    PUT SKIP LIST('POWERS OF 2');
    statement
    statement
    END;
```

We can apply rules 2b, 7, 4, 5b and 8 to transform the
"statement" following PUT SKIP LIST to the desired form:

```
         statement
         variable=expression;       (produced using rule 2b)
         I=expression;              (produced using rule 7)
         I=value;                   (produced using rule 4)
         I=1;                       (produced using rules 5b,8)
```

We can now transform the last "statement" to the desired DO WHILE
loop:

```
         statement

         DO WHILE(expression<=expression);   (rule 2c)
            statement
            statement
            END;

         DO WHILE(I<=8);                (rules 2a, 2b, 3a, 4, 5, 6, 7 and 8)
            PUT SKIP LIST(I);
            I=I+I;
            END;
```

We have now used the syntax rules to produce the example program
that prints powers of 2. Since this program can be produced
using the syntax rules, it is syntactically correct.

Syntax rules provide a concise way of describing a language.
They do not completely describe a language. For example, the
syntax rules for PSP/3 do not imply that every variable used in
the program must be declared. The syntax rules for PSP/3
describe all legal PSP/3 programs, but they describe some illegal
ones as well, in particular the ones with undeclared variables.

One of the most important uses of syntax rules is for
specifying a high-level language so that a compiler can be
written for the language. In the next sections we develop a
complete compiler for PSP/3. Because of the level of detail in

these sections, some readers may choose to skim them or to skip them altogether.

ACTIONS OF THE COMPILER

To keep our compiler simple, we will make several assumptions about PSP/3 programs. We will assume that <u>PSP/3 programs</u> <u>never</u> <u>contain errors</u>, so our compiler will not need to check for such errors. In the real world of programming, this would be a disastrous assumption; we are making it only so the example compiler can be smaller.

We will assume that every PSP/3 program is surrounded by the control cards %JOB and %DATA in this manner:

```
%JOB
   PSP/3 program
%DATA
```

Our compiler will use the %DATA card to detect the end of a PSP/3 job; it will ignore the %JOB card.

We will assume that each card is blank following a semicolon that is not in a literal. To present the compiler we will consider each of the following six types of lines separately; they will appear on separate cards in a PSP/3 program.

```
T:PROCEDURE OPTIONS(MAIN);
DECLARE(...)FIXED;
PUT SKIP LIST(...);
variable=expression;
DO WHILE(...);
END;
```

We will assume there are no cards that are all blank. Since every PSP/3 program begins with the same line,

```
T:PROCEDURE OPTIONS(MAIN);
```

this line can be ignored by our compiler.

A real PL/1 compiler analyzes declarations to determine the attributes of variables and to see that memory space is set aside to represent the variables. Our compiler takes advantage of the fact that all PSP/3 variables are FIXED and must be named A, B, C, ... or Z. Our compiler always sets aside enough memory for all 26 possible PSP/3 variables, regardless of whether they are used in the particular program. This wastes memory, but it makes our compiler simpler. The only purpose of the declarations in PSP/3 is so that PSP/3 programs are legal SP/k programs.

The PSP/3 compiler can simply ignore the first three cards:

```
%JOB
 T:PROCEDURE OPTIONS(MAIN);
    DECLARE(...)FIXED;
```

Having skipped these three cards, the compiler must translate each of the following four types of cards to machine language:

```
    PUT SKIP LIST(...);
    variable=expression;
    DO WHILE(...);
    END;
```

When the compiler reads each of these cards, it should take these actions:

Type of Card	Action by Compiler
PUT SKIP LIST(output item);	If the output item is a literal, then an instruction is generated to print the literal. Otherwise instructions are generated to find the value of the expression and print it.
variable=expression;	Instructions are generated to find the value of the expression and to store it in the variable's memory location.
DO WHILE(expr<=expr);	Instructions are generated to find the values of the two expressions. Then instructions are generated to compare their values, and either to execute the body of the loop or to jump beyond the body of the loop.
END;	If the END is for a DO WHILE loop, then a JUMP instruction is generated to repeat the loop. If it is the final END of the program, a HALT instruction is generated.

We can modularize our compiler by defining four procedures to carry out the above actions:

```
    COMPILE_PUT_SKIP_LIST
    COMPILE_ASSIGNMENT
    COMPILE_DO_WHILE
    COMPILE_END
```

After reading a card, the compiler can decide which of these procedures to call by inspecting the first word on the card. We will define the procedure:

```
    SCAN_WORD - skips blanks and finds the first (or next) word
        on a card and records it in NEXT_WORD.
```

Since each PSP/3 identifier consists of one letter, our compiler can recognize an assignment statement by seeing if the length of the first word on the card is 1. Using these procedures, we can now give the structure of our compiler:

```
Do any required initialization;
Read and print three cards (%JOB, T:PROC... and DECLARE...);
DO WHILE(CARD¬='%DATA');
   Read and print a card;
   CALL SCAN_WORD;
   IF NEXT_WORD='PUT' THEN
      CALL COMPILE_PUT_SKIP_LIST;
   IF LENGTH(NEXT_WORD)=1 THEN
      CALL COMPILE_ASSIGNMENT;
   IF NEXT_WORD='DO' THEN
      CALL COMPILE_DO_WHILE;
   IF NEXT_WORD='END' THEN
      CALL COMPILE_END;
   END;
```

SCANNING WORDS AND CHARACTERS

Within a compiler, it is often necessary to determine the next word or character on a card. The part of the compiler that does this work is called the scanner. Our scanner includes the SCAN_WORD procedure and the two procedures:

SCAN_CHAR - sets NEXT_CHAR to the next character on the card. (NEXT_CHAR may be set to a blank).

SCAN_NON_BLANK_CHAR - sets NEXT_CHAR to the next non-blank character on the card.

COMPILING ASSIGNMENT STATEMENTS

We will now explain how the COMPILE_ASSIGNMENT procedure works. Given a card such as

```
I=1;
```

this procedure must generate machine language:

```
1   91    (LOAD ONE)
2   59    (STORE I)
```

We set aside memory locations 51 through 76 to hold variables A through Z, so variable I corresponds to 59. We set aside memory locations 90 through 99 to hold the allowed PSP/3 constants 0 through 9. There is no special significance to locations 51 to 76 and 90 to 99; we could have used other locations.

If PSP/3 allowed constants other than 0 to 9, our compiler would need to reserve locations for each new constant it encountered. We have avoided this complication by allowing only constants 0 to 9. If you wish, you can augment our compiler so it could accept other constants.

To generate machine language for assignment statements, the COMPILE_ASSIGNMENT procedure uses three other procedures:

COMPILE_EXPRESSION - generates instructions to find the value of an expression and leave that value in the accumulator.

COMPILE_VARIABLE - determines the location corresponding to a given variable. For example, 59 is returned for variable I.

EMIT_INSTRUCTION - places one machine instruction in memory. This procedure accepts two parameters, an operator and an operand, and places these in two memory locations just after the last generated machine instruction. This procedure uses a variable called INSTRUCTION_POINTER to keep track of the next location to receive an instruction. INSTRUCTION_POINTER is initialized to zero. Do not confuse this INSTRUCTION_POINTER with the one used by the simulator in the last chapter. They are two quite different things.

When the COMPILE_ASSIGNMENT procedure is entered, NEXT_WORD holds the name of the variable to be assigned a value. The procedure will do the following:

Skip over the '=' sign;
Find the beginning of the expression;
Generate instructions to place the value of the expression
    in the accumulator;
Generate a STORE instruction to assign the accumulator
    to the location corresponding to the variable
    in NEXT_WORD;

When we write this in PL/1, we get the COMPILE_ASSIGNMENT procedure.

```
COMPILE_ASSIGNMENT:PROCEDURE;
    /* SKIP '=' AND FIND START OF EXPRESSION */
    CALL SCAN_NON_BLANK_CHAR;
    CALL SCAN_NON_BLANK_CHAR;
    CALL COMPILE_EXPRESSION;
    CALL EMIT_INSTRUCTION(STORE,COMPILE_VARIABLE(NEXT_WORD));
    END;
```

As was done in the last chapter, the names of the machine instructions, LOAD, STORE, and so on are declared as variables and initialized to their appropriate numeric values. This allows us to write STORE in the call to EMIT_INSTRUCTION when we want to specify operator 2.

COMPILING PUT SKIP LIST STATEMENTS

The COMPILE_PUT_SKIP_LIST procedure is not much more complicated than COMPILE_ASSIGNMENT. If the output item to be printed is an expression, then the COMPILE_EXPRESSION procedure is called to generate instructions to place the expression's value in the accumulator. The PUT_INTEGER instruction will print the value in the accumulator; this instruction is generated by executing:

    CALL EMIT_INSTRUCTION(PUT_INTEGER,0);

Since the PUT_INTEGER instruction uses no operand, a dummy operand of zero is used.

If the output item is a literal, then the characters of the literal are collected and placed in the next available string location in the VS computer's special string memory. Then the PUT_STRING instruction is generated by

    CALL EMIT_INSTRUCTION(PUT_STRING,STRING_NUMBER);

The variable STRING_NUMBER gives the location of the literal.

COMPILING DO WHILE AND END

There are two complications in compiling DO WHILE and END. The first has to do with using the accumulator to evaluate two different expressions, without losing the value of either. The second has to do with making JUMP instructions transfer control to appropriate locations. We will now consider the first of these complications.

When our compiler encounters a card such as

    DO WHILE(I+1 <= J-K);

it must see that instructions are generated to evaluate both expressions, I+1 and J-K, before the comparison is made. The difficulty is that both evaluations use the accumulator. After I+1 is evaluated, its result, which will reside in the accumulator, is temporarily saved while J-K is evaluated in the accumulator. The following sequence of instructions performs the evaluations, the temporary saving of one value, the comparison and the conditional jump beyond the end of the DO WHILE loop.

```
LOAD       I
ADD        ONE
STORE      TEMPORARY          (save value of I+1)
LOAD       J
SUBTRACT   K
SKIP_LE    TEMPORARY          (compare values of I+1 and J-K)
JUMP       LOOPEND
```

These instructions are followed immediately by the body of the
loop. The value I+1 is saved in the location called TEMPORARY;
in our compiler we will arbitrarily make TEMPORARY correspond to
location 80.

The COMPILE_DO_WHILE procedure can generate the above
sequence of instructions by first executing

```
CALL COMPILE_EXPRESSION;     (generates LOAD I and ADD ONE)
CALL EMIT_INSTRUCTION(STORE,TEMPORARY);
```

Next, '<=' is skipped over and this is executed:

```
CALL COMPILE_EXPRESSION;      (generates LOAD J and SUBTRACT K)
CALL EMIT_INSTRUCTION(SKIP_LE,TEMPORARY);
```

Finally, this is executed:

```
CALL EMIT_INSTRUCTION(JUMP,0);
```

This leads us to the second complication in compiling DO WHILE
and END. When the JUMP instruction for DO WHILE is generated,
the compiler does not yet know where the end of the loop will be.
The operand of the JUMP is temporarily set to the dummy value of
zero.

Our compiler records the location of this JUMP instruction,
so its operand can be corrected when the END of the loop is
found. The COMPILE_END procedure corrects the operand of this
JUMP. It also generates a JUMP instruction to return to the
beginning of the loop. The COMPILE_END procedure must know the
location of the beginning of the loop so it can make the JUMP
instruction transfer to the correct location.

If PSP/3 programs were allowed to contain at most a single
un-nested DO WHILE loop, then we could easily produce the
required JUMP operands by using two variables:

```
DO_START - records location of beginning of loop.
DO_JUMP - records location of operand of JUMP at beginning
          of loop.
```

The COMPILE_DO_WHILE procedure would set DO_START to
INSTRUCTION_POINTER, which gives the location of the instruction
to be generated next, before generating instructions to evaluate
the left expression of the comparison. The COMPILE_DO_WHILE
procedure would set DO_JUMP to INSTRUCTION_POINTER+1 just before

generating the instruction JUMP 0.   The COMPILE_END procedure
would then execute

```
CALL EMIT_INSTRUCTION(JUMP,DO_START);
MEMORY(DO_JUMP)=INSTRUCTION_POINTER;
```

This generates a JUMP to the start of the loop and then corrects
the JUMP instruction at the beginning of the loop to transfer
control beyond the just generated JUMP instruction.

Things are not this simple in PSP/3, because DO WHILE loops
can be nested inside DO WHILE loops.   Whenever our compiler
encounters the END of a loop, it must match it with the nearest
preceding DO WHILE. It needs to keep track of the locations of
the DO WHILEs on a last-in-first-out basis. The last encountered
DO WHILE is the next one to be matched with an END.   Once the
compiler matches a DO WHILE to an END and produces the
appropriate JUMPs, it can discard the location of that DO WHILE.

We need a data structure that allows us to save the locations
of DO WHILEs until they are needed. What we need is a stack, as
was described in Chapter 17. We can establish a stack by the
declaration

```
DECLARE(STACK(20),STACK_TOP)FIXED;
```

We will initialize STACK_TOP to zero to indicate that the stack
is empty.

Before the COMPILE_DO_WHILE procedure generates any
instructions, it places the value of the INSTRUCTION_POINTER on
top of the stack. Just before it generates the JUMP instruction
that transfers control beyond the end of the loop, it places the
value of INSTRUCTION_POINTER+1 on top of the stack.   The
COMPILE_END procedure uses these stacked locations in this way:

```
/* CORRECT OPERAND OF JUMP AT BEGINNING OF LOOP */
MEMORY(STACK(STACK_TOP))=INSTRUCTION_POINTER+2;
STACK_TOP=STACK_TOP-1;
/* EMIT JUMP TO GO BACK TO BEGINNING OF LOOP */
CALL EMIT_INSTRUCTION(JUMP,STACK(STACK_TOP));
STACK_TOP=STACK_TOP-1;
```

Before executing these statements, the COMPILE_END procedure
checks to see if the stack is empty.   If it is empty, this
indicates that the END does not correspond to a DO WHILE.
Instead, it is the final END of the PSP/3 program, and a HALT
instruction is generated.

THE COMPILER

We have now described the modules of our compiler. We can put these modules together to make a procedure that compiles PSP/3 programs. Our compiler has this overall structure:

```
COMPILER:PROCEDURE;
    (declare the variables INSTRUCTION_POINTER, STRING_NUMBER,
        STACK, STACK_TOP, CARD, NEXT_WORD and NEXT_CHAR)
    (define the procedure READ_AND_PRINT_CARD)
    (define the scanner procedures SCAN_WORD, SCAN_CHAR
        and SCAN_NON_BLANK_CHAR)
    (define the procedure EMIT_INSTRUCTION)
    (define the procedures COMPILE_VARIABLE, COMPILE_VALUE,
        COMPILE_EXPRESSION, COMPILE_PUT_SKIP_LIST,
        COMPILE_ASSIGNMENT, COMPILE_DO_WHILE and COMPILE_END)
    Initialize INSTRUCTION_POINTER, STRING_NUMBER and STACK_TOP;
    Read and print three cards (%JOB, T:PROC ... and DECLARE ...);
    DO WHILE(CARD¬='%DATA');
        Read and print a card;
        CALL SCAN_WORD;
        Call the appropriate procedure among
            COMPILE_PUT_SKIP_LIST, COMPILE_ASSIGNMENT,
            COMPILE_DO_WHILE and COMPILE_END;
        END;
    END;
```

Our compiler must have access to arrays representing the regular and string memory of the VS computer. These arrays can be declared to be global to the compiler procedure via

```
DECLARE(MEMORY(0:99))FIXED;
DECLARE(STRING(10))CHARACTER(78)VARYING;
```

As we have explained, our compiler uses the words in the VS computer's memory as follows:

```
Locations 0 to 50 - used for instructions.
Locations 51 to 76 - used for variables A to Z.
Location 80 - used for TEMPORARY (saves the value of the left
            expression in a comparison).
Locations 90 to 99 - used for constants 0 to 9.
```

The compiler must have access to variables for each of the VS instructions

```
DECLARE(LOAD,STORE,...,HALT)FIXED;
```

These variables must be initialized to their corresponding machine language numeric values:

```
LOAD=1;
STORE=2;
...
HALT=9;
```

Here is the complete procedure that translates PSP/3 programs
into VS machine language:

```
/* THIS PROCEDURE COMPILES A PSP/3 PROGRAM */
COMPILER:PROCEDURE;
    DECLARE(INSTRUCTION_POINTER,STRING_NUMBER)FIXED;
    DECLARE(STACK(20),STACK_TOP)FIXED;
    DECLARE (CARD, NEXT_WORD) CHARACTER (80) VARYING,
        (NEXT_CHAR)CHARACTER(1)VARYING;

    READ_AND_PRINT_CARD:PROCEDURE;
        /* FOR PSP/3 PUNCH CARDS NOT IN QUOTES USE: */
        /* GET SKIP EDIT (CARD) (A(80));        */
        GET LIST(CARD);
        PUT SKIP LIST(CARD);
        END;

    SCAN_WORD:PROCEDURE;
        DO WHILE(SUBSTR(CARD,1,1)=' ');
            CARD=SUBSTR(CARD,2);
            END;
        NEXT_WORD='';
        DO WHILE(SUBSTR(CARD,1,1)>='A' & SUBSTR(CARD,1,1)<='Z');
            NEXT_WORD=NEXT_WORD||SUBSTR(CARD,1,1);
            CARD=SUBSTR(CARD,2);
            END;
        END;

    SCAN_CHAR:PROCEDURE;
        NEXT_CHAR=SUBSTR(CARD,1,1);
        CARD=SUBSTR(CARD,2);
        END;

    SCAN_NON_BLANK_CHAR:PROCEDURE;
        DO WHILE(SUBSTR(CARD,1,1)=' ');
            CARD=SUBSTR(CARD,2);
            END;
        NEXT_CHAR=SUBSTR(CARD,1,1);
        CARD=SUBSTR(CARD,2);
        END;

    /* PUT AN INSTRUCTION INTO THE MEMORY */
    EMIT_INSTRUCTION:PROCEDURE(OPERATOR,OPERAND);
        DECLARE(OPERATOR,OPERAND)FIXED;
        MEMORY(INSTRUCTION_POINTER)=OPERATOR;
        MEMORY(INSTRUCTION_POINTER+1)=OPERAND;
        INSTRUCTION_POINTER=INSTRUCTION_POINTER+2;
        END;
```

```
/* FOR IDENTIFIERS A TO Z, THIS WILL RETURN 51 TO 76, */
/* RESPECTIVELY                                        */
COMPILE_VARIABLE:PROCEDURE(LETTER)RETURNS(FIXED);
   DECLARE(LETTER)CHARACTER(*)VARYING;
   DECLARE(I)FIXED;
   I=1;
   DO WHILE(LETTER ¬=
          SUBSTR('ABCDEFGHIJKLMNOPQRSTUVWXYZ',I,1));
      I=I+1;
      END;
   RETURN(I+50);
   END;

/* FIND MEMORY LOCATION OF NEXT VARIABLE OR INTEGER ON */
/* CARD                                                */
COMPILE_VALUE:PROCEDURE RETURNS(FIXED);
   DECLARE(LOCATION)FIXED;
   IF NEXT_CHAR>='A' & NEXT_CHAR<='Z' THEN
      LOCATION=COMPILE_VARIABLE(NEXT_CHAR);
   ELSE
      DO;
         LOCATION=1;
         DO WHILE(NEXT_CHAR¬=SUBSTR('0123456789',
             LOCATION,1));
            LOCATION=LOCATION+1;
            END;
         /* INTEGERS 0 TO 9 ARE IN LOCATIONS 90-99 */
         LOCATION=LOCATION+89;
         /* PUT THE INTEGER'S VALUE INTO ITS LOCATION*/
         MEMORY(LOCATION)=LOCATION-90;
         END;
   CALL SCAN_NON_BLANK_CHAR;
   RETURN(LOCATION);
   END;

/* GENERATE CODE FOR NEXT EXPRESSION ON CARD */
COMPILE_EXPRESSION:PROCEDURE;
   DECLARE(PLUS_MINUS)CHARACTER(1)VARYING;
   CALL EMIT_INSTRUCTION(LOAD,COMPILE_VALUE);
   DO WHILE(NEXT_CHAR='+'|NEXT_CHAR='-');
      PLUS_MINUS=NEXT_CHAR;
      CALL SCAN_NON_BLANK_CHAR;
      IF PLUS_MINUS='+' THEN
         CALL EMIT_INSTRUCTION(ADD,COMPILE_VALUE);
      ELSE
         CALL EMIT_INSTRUCTION(SUBTRACT,COMPILE_VALUE);
      END;
   END;
```

```
COMPILE_PUT_SKIP_LIST:PROCEDURE;
   DECLARE(OUTPUT_STRING)CHARACTER(78)VARYING;
   /* IGNORE 'SKIP LIST('. FIND START OF OUTPUT ITEM. */
   CALL SCAN_WORD;
   CALL SCAN_WORD;
   CALL SCAN_NON_BLANK_CHAR;
   CALL SCAN_NON_BLANK_CHAR;
   /* SEE IF NEXT CHARACTER IS A QUOTE */
   IF NEXT_CHAR='''' THEN
      DO;
         CALL SCAN_CHAR;
         OUTPUT_STRING='';
         DO WHILE(NEXT_CHAR¬='''');
            OUTPUT_STRING=OUTPUT_STRING||NEXT_CHAR;
            CALL SCAN_CHAR;
            END;
         STRING(STRING_NUMBER)=OUTPUT_STRING;
         CALL EMIT_INSTRUCTION(PUT_STRING,STRING_NUMBER);
         STRING_NUMBER=STRING_NUMBER+1;
         END;
   ELSE
      DO;
         CALL COMPILE_EXPRESSION;
         CALL EMIT_INSTRUCTION(PUT_INTEGER,0);
         END;
   END;

COMPILE_ASSIGNMENT:PROCEDURE;
   /* SKIP '=' AND FIND START OF EXPRESSION */
   CALL SCAN_NON_BLANK_CHAR;
   CALL SCAN_NON_BLANK_CHAR;
   CALL COMPILE_EXPRESSION;
   CALL EMIT_INSTRUCTION(STORE,COMPILE_VARIABLE(NEXT_WORD));
   END;

COMPILE_DO_WHILE:PROCEDURE;
   DECLARE(TEMPORARY)FIXED;
   TEMPORARY=80;
   /* SKIP 'WHILE('. FIND START OF LEFT EXPRESSION */
   CALL SCAN_WORD;
   CALL SCAN_NON_BLANK_CHAR;
   CALL SCAN_NON_BLANK_CHAR;
   /* RECORD LOCATION OF BEGINNING OF LOOP ON TOP OF STACK */
   STACK_TOP=STACK_TOP+1;
   STACK(STACK_TOP)=INSTRUCTION_POINTER;
   CALL COMPILE_EXPRESSION;
   CALL EMIT_INSTRUCTION(STORE,TEMPORARY);
   /* SKIP OVER '<=' */
   CALL SCAN_NON_BLANK_CHAR;
   CALL SCAN_NON_BLANK_CHAR;
   CALL COMPILE_EXPRESSION;
   CALL EMIT_INSTRUCTION(SKIP_LE,TEMPORARY);
   /* RECORD LOCATION OF JUMP SO ITS OPERAND CAN BE CORRECTED */
   STACK_TOP=STACK_TOP+1;
   STACK(STACK_TOP)=INSTRUCTION_POINTER+1;
   CALL EMIT_INSTRUCTION(JUMP,0);
```

```
            END;

    COMPILE_END:PROCEDURE;
        /* SEE IF STACK HOLDS LOCATION OF 1 OR MORE DO WHILE'S */
        IF STACK_TOP>0 THEN
            DO;
                /* CORRECT OPERAND OF JUMP AT BEGINNING OF LOOP */
                MEMORY(STACK(STACK_TOP))=INSTRUCTION_POINTER+2;
                STACK_TOP=STACK_TOP-1;
                /* EMIT JUMP TO GO BACK TO BEGINNING OF LOOP. */
                CALL EMIT_INSTRUCTION(JUMP,STACK(STACK_TOP));
                STACK_TOP=STACK_TOP-1;
                END;
        ELSE
            /* THIS IS THE FINAL 'END' OF THE PSP/3 PROGRAM */
            CALL EMIT_INSTRUCTION(HALT,0);
        END;

    /* BODY OF PROCEDURE THAT COMPILES PSP/3 PROGRAMS */
    /* SKIP %JOB, T:PROC... AND DECLARE... */
    CALL READ_AND_PRINT_CARD;
    CALL READ_AND_PRINT_CARD;
    CALL READ_AND_PRINT_CARD;
    /* INITIALIZE INSTRUCTION_POINTER, STRING_NUMBER, STACK_TOP */
    INSTRUCTION_POINTER=0;
    STRING_NUMBER=1;
    STACK_TOP=0;
    DO WHILE(CARD¬='%DATA');
        CALL READ_AND_PRINT_CARD;
        CALL SCAN_WORD;
        IF NEXT_WORD='PUT' THEN
            CALL COMPILE_PUT_SKIP_LIST;
        IF LENGTH(NEXT_WORD)=1 THEN
            CALL COMPILE_ASSIGNMENT;
        IF NEXT_WORD='DO' THEN
            CALL COMPILE_DO_WHILE;
        IF NEXT_WORD='END' THEN
            CALL COMPILE_END;
        END;

END /* OF COMPILER */;
```

RUNNING THE COMPILED PROGRAM

We can have a PSP/3 program executed by translating it using our compiler, and then placing the machine language version of our program in the memory of a VS computer. The electronic circuitry of the VS computer would carry out the machine instructions corresponding to our program. By analogy, the PL/C compiler translates PL/1 programs to IBM 360 machine language and then has the IBM 360 computer execute the translated program.

Unfortunately, we do not have a VS computer. But we do have a simulator for VS machine language, which we developed in the last chapter, and we could use it to execute our translated PSP/3 program. This is accomplished by the following job, which both compiles and executes a PSP/3 program:

```
$JOB ID='MARG KIMBALL'
 /* COMPILE AND EXECUTE A PSP/3 PROGRAM */
 RUNPSP3:PROCEDURE OPTIONS(MAIN);
    DECLARE(MEMORY(0:99))FIXED;
    DECLARE(STRING(10))CHARACTER(78)VARYING;
    DECLARE(LOAD,STORE,...,HALT)FIXED;
    COMPILER:PROCEDURE;
        (PSP/3 compiler as given in this chapter)
        END;
    SIMULATOR:PROCEDURE;
        (simulator for VS computer as given in last chapter)
        END;
    LOAD=1;
    STORE=2;
    ...
    HALT=9;
    CALL COMPILER;
    CALL SIMULATOR;
    END;
$DATA
'%JOB                                           '
'T:PROCEDURE OPTIONS(MAIN);                      '
'    DECLARE(I)FIXED;                            '
'    PUT SKIP LIST(''POWERS OF 2'');             '
'    I=1;                                        '
'    DO WHILE(I<=8);                             '
'        PUT SKIP LIST(I);                       '
'        I=I+I;                                  '
'        END;                                    '
'    END;                                        '
'%DATA                                           '
```

If you want to run a PSP/3 program, make sure that your PSP/3 program has no errors. Remember, the compiler was simplified by ignoring the possibility of errors; it may fail miserably if it encounters a syntax error in a PSP/3 program.

CHAPTER 20 SUMMARY

In this chapter we showed how a program, called a compiler, can translate from a high-level language like PL/1 to machine language. A simple language called PSP/3 was defined to illustrate points about syntax, language specification and translation. We presented a compiler written in PL/1 that translates error-free PSP/3 programs to the machine language for the VS computer described in the last chapter. If this compiler is combined with the VS computer simulator given in the last chapter, we have a program that compiles and executes PSP/3 programs. The following important terms were discussed in this chapter:

Syntax (or grammar) - a set of rules that specify the legal forms of programs in a particular programming language.

Non-terminal symbol - a symbol such as "statement" used in syntax rules to represent a set of possibilities. Non-terminal symbols do not appear in the final program.

Terminal symbol - a symbol such as "PROCEDURE", ";" or "I" that appears in the final program.

Producing a program - using the syntax rules to create a program by successively replacing non-terminal symbols until only terminal symbols remain.

Recursive definition - defining a term in a way that uses the term. For example, in PSP/3 a DO WHILE loop is defined recursively as a statement with the form

```
DO WHILE(expression<=expression);
    {statement}
END;
```

This is recursive because a statement inside a DO WHILE loop can be a DO WHILE loop.

Stack - a data structure providing last-in-first-out manipulation of data, as described in Chapter 17. Stacks are used in compilers for keeping track of nested structures, including DO WHILE loops and parenthesized expressions.

CHAPTER 20 EXERCISES

1. The PSP/3 compiler given in this chapter requires the following six types of lines to be on separate cards:

```
(1) T:PROCEDURE OPTIONS(MAIN);
(2) DECLARE(...)FIXED;
(3) PUT SKIP LIST(...);
(4) DO WHILE(...);
(5) END;
(6) variable=expression;
```

Modify the PSP/3 compiler so that more than one of these can appear on a card.

2. Modify the PSP/3 compiler and VS simulator so that any attempt to use an uninitialized variable is detected. For example, the following job should be stopped by the simulator in line 4 when the uninitialized value of J is accessed.

```
1     %JOB
2     T:PROCEDURE OPTIONS(MAIN);
3        DECLARE(I,J)FIXED;
4        I=J;
5        PUT SKIP LIST(I);
6        END;
7     %DATA
```

The use of an uninitialized variable can be detected in the following manner. Before the program begins execution, the values of all variables are set to some special value, say 99999. When the simulator executes the LOAD instruction, it checks to see if the loaded value is 99999. If so, the program is stopped and an error message is printed. (The SP/k and PL/C compilers use a technique similar to this for detecting the use of uninitialized variables.)

3. Modify the PSP/3 compiler as given in this chapter so that it prints an error message if a variable is used but not declared. This can be done in the following manner. An array having 26 elements is declared and initialized so that all elements are zero. When the compiler reads the declaration, the elements of the array corresponding to declared variables are set from zero to one. Whenever a variable is encountered in the remainder of the PSP/3 program, a check is made to see if the corresponding array element is zero or one. If it is zero, an error message is printed.

APPENDIX 1

SPECIFICATIONS FOR THE
SP/k LANGUAGE

SP/k is a sequence of subsets of the PL/1 language that has been developed for the purpose of teaching computer programming. SP/k was designed at the University of Toronto, and this appendix is an adaption of a technical report by Richard C. Holt and David B. Wortman.

Since SP/k is a compatible subset of PL/1, SP/k programs can be run under a variety of compilers, including the University of Toronto's SP/k compiler and Cornell University's PL/C compiler. Details about running SP/k programs under the SP/k compiler are given in Appendix 4.

In the interest of making PL/1 more suitable for pedagogic purposes, SP/k restricts or eliminates many PL/1 features. In SP/k every variable must be declared. Declarations are not allowed to specify number bases (binary versus decimal) or precisions; this avoids problems arising from the precision rules of full PL/1. Implicit conversions are not allowed among numeric, logical and character types, thereby eliminating conversion anomalies.

Features implied by the following keywords are not in SP/k: binary, complex, initial, external, pointer, goto, on, and begin. The following PL/1 features are eliminated: fixed-length character strings, label variables, operations on entire arrays, pseudo variables, data directed input-output, static allocation, controlled allocation, based allocation, multitasking, and compile-time processing.

Instead of giving a complete list of the omitted PL/1 features, we will specify SP/k by giving a list of included features. Language features introduced by subsets SP/1 to SP/8 are summarized in the following table.

Subset   Features Introduced

SP/1   Characters: letters, digits and special characters
        Constants: fixed, float and character string
        Expressions: +, -, *, /, fixed to float conversion

```
                Simple output:  put list
                Mathematical built-in functions:  mod, sin, cos, atan,
                    log, exp, sqrt

SP/2            Identifiers and variables
                Declarations:  fixed and float
                Assignment statements (with float to fixed conversion)
                Simple input:  get list

SP/3            Comparisons: <, >, =, <=, >=, ¬=
                Logical expressions:  &, |, and ¬
                Selection:  if-then-else and non-iterative do group
                Repetition:  do while loop and indexed do loop
                Paragraphing
                Logical constants:  '0'B (false) and '1'B (true)
                Logical variables:  the bit attribute

SP/4            Character string expressions: concatenation
                Character string variables (varying length only)
                Character string comparison and blank padding
                Character string built-in functions:  length and substr

SP/5            Arrays (including multiple dimensions)

SP/6            Procedures:  subroutines and functions
                Calling and returning
                Arguments and parameters
                Side effects and dummy arguments
                Arrays and character strings as arguments

SP/7            Detailed control of input and output: get and put edit

SP/8            Records (PL/1 structures) (one level only)
                Files: open and close
                Record oriented input and output: read and write
```

The following sections give detailed specifications for each subset. In describing the subsets, we will use this notation:

```
        [item] means the item is optional
        [item] means the item can appear zero or more times
```

When presenting the syntax of language constructs, items written in <u>upper case</u> letters, for example,

```
        PROCEDURE
```

denote keywords; these items must appear in SP/k jobs exactly as presented. Items written in <u>lower case</u> letters, for example,

```
        statement
```

denote one of a class of constructs; each such item is defined below as it is introduced.

SP/1: INTRODUCTION OF EXPRESSIONS AND OUTPUT

We now begin the specification of the first subset.

A <u>character</u> is a letter or a digit or a special character.

A <u>letter</u> is one of the following:

    A B C D E F G H I J K L M N O P Q R S T U V W X Y Z $ # ∂

A <u>digit</u> is one of the following:

    0 1 2 3 4 5 6 7 8 9

A <u>special</u> <u>character</u> is one of the following:

    + - * / ( ) = < > . : ; , ? % & | ¬
    b (blank)
    ' (apostrophe or single quote)
    _ (break character or underscore)

A <u>fixed</u> <u>constant</u> is one or more digits (without embedded blanks),
for example:

    4 19 243 92153

A <u>float</u> <u>constant</u> consists of a mantissa followed by an exponent
(without embedded blanks). The <u>mantissa</u> must be one or more
digits with an optional decimal point. The <u>exponent</u> must be the
letter E, followed by an optional plus or minus sign followed by
one or more digits. The following are examples of float
constants.

    5.16E+00 50E0 .9418E24 1.E-2

Note that fixed constant must <u>not</u> contain a decimal point. Note
also that a float constant need not contain a decimal point, but
<u>must</u> contain an exponent.

There is a maximum allowed number of digits in a fixed
constant. There is a maximum allowed number of digits in the
mantissa of a float constant and a maximum allowed magnitude of
exponent. (These maximum values will vary from compiler to
compiler; see Appendix 4.)

A <u>literal</u> (or <u>character</u> <u>string</u> <u>constant</u>) is a single quote (an
apostrophe), followed by zero or more occurrences of non-single-
quote characters or twice repeated single quotes, followed by a
single quote. The following are examples of literals:

    'FRED' 'X=24' 'MR. O''REILLY'

There is a maximum length of character strings (see Appendix 4).

Each constant must appear entirely on one card, i.e., constants must not cross card boundaries.

In SP/1, an <u>expression</u> is one of the following:

```
fixed constant
float constant
literal
+expression
-expression
expression + expression
expression - expression
expression * expression
expression / expression
(expression)
built-in function
```

Float and fixed values may be combined in expressions. When a fixed value is combined with a float value, the result is a float value.

Evaluation of expressions proceeds from left to right, with the exceptions that multiplications and divisions have higher precedence than (i.e., are evaluated before) additions and subtractions and that parenthesized sub-expressions are evaluated before being used in arithmetic operations. Unary operations (+ and -) are evaluated before binary operations. Division (/) can be used only when one or both of the operands are float values. Division of a fixed value by a fixed value is not allowed. The following are examples of legal expressions.

$$-4+20 \quad 2*8.5E+00 \quad (4.0E+01-12.0E+01)/-2$$

The values of these three expressions are, respectively, 16, 17.0E+00, and 4.0E+01.

Character strings cannot be used in arithmetic operations. In SP/k there are no implicit conversions from numeric values to character string values or vice versa.

An SP/1 built-in function call is one of the following:

```
MOD( expression , expression )
SIN( expression )
COS( expression )
ATAN( expression )
LOG( expression )
EXP( expression )
SQRT( expression )
```

The MOD function accepts two fixed expressions as arguments and produces a fixed result. The SIN, COS, ATAN, LOG, EXP, and SQRT mathematical functions accept a single fixed or float expression as an argument and produce a float result. Appendix 3 gives a more detailed description of SP/k built-in functions.

An SP/1 <u>statement</u> is one of the following:

```
PUT [SKIP] LIST(expression {,expression} );
PUT PAGE LIST(expression {,expression} );
```

An SP/1 <u>program</u> is: T:PROCEDURE OPTIONS(MAIN);
                               {statement}
                             END;

Remember that the notation {statement} means zero or more statements. The following is an example of an SP/1 program:

```
T:PROCEDURE OPTIONS(MAIN);
  PUT SKIP LIST(2, 'PLUS', 3, 'MAKES', 2+3);
  END;
```

The output from this example is: 2   PLUS   3   MAKES   5

Output produced by the PUT LIST statement is placed in successive "fields" across the print line. All fields have the same width. A new print line is started when all fields on the preceding line have been used, or when SKIP (or PAGE) is used in the PUT LIST statement. (See Appendix 4 for the number of and size of these fields.)

When a literal is printed by a PUT LIST statement, its enclosing single quotes are removed. In addition, twice repeated single quotes in a literal are printed as one single quote. A long string may use several fields. If the printed string exactly fills all the columns of a field, then the next field is skipped.

There may be slight differences in the handling of certain aspects of the SP/1 subset by different compilers. These differences include the following:

1. Length of character strings. Most compilers allow character strings to be at least 127 characters long.

2. Number of digits in fixed numbers. Most compilers allow at least 5 digits.

3. Number of digits in the mantissa of a float number. Most compilers allow at least 6 mantissa digits.

4. Magnitude of float numbers. Most compilers allow the magnitude of float numbers to be at least 1E36.

5. Use of columns of punch cards for programs. Some compilers allow only columns 2 through 72 of a punch card to be used for the program. Of course, this restriction does not apply to mark sense cards. All 80 columns of a punch card can be used for data.

(See Appendix 4 for more details on the above points.)

SP/2: INTRODUCTION TO VARIABLES, INPUT AND ASSIGNMENT

We now begin the specifications of the second subset, SP/2.

An identifier is a letter followed by zero or more letters, digits, or break characters (underscores). An identifier cannot contain embedded blanks. Most compilers allow identifiers to be at least 31 characters long. Some compilers limit the identifier which names a program to 7 characters.

An SP/2 program is: identifier:PROCEDURE OPTIONS(MAIN);
                          {declaration}
                          {statement }
                       END;

A declaration is: DECLARE(variable {,variable})attribute
                       {,(variable {,variable})attribute};

An attribute is one of the following:
                       FIXED
                       FLOAT

A statement is one of the following:
                       PUT [SKIP] LIST(expression {,expression});
                       PUT PAGE LIST(expression {,expression});
                       variable = expression;
                       GET [SKIP] LIST(variable {,variable});

In SP/2, each variable is simply an identifier. (There are no arrays in SP/2.) In SP/k all variables must be declared. In SP/2 an expression may be a variable.

In SP/2 an expression may be a variable.

Float values may be assigned to fixed variables. Any non-integer part of such a float value is truncated toward zero before the assignment without a warning message. Fixed values may be assigned to float variables with automatic conversion.

The items in the data (the input stream) read by GET LIST statements must be separated by one or more blanks. When a GET LIST statement is executed, one data item is read for each variable in the statement.

Each item in the input stream must be a literal, a float constant, a fixed constant or a non-integer fixed constant. An optional minus sign can precede each item. A non-integer fixed constant is one or more digits with a decimal point. The follow-ing are examples of non-integer fixed constants:

                3.14159   243.12

Non-integer fixed constants should not appear in programs, but can appear in data.

Any numeric constant (float, fixed or non-integer fixed) can be read (and will be automatically converted if necessary) into a float variable. Similarly, any numeric constant can be read (and will be automatically truncated if necessary) into a fixed variable. There are no automatic conversions from character string values to numeric values or vice versa.

A keyword is any of the special identifiers, e.g., PROCEDURE, GET, and LIST, that are part of the SP/k syntax. A variable must not be given the same name as a keyword.

Any number of blanks (or card boundaries) can appear between symbols, e.g., between constants, keywords, identifiers, operators +, -, *, / and the parentheses (and). When constants, keywords or identifiers are adjacent, for example, the adjacent keywords PUT and LIST, they must be separated by at least one blank.

A comment consists of the characters /* followed by any characters except the combination */ followed by the characters */. A blank cannot appear between the / and * or between the * and /. Comments can appear wherever blanks can appear. A comment must not cross a card boundary. Hence, any comment which would cross a card boundary should be closed by */ at the end of one card and continued by /* on the next card. In general, it is good practice for comments to appear on separate lines or at the ends of lines. Some compilers do not allow the initial /* of a comment to start in card column 1. Comments cannot appear in the data.

SP/3: INTRODUCTION OF LOGICAL EXPRESSIONS, SELECTION AND REPETITION

A <u>condition</u> is one of the following:

```
'0'B
'1'B
¬condition
condition & condition
condition | condition
comparison
(condition)
logical variable
```

A condition is sometimes called a <u>logical expression</u>. The constant '0'B means "false" and '1'B means "true".

A <u>comparison</u> is one of the following:

```
expression < expression
expression > expression
expression = expression
expression <= expression
expression >= expression
expression ¬= expression
```

An <u>attribute</u> is one of the following:

```
FIXED
FLOAT
BIT
```

Variables declared to have the BIT attribute are called <u>logical variables</u>. Logical variables can be operands in the logical operations of <u>and</u> (&), <u>or</u> (|) and <u>not</u> (¬). Float and fixed values cannot be operands in logical operations.

(Some compilers, namely, PL/C and PL/1 F, do not allow logical variables to be declared as simply BIT. For these compilers, the attribute BIT(1) must be used instead.)

The <u>and</u> operator (&) has higher priority than the <u>or</u> operator (|). Logical variables can be compared, assigned, read, and printed. Logical variables can be compared only for equality or inequality.

There is no implicit conversion between numeric values (fixed and float) and logical values. Logical values cannot participate in arithmetic operations.

An SP/3 <u>statement</u> is one of the following:

```
PUT [SKIP] LIST(expression {,expression} );
PUT PAGE LIST(expression {,expression} );
variable = expression;
GET [SKIP] LIST(variable {,variable} );
IF condition THEN
   statement
[ELSE
   statement]
DO WHILE(condition);
   {statement}
   END;
DO identifier = expression TO expression [BY expression];
   {statement}
   END;
DO;
   {statement}
   END;
```

In the indexed DO group (second DO group above), the index variable (identifier) must have been declared to be a fixed variable. (Even after arrays are introduced, the index must still be simple, i.e., not an array element.) Each of the expressions is evaluated once at the beginning of the execution of the loop. The BY clause specifies a step size. If the BY clause is omitted, a step size of 1 is assumed.

When the third expression (step size) is positive, the indexed DO group is equivalent to the following:

```
start = first expression;
limit = second expression;
step = third expression (or 1 if no by clause);
identifier = start;
DO WHILE(identifier <= limit);
   {statement}
   identifier = identifier + step;
   END;
```

If the third expression is negative, the comparison in the above DO WHILE group becomes >=.

The following is an example of an SP/3 program.

```
SP3:PROCEDURE OPTIONS(MAIN);
   DECLARE(N,X,TOTAL)FIXED;
   TOTAL=0;
   GET LIST(N);
   DO WHILE(N>0);
      GET LIST(X);
      TOTAL=TOTAL+X;
      N=N-1;
      END;
   PUT LIST('TOTAL IS',TOTAL);
   END;
```

<u>Paragraphing</u> <u>rules</u> are standard conventions for indenting
program lines. Some compilers provide automatic paragraphing of
programs. If this feature is available, it should be used.

A set of paragraphing rules can be inferred from the method
used to present SP/k constructs. For example, the DO WHILE group
was presented in the following form:

```
DO WHILE(condition);
   {statement}
   END;
```

This form means that the statements enclosed in a DO WHILE group
should be indented beyond the level of the opening "DO WHILE"
line. The construct "END;" which closes the group should be
indented to the same level as the enclosed statements.

Comments should be indented to the same level as their
corresponding program lines. The continuation(s) of a long
program line should be indented beyond the line's original
indentation. If the level of indentation becomes too deep, it
may be necessary to abandon indentation rules temporarily,
maintaining a vertical positioning of lines.

SP/4: INTRODUCTION OF CHARACTER STRING VARIABLES AND EXPRESSIONS

An <u>attribute</u> is one of the following:

    FIXED
    FLOAT
    CHARACTER(maximum length)VARYING
    BIT

Variables declared to have the attribute CHARACTER(maximum length)VARYING are called <u>character</u> <u>string</u> <u>variables</u>. In the declaration of character string variables, <u>maximum length</u> must be a fixed constant. The concatenation operator (||) can be used to join two strings together. Both of its operands must be character strings.

There are two built-in functions, SUBSTR and LENGTH, which operate on character string values. The SUBSTR built-in function can accept two or three arguments. (SUBSTR cannot be used as a PL/1 pseudo variable.) See Appendix 3 for a detailed description of SUBSTR.

The LENGTH built-in function has one argument which must be a character string expression. Character strings can be compared, assigned, read and printed. When character strings of different lengths are compared, the shorter string is automatically extended (on the right) with blanks to the length of the longer string.

In general, a character string variable assumes the length of the string which is assigned to it (or read into it via a get list statement). However, if the maximum length of the variable being assigned to is less than the length of the string being assigned, then before assignment the assigned value is automatically truncated (on the right) to this maximum length.

There is no implicit conversion between character string values and numeric or logical values.

SP/5: INTRODUCTION OF ARRAYS

The form of declaration remains as it was:

A <u>declaration</u> is: DECLARE(variable {,variable})attribute
                        {,(variable {,variable})attribute};

However, the form of <u>variable</u> is now allowed to specify array bounds. In a declaration, a variable is now:

identifier [(range {,range})]

A <u>range</u> is one of the following:

fixed constant
[-] fixed constant : [-] fixed constant

The first form of range assumes the lower bound is 1, and specifies the upper bound. The second form specifies both the lower and upper bounds.

In an expression, or in a GET LIST statement, a variable has the form:

identifier [(expression {,expression})]

Each array index expression must have a numeric value. A float value used as an array index will be truncated to a fixed value.

Array elements may be compared, assigned, read, and printed on an element by element basis, in the same way as scalar variables with similar attributes.

SP/6: INTRODUCTION OF PROCEDURES

In SP/6 the form of <u>program</u> is extended to allow the definition of (internal) procedures.

A SP/6 <u>program</u> is: identifier:PROCEDURE OPTIONS(MAIN);
                            {declaration}
                            {definition }
                            {statement }
                            END;

A <u>definition</u> is: identifier:PROCEDURE [(identifier {,identifier})]
                            [RETURNS(attribute)];
                            {declaration}
                            {definition }
                            {statement }
                            END;

Two new statements are added:

                            CALL procedure name [(expression {,expression})];
                            RETURN [(expression)];

All parameters to a procedure must be declared. Parameters are passed to procedures "by reference"; this means that when a procedure assigns a value to a parameter, the corresponding argument in the call to the procedure actually receives the value. If an array is a parameter, then the ranges for each array index must be declared by an asterisk (*) in the procedure. If a character string is a parameter, then the maximum length of the character string must be declared by an asterisk (*) in the procedure. This example illustrates these requirements:

        SUPERSTR:PROCEDURE(S,I);
            DECLARE(S)CHARACTER(*)VARYING;
            DECLARE(I(*,*))FIXED;
            ...
            END;

A <u>subroutine</u> is a procedure which does not have the RETURNS clause in its definition. A subroutine can be invoked only by the CALL statement. Return from a subroutine must be (a) via a RETURN statement without the optional RETURN expression or (b) via the last statement of the subroutine (when the last statement is not a RETURN statement).

A <u>function</u> is a procedure which has the RETURNS clause in its definition. A function can be invoked only by using its name (with arguments if required) in an expression. Return from a function must be via a RETURN statement having an expression whose attribute matches the attribute given in the RETURNS clause. (It is legal to have a fixed value as the RETURN expression in a float function and vice versa; automatic conversion of returned values will take place for these cases.)

SP/7: INTRODUCTION OF EDIT DIRECTED INPUT AND OUTPUT

Statements giving explicit control of the format of input and output data are introduced.

A <u>statement</u> is one of the following:

a. PUT SKIP [(lines to skip)];
b. PUT [SKIP[(lines to skip)]] LIST (expression
      {,expression});
c. PUT PAGE LIST (expression {,expression});
d. PUT [SKIP[(lines to skip)]] EDIT (expression
      {,expression})(format item {,format item});
e. PUT PAGE EDIT (expression {,expression})
      (format item {,format item});
f. PUT PAGE;
g. variable = expression;
h. GET SKIP [(cards to skip)];
i. GET [SKIP[(cards to skip)]] LIST (variable
      {,variable});
j. GET [SKIP[(cards to skip)]] EDIT (variable
      {,variable})(format item {,format item});
k. IF condition THEN
      statement
   [ELSE
      statement]
l. DO WHILE (condition);
      {statement}
      END;
m. DO identifier=expression TO expression
      [BY expression];
      {statement}
      END;
n. DO;
      {statement}
      END;
o. CALL procedure name [(expression {,expression})];
p. RETURN [(expression)];

PUT EDIT statements (forms d and e above) allow the specification of a particular number of columns to be printed. When successive items are printed via a PUT EDIT statement, each item is printed immediately next to the preceding item. This is in contrast to PUT LIST statements, which cause items to be printed in equal fields across the page. GET EDIT statements (form j above) are analogous and allow the specification of particular card columns to be read. This means that EDIT data items need not be separated by blanks or commas.

It is possible to use both LIST directed input-output and EDIT directed input-output in the same program. To avoid confusion, LIST and EDIT directed input-output should not be mixed in printing a particular line, or in reading a particular card. Those who insist upon mixing the two for printing a single line should understand the following details. LIST output always proceeds to the next standard output field, while EDIT output always starts at the current position. LIST output actually prints a blank after each item; hence, when an EDIT item follows a LIST item on a print line, the two will be separated by a blank. Those who insist upon mixing LIST and EDIT directed input when reading a single card should understand the following details. Each LIST data item must be followed immediately by a comma or blank. If the next read is via a GET EDIT statement, the current position is taken to be that just beyond this blank or comma. Following the reading of a data item via GET EDIT, scanning for a LIST data item begins just beyond the EDIT item.

In the PUT SKIP forms (a, b, and d above), <u>lines to skip</u> can be any numeric expression; if the value is float, it is truncated to fixed. If the <u>lines to skip</u> clause is omitted from the SKIP clause, then the remainder of the current line is left blank and output continues on the next line.

If the value of <u>lines to skip</u>, call it x, is positive, then the printer will return to column 1 while performing x line ejects. Putting this another way, the remaining columns (if any) of the current line will be left blank, and x-1 blank lines will then be printed. If x is zero (or negative), the effect is a return to column 1 of the current line (with no line eject). Note: when x is equal to 1, it is equivalent to omitting the <u>lines to skip</u> clause.

In the GET SKIP forms (h, i, and j above), if the <u>cards to skip</u> clause is omitted from the SKIP clause, the remainder of the current card is ignored, and input continues from the next card.

In the GET SKIP forms, <u>cards to skip</u> can be an expression. If it is a float value, it is truncated to a fixed value. This fixed value, call it x, must be at least 1. The next x cards (where the remainder of the current card counts as one card) will be ignored. Note: SKIP(1) is equivalent to SKIP with <u>cards to skip</u> omitted.

If a SKIP clause is specified and the current card or line is positioned after the last valid data column, then one card or line is counted as having been skipped by moving to the next card or line even though there were no available data columns to be skipped.

A <u>format item</u> is one of the following:

X(width)	(to skip columns)
COLUMN(position)	(to skip columns)
F(width [,fractional digits])	(for numeric values)
E(width, fractional digits)	(for numeric values)
A[(width)]	(for character strings)
B(width)	(for logical values)
P picture specification	(to print dollars)

The X and COLUMN format items are used only for control of
the format (skipping columns). The other format items, F, E, A,
B, and P, are data transferring items. In the EDIT forms (d, e,
and j above) there must be the same number of data transferring
format items as there are data items to be transferred. The last
format item of a list must be a data transferring item and can
not be X or COLUMN.

The terms <u>position</u>, <u>width</u>, or <u>fractional digits</u> must be
arithmetic expressions; usually these are fixed constants. If
the value is float, it is truncated to a fixed value.

The format item X(width) causes <u>width</u> columns to be skipped
on input, or <u>width</u> blanks to be printed on output. If <u>width</u> is
negative it is treated as zero. (Note: punch cards have 80
columns. Lines have 120 columns on many printers; however, other
printers may provide, for example, 72, 80 or 132 columns.)

The COLUMN format item causes skipping of columns until the
column numbered <u>position</u> is reached. If <u>position</u> is zero or
negative, or if <u>position</u> is greater than the size of the card or
line, it is replaced by one. If the current card or line is
already positioned after column <u>position</u>, a skip to the next card
or line is performed, followed by skipping columns until the
column numbered <u>position</u> is reached.

The F and E format items are used to read and write either
FIXED and FLOAT variables.

For E and F format items on output, fractions are rounded and
not truncated when insufficient space is allocated for the
fractional digits. The values printed under control of E and F
format items are right-justified and padded on the left with
blanks.

On input, the F format item causes the next <u>width</u> columns to
be read as a fixed number. If <u>fractional digits</u> is given in the
format item, it must be at least one and it specifies the
insertion of a decimal point the given number of places from the
right of the number, producing a non-integer fixed constant; the
effect is that if the decimal point is omitted from the data,
scaling occurs. If <u>fractional digits</u> is omitted, the data is
assumed to be an integer fixed constant. If a decimal point
appears in the input data, then the actual value of the data is
used, ignoring the specified <u>fractional digits</u>. The number being
read may be preceded or followed by blanks. A completely blank
field is read as zero. (Note: when a non-integer fixed constant
is read into a FIXED variable, the value is truncated to an
integer.) On output, if <u>fractional digits</u> is not specified, an
integer is printed with no decimal point, but if it is specified,
a non-integer fixed constant is printed with the designated
precision of fraction. In no case does the F format item cause
scaling on output.

The E format item on input causes the reading of a field of
size <u>width</u> containing a float constant. If a decimal point is

present in the float constant, the specification of <u>fractional</u>
<u>digits</u> is ignored. Otherwise, a decimal point is inserted
<u>fractional</u> <u>digits</u> from the right of the mantissa (the effect is
that if the decimal point is omitted in the data, scaling
occurs). If the field is completely blank, this is an error.
The exponent can be omitted from values read under control of the
E format item. On output, the number is printed as a float
constant. (Note: the <u>fractional</u> <u>digits</u> field must be specified
in the E format item.)

When using an E format item on output, the field width must
be at least large enough to print the float value. In particular,
the number of columns specified by <u>width</u> should be at least seven
plus <u>fractional</u> <u>digits</u>. (The float value is printed in the form
mD.{f}Esdd where m is a possible leading minus sign, D is a non-
zero digit (unless the float value is zero), {f} is the string of
fractional digits, s is a plus or minus sign, and dd is the
exponent magnitude.)

The A format item is used for the transfer of character data.
The specified number of characters are transferred. On input,
quotes are not required around the data item. On output, if the
field is wider than the data item, the item is left-justified and
padded with blanks on the right; if the field is not as wide as
the data item, the item is truncated on the right. On output
<u>width</u> can be omitted and then the current length of the data item
is used. (The <u>width</u> field must be specified for input.)

The B format item is used for transfer of logical (declared
BIT) data items. On input, the value can be preceded or followed
by blanks. On output, the value is printed left-justified and
padded on the right with blanks. Logical data values are 0 or 1
(not '0'B or '1'B as they are within a program and for LIST
input-output).

For format items F, E, A, and B, <u>width</u> must be greater than
zero.

The P format item is used for writing numbers, usually as
dollar values. Numbers cannot be read using the P format item.
Only FIXED values can be written using this format item. Each P
format item consists of the letter P followed by a sequence of
<u>picture</u> <u>elements</u> in quotes. For example, P'$ZZ,ZZ9.99DB' is a P
format item whose sequence of picture elements is $ZZ,ZZ9.99DB.
The following picture elements can be used.

element	use
.	period insertion
,	comma insertion
$	floating dollar sign
Z	digit position, suppress zero
9	digit position
CR	negative indicator
DB	negative indicator

These elements must appear in a picture specification in this order. First, zero or more dollar signs with optional periods and commas. Next, zero or more Zs with optional periods and commas. Next, one or more 9s with optional periods and commas. Finally, an optional CR or DB; this is printed for negative numbers.

The period is printed where specified if a digit is to be printed to its immediate left, otherwise a blank is printed.

(Note: since FIXED variables must have integer values in SP/k, dollar values should be represented internally as cents. When printing such a value, the decimal point for dollars can be inserted using a period in a picture specification.)

Similarly, a comma is printed where specified if a digit is to be printed to its immediate left, otherwise a blank is printed.

The dollar sign indicates that a digit may be printed, unless the digit is a leading zero in which case blank is printed, except for the rightmost of a series of such dollar sign positions, and here a dollar sign is printed. The dollar sign will also "float" across commas and periods that are embedded in a series of dollar signs.

The Z signifies printing of a digit unless it would be a leading zero, in which case a blank is printed. The nine signifies that a digit (0 to 9) is to be printed. The credit symbol (CR) or debit symbol (DB) is printed only if the number is negative. If a negative number is to be printed, then DB or CR must be present.

The following is an example of the use of a picture format item:

    PUT EDIT(21612)(P'$ZZ,ZZ9.99DB');

This statement will print $bbb216.12bb (the letter b is used here to represent a blank). Now consider this statement:

    PUT EDIT(PROFIT)(P'$$,$$9.99DB');

This table gives the output for selected values of PROFIT:

PROFIT	output
259271	$2,592.71
39100	$391.00
2516	$25.16
5	$0.05
-481	$4.81DB

some compilers such as PL/C disallow P format items.

SP/8: INTRODUCTION OF STRUCTURES AND FILES

The form of <u>declaration</u> is extended to allow definition of structures and files.

A <u>declaration</u> is one of the following:

a. DECLARE (variable {,variable})attribute
       {,(variable {,variable})attribute};
b. DECLARE 1 variable,
             2 variable attribute
             {,2 variable attribute};
c. DECLARE 1 variable LIKE identifier;

The form b allows the definition of structures. A structure is an aggregate of several <u>fields</u> or data items. The fields can have different attributes, and any field can be an array. Arrays of structures are defined by including <u>ranges</u> in the <u>variable</u> following the integer 1 in the declaration. Structures cannot contain other structures as fields and thus are of only one level.

The form c allows the definition of a structure or array of structures with the same <u>template</u> (field names and attributes) as another structure. The <u>identifier</u> must be a structure identifier. The newly-declared structure variable only inherits the template of <u>identifier</u>, not its dimensionality. If the structure variable is to represent an array, the ranges must be explicitly given. The structure referred to by LIKE must not itself have been declared using LIKE.

An <u>attribute</u> is one of the following:

FIXED
FLOAT
CHARACTER (maximum length) VARYING
BIT
RECORD FILE

A variable with the attribute RECORD FILE allows access to a collection of records external to the main memory of the computer. A field of a structure cannot have the attribute RECORD FILE. This collection is called a <u>dataset</u> or <u>file</u>. Arrays of files are not allowed, and files cannot be assigned, compared, or passed as parameters. Each record corresponds to a structure. The data set consists of records all of the same template. Some compilers restrict the name of a file to be at most seven characters long. One record at a time can be transferred from the dataset to a structure or from a structure to the dataset by using READ and WRITE statements, respectively.

The following statements are introduced:

a. OPEN FILE(file name)INPUT;

```
b. OPEN FILE(file name)OUTPUT;
c. CLOSE FILE(file name);
d. READ FILE(file name)INTO(structure name)
e. WRITE FILE(file name)FROM(structure name)
```

The parenthesized file name following the keyword FILE in the forms a to e must have been declared with the attribute RECORD FILE.

Files allow sequential access to datasets. The OPEN statement establishes a communication path between the file variable and an external dataset. When an OPEN statement is executed, the file is positioned at the first record of the dataset. An OPEN must be the first operation performed on any file.

A file opened for INPUT can only have READ or CLOSE performed on it. A file opened for OUTPUT can only have WRITE or CLOSE performed on it.

The CLOSE statement dissolves the communication path between the file variable and the associated external dataset. A file can be closed and reopened in a program, and the mode (INPUT or OUTPUT) is independent of previous usage of the file. Within a given program, all structures transferred to and from a particular file must be LIKE each other, or LIKE the same structure.

A field of a structure is always referred to by the name of its containing structure, followed by a period, followed by the field name. If either the structure or the field is an array, parenthesized subscripts must immediately follow the corresponding name(s).

The following is an example of a declaration of a structure:

```
DECLARE 1 OBSERVATION(100),
          2 TIME FIXED,
          2 SIZE FIXED;
```

This statement assigns 12 to the TIME field of the 23rd structure:

```
OBSERVATION(23).TIME=12;
```

Structures can be read into, written from, assigned, and passed as parameters. No other operations can be performed on structures. One structure can be assigned to another only if one is LIKE the other or both are LIKE the same structure. Similarly, if a structure is passed as a parameter, the formal parameter that it corresponds to must be LIKE it, or they must both be LIKE the same structure.

Fields of structures can be used in LIST or EDIT input and output statements, but whole structures cannot be transferred by these statements.

The following is an example of an SP/8 program. This program reads a dataset into an array of structures, sorts these structures into ascending order by TIME and writes the sorted array to a new file.

```
1     SORT:PROCEDURE OPTIONS(MAIN);
2        DECLARE(NUMBER_OF_RECORDS)FIXED,
3           (I,J)FIXED;
4        DECLARE(INFILE,OUTFILE)RECORD FILE;
5        DECLARE 1 OBSERVATION(100),
6                  2 TIME FIXED,
7                  2 SIZE FIXED;
8        DECLARE 1 WORK_RECORD LIKE OBSERVATION;
9        /* READ IN THE UNSORTED STRUCTURES */
10       GET LIST(NUMBER_OF_RECORDS);
11       OPEN FILE(INFILE)INPUT;
12       DO I=1 TO NUMBER_OF_RECORDS;
13          READ FILE(INFILE)INTO(OBSERVATION(I));
14          END;
15       CLOSE FILE(INFILE);
16       /* SORT THE VECTOR OF STRUCTURES */
17       DO I=1 TO NUMBER_OF_RECORDS-1;
18          DO J=1 TO NUMBER_OF_RECORDS-I;
19             IF OBSERVATION(J).TIME>OBSERVATION(J+1).TIME THEN
20                DO;
21                   WORK_RECORD=OBSERVATION(J);
22                   OBSERVATION(J)=OBSERVATION(J+1);
23                   OBSERVATION(J+1)=WORK_RECORD;
24                   END;
25             END;
26          END;
27       /* WRITE OUT THE SORTED VECTOR */
28       OPEN FILE(OUTFILE)OUTPUT;
29       DO I=1 TO NUMBER_OF_RECORDS;
30          WRITE FILE(OUTFILE)FROM(OBSERVATION(I));
31          END;
32       CLOSE FILE(OUTFILE);
33       END;
```

Some PL/1 compilers such as PL/C do not support LIKE in declarations. To run under such a compiler, line 8 of the example program could be changed to:

```
DECLARE 1 WORK_RECORD,
          2 TIME FIXED,
          2 SIZE FIXED;
```

Some compilers such as PL/C do not allow READ and WRITE to transfer elements of an array of structures. To run under such a compiler, line 13 could be changed to:

```
READ FILE(INFILE)INTO(WORK_RECORD);
OBSERVATION(I)=WORK_RECORD;
```

In a similar way, line 30 could be changed.

APPENDIX 2

THE STATEMENT SYNTAX OF SP/6

A <u>job</u> is: $JOB
                    program
                    $DATA
                    [data]

A <u>program</u> is: identifier:PROCEDURE OPTIONS(MAIN);
                         {declaration}
                         {definition }
                         {statement }
                    END;

A <u>declaration</u> is: DECLARE(variable {,variable})attribute
                         {,(variable {,variable})attribute};

An <u>attribute</u> is one of the following:
                    FIXED
                    FLOAT
                    CHARACTER(maximum length)VARYING
                    BIT

A <u>definition</u> is: identifier:PROCEDURE[(identifier {,identifier})]
                         [RETURNS(attribute)];
                         {declaration}
                         {definition }
                         {statement }
                    END;

A <u>statement</u> is one of the following:
```
PUT [SKIP] LIST(expression {,expression} );
PUT PAGE LIST(expression {,expression} );
GET [SKIP] LIST(variable {,variable} );
variable = expression;
IF condition THEN
   statement
[ELSE
   statement]
DO WHILE(condition);
   {statement}
   END;
DO identifier = expression TO expression
   [BY expression];
   {statement}
   END;
DO;
   {statement}
   END;
CALL procedure name [(expression {,expression})];
RETURN [(expression)];
```

Notation: [item] means the item is optional.
             {item} means the item is repeated zero or more times.

APPENDIX 3

BUILT-IN FUNCTIONS IN SP/k

a. <u>An arithmetic built-in function</u>.

MOD(i,j): remainder of i divided by j; i and j must be fixed
values. The result is fixed.

b. <u>Mathematical built-in functions</u>.

For these functions, the arguments may be float or fixed.
The result is float.

SIN(x) - sine of x radians.
COS(X) - cosine of x radians.
ATAN(x) - arctangent of x in radians.
LOG(x) - natural logarithm of x.
EXP(x) - e to the x power.
SQRT(x) - square root of x.

c. <u>String built-in functions</u>.

LENGTH(s) - number of characters (currently) in string s.
SUBSTR(s,i [,j]) - substring of s from i-th to last character
     [or from i-th character for a length of j characters].

In SUBSTR, s must be a character string; i [and j] must be
fixed or float; the result is a character string. The values of
i and j are truncated to fixed values when given as float. The
substring selected by i [and j] must be contained entirely within
s. This means that i should be at least one, j should be
positive or zero and i plus j minus one should not exceed the
length of string s; otherwise there is an error. Some compilers,
such as PL/C, require that i must be at most equal to the length
of s. Other compilers, such as Toronto's SP/k compiler, allow i
to be one more than the length of s when j is zero or j is
omitted.

APPENDIX 4

THE SP/k COMPILER

A special compiler has been developed at the University of Toronto to support the SP/k language; Appendix 1 gives the specifications for the SP/k language. Generally, an SP/k program that runs without errors under the SP/k compiler will run with the same results under other PL/1 compilers such as PL/C or the IBM PL/1 compilers.

As of summer 1975 there exist versions of the SP/k compiler that run on either the IBM 360/370 computers or the DEC PDP-11 computers. Either punch cards or mark sense cards can be accepted. Persons interested in obtaining an SP/k compiler should contact: SP/k Distribution Manager, Computer Systems Research Group, University of Toronto, Toronto, Canada. These compilers support SP/k subsets SP/1 to SP/6; they may or may not support subsets SP/7 and SP/8.

SP/k JOB CARD PARAMETERS

The first card of an SP/k job is called the job card, for example

    $JOB ID='JOHN WALSH'

In some computer installations, the characters $JOB are not used, and are replaced by other characters. For example, on the University of Toronto High Speed Job Stream, $JOB must be replaced by $JOBK. The ID parameter as shown in this example job card causes the name JOHN WALSH to be printed in a header box preceding the printing of the SP/k program. The three characters ID= are optional, so the above job card is equivalent to

    $JOB 'JOHN WALSH'

Other parameters can be given on the job card, as we show in this example:

    $JOB ID='GLEN BONHAM',STMTS=10000,LINES=300

The parameter STMTS=10000 specifies that the job is to be allowed
to execute 10000 statements before being terminated for excess
running time. The parameter LINES=300 specifies that the job is
to be allowed to print, via PUT statements, 300 lines before
being terminated for excess lines. STMTS can be abbreviated as S
and LINES can be abbreviated as L. Individual computer centers
may have different job card parameters.

HANDLING ERRORS IN SP/k PROGRAMS

When an error is found in an SP/k program, the SP/k compiler
generally makes an attempt to repair the error. The programmer
is warned that these repairs are not to be taken as intelligent
advice for producing a correct program, but instead as a method
of allowing processing to continue. This strategy of automatic
error repair is intended to minimize programmer frustration and
required computer runs.

We will now show how a number of common errors are handled.
Since compilers are always being modified, the treatment of these
errors by a particular version of the SP/k compiler may differ
slightly from what we present.

Here is the listing of a simple SP/k program in which the
PROCEDURE OPTIONS(MAIN) line has been forgotten.

```
    1
      ?
****     SYNTAX ERROR IN PREVIOUS LINE.   LINE IS REPLACED BY:
    1 $NIL:PROCEDURE OPTIONS(MAIN);

    2     PUT LIST('HELLO');
    3     END;
```

As you can see, the missing line is supplied by the compiler and
the program is given the name $NIL. The program is executed and
prints HELLO. If the programmer forgets a semicolon, the
compiler is often able to insert it, as is shown here:

```
    2     PUT LIST('HELLO')
                              ?
****     SYNTAX ERROR IN PREVIOUS LINE.   LINE REPLACED BY:
    2     PUT LIST('HELLO');
```

If the programmer forgets the right-hand quote mark from a
literal, the compiler inserts a quote mark, although probably not
in the desired place. In the following example, the quote mark
between the O of HELLO and the right parenthesis has been
omitted. The compiler inserts a quote mark after the semicolon.
As a result, the line requires a new right parenthesis and
semicolon because the original right parenthesis and semicolon
were absorbed into the literal. Note that the right quote mark
was not present on the card, but was inserted by the compiler.

```
2      PUT LIST('HELLO); '
```

```
****      STRING IS ENDED WITH QUOTE(')
```

```
****      SYNTAX ERROR IN PREVIOUS LINE.  LINE IS REPLACED BY:
2      PUT LIST('HELLO); ');
```

When this program runs, it will print HELLO); instead of HELLO.

In the next example, a forgotten right parenthesis is inserted by the compiler.

```
2      PUT LIST('HELLO';
                          ?
****      SYNTAX ERROR IN PREVIOUS LINE.  LINE IS REPLACED BY:
2      PUT LIST('HELLO');
```

In the next example, the keyword PROCEDURE has been misspelled.

```
1 SAMPLE:PROCDEURE OPTIONS(MAIN);
             ?
****      SYNTAX ERROR IN PREVIOUS LINE.  LINE IS REPLACED BY:
1 SAMPLE:PROCEDURE OPTIONS(MAIN);
```

The following SP/k program does not make sense because it tries to use the value of the variable named INCHES, but INCHES is never given a value. To allow the program to execute, INCHES is given the value 1.

```
1 SP2:PROCEDURE OPTIONS(MAIN);
2      DECLARE(CENTIMETERS,INCHES)FLOAT;
3      CENTIMETERS=2.54E0*INCHES;
4      PUT LIST('LENGTH IS',CENTIMETERS);
5      END;
****ERROR IN LINE 5: FLOAT VARIABLE HAS NO VALUE; 1.0E+00 USED
LENGTH IS          2.54000E+00
```

The next program attempts to read data items into two variables: WIDTH and HEIGHT. The data as provided by the programmer contains only one data item, so the program is stopped because it attempts to read beyond the end of the data.

```
1 SP2:PROCEDURE OPTIONS(MAIN);
2      DECLARE(WIDTH,HEIGHT)FLOAT;
3      GET LIST(WIDTH,HEIGHT);
4      PUT LIST('AREA IS',WIDTH*HEIGHT);
5      END;
****ERROR IN LINE 3: NO MORE INPUT DATA
```

The next program has WEIGHT misspelled as WIEGHT in line 4. The compiler assumes (wrongly) that WEIGHT and WIEGHT are different variables; fortunately, it warns us about its wrong assumption. Note that the value of WEIGHT remains as 7.5E0.

```
1 SP2:PROCEDURE OPTIONS(MAIN);
2    DECLARE(WEIGHT)FLOAT;
3    WEIGHT=7.5E0;
4    WIEGHT=2.2E0*WEIGHT;
5    PUT LIST('WEIGHT IS',WEIGHT);
6    END;
****ERROR IN LINE 4: UNDECLARED VARIABLE ASSUMED FIXED
WEIGHT IS      7.50000E+00
```

In the next program, it was forgotten to read values of
NUMBER inside the loop. As the program now stands, there is an
infinite loop because NUMBER is not changed inside the loop.

```
1 SP3:PROCEDURE OPTIONS(MAIN);
2    DECLARE(NUMBER,SUM)FIXED;
3    SUM=0;
4    NUMBER=0;
5    DO WHILE(NUMBER¬=-99999);
6       SUM=SUM+NUMBER;
7       END;
8    PUT LIST('SUM IS',SUM);
9    END;
****ERROR IN LINE 6: EXECUTION LIMIT EXCEEDED
```

The next program tries to find the last name of Bill
McKeeman, but since the name McKeeman contains 8 letters and not
9 letters, the substring does not lie within the string.

```
1 SP4:PROCEDURE OPTIONS(MAIN);
2    DECLARE(NAME,LAST_NAME)CHARACTER(20)VARYING;
3    NAME='BILL MCKEEMAN';
4    LAST_NAME=SUBSTR(NAME,6,9);
5    PUT LIST('LAST NAME IS',LAST_NAME);
6    END;
****ERROR IN LINE 4: SPECIFIED SUBSTRING NOT WITHIN STRING
LAST NAME IS    ?
```

In the next program the NAME array contains elements NAME(1),
NAME(2), NAME(3), and NAME(4). The program is supposed to read
four names followed by the dummy name ZZZ. When the program
runs, there is an error because an attempt is made to read ZZZ
into NAME(5), but NAME(5) does not exist. The error can be
corrected by increasing the declared upper bound of NAME to 5.

```
 1 SP5:PROCEDURE OPTIONS(MAIN);
 2    DECLARE(NAME(4))CHARACTER(20)VARYING;
 3    DECLARE(I)FIXED;
 4    I=1;
 5    GET LIST(NAME(I));
 6    DO WHILE(NAME(I)¬='ZZZ');
 7       PUT LIST(NAME(I));
 8       I=I+1;
 9       GET LIST(NAME(I));
10       END;
11    END;
```
(Four names printed here.)
****ERROR IN LINE 9: SUBSCRIPT OUT OF RANGE; LOWER BOUND USED

CHARACTERISTICS OF THE SP/k COMPILER

The various compilers for PL/1 differ in their treatment of certain constructs of the PL/1 language. Generally, conservative use of these constructs results in programs that work as well under most of the compilers. In this section we list limits of the SP/k compiler and those language aspects that it may handle in its own particular way.

Error Recovery. A large number of errors in programs will be automatically "repaired".

Card boundaries. Identifiers, keywords, constants and comments cannot cross card boundaries in a program. Constants read by GET LIST cannot cross card boundaries. If a constant uses the last columns of one card and another constant uses the first columns of the next card, the two constants are read separately. Persons using mark sense cards are provided with a convention for suppressing card boundaries when desired.

Use of card columns for programs. When a program is presented using punch cards, all 80 columns are used.

Reserving of keywords. Keywords must not be used as the names of variables. Variables must not begin with the characters $JOB or $DATA.

Two character operators. This compiler does not in general enforce the convention that blanks may not be embedded in two character operators such as >=. (In fact, it allows blanks in >=, <= and ¬= but not in ||.)

Length of identifiers. Identifiers can be at most 31 characters long.

Width of print fields. For printers with 120 or 132 columns, there are 5 fields per print line with 24 columns per field. For printers with 72 or 80 columns, there are 5 fields per line with 14 columns per field.

Form of printed numbers. Each fixed or float value printed by a PUT LIST statement is right-justified in the first 12 columns of the next print field. Float values are printed in the form mD.dddddEsdd where m is an optional minus sign, D is a non-zero digit, each d is a digit, and s is a plus or minus sign. (Exception: D is zero when the float value is zero.)

Range of fixed values. Fixed values have a maximum magnitude of 999999999.

Non-integer fixed constants. Non-integer fixed constants, e.g., 214.8, are flagged as errors in programs and are automatically converted to float. Non-integer fixed constants are accepted (without error messages) in data.

Range of float values. Float values have a maximum magnitude of 1E36.

Precision of float arithmetic. Float arithmetic is accurate to approximately 6 significant figures.

Length of character strings. Character strings can be, at most, 127 characters long.

Definition before use. The definition of a procedure must appear before its invocation. (Calling of a following procedure which has the same name and parameter attributes as a global procedure will result in a call to the global procedure instead of a call to the following procedure; no error message will be issued.)

Checks for recursion. Any procedure (except the main procedure) can be called recursively.

Conversion of arguments. Conversion of fixed scalar arguments to float scalar formal parameters (and vice versa) is automatic and creates a dummy argument.

Dummy arguments. Arguments preceded by a unary plus or enclosed in parentheses will have a dummy argument created. Assignment of a value to a parameter having a dummy argument does not change the value of the actual argument.

Division of fixed values. Division of fixed values, for example 7/3, results in an error message, and the truncated value of the quotient is used.

Collating sequence. The version of the SP/k compiler that runs on the IBM 360/370 has IBM standard (EBCDIC) order of characters for comparisons:

b.<(+|&$*);¬-/,%_>?:#@'=ABCDEFGHIJKLMNOPQRSTUVWXYZ0123456789

The version of the SP/k compiler that runs on the DEC PDP-11 has the international standard (ASCII) order of characters for comparisons:

b|#$%&'()*+,-./0123456789:;<=>?@ABCDEFGHIJKLMNOPQRSTUVWXYZ_¬

Since the characters | and ¬ are not standard ASCII characters, they are printed as the exclamation point and the caret.

Reserved words. The following are keywords in SP/k and must not be used as names of variables or procedures.

BIT	ELSE	INPUT	PAGE	THEN
BY	END	INTO	PROCEDURE	TO
CALL	FILE	LIKE	PUT	VARYING
CHARACTER	FIXED	LIST	READ	WHILE
CLOSE	FLOAT	MAIN	RECORD	WRITE
DECLARE	FROM	OPEN	RETURN	$DATA
DO	GET	OPTIONS	RETURNS	$JOB
EDIT	IF	OUTPUT	SKIP	

Recursion. Procedures can call themselves directly or indirectly, subject to the constraint that a procedure name must be defined before being called. The PL/1 keyword RECURSIVE is neither required nor allowed.

Overflow. All runtime FIXED computations yielding results in the supported FIXED range give mathematically correct results. All overflows produce error messages. Runtime FLOAT computations are similar except that FLOAT results have a limited precision and are not necessarily exact. Exponent underflow yields a result of zero with no warning message.

Bibliography

1. Holt, Richard C., "Teaching the Fatal Disease (or) Introductory Computer Programming Using PL/1", Assoc. for Computing Machinery SIGPLAN Notices, 8, 5 (May 1973) 8-23.

2. Conway, Richard and Gries, David, An Introduction to Programming: A Structured Approach Using PL/1 and PL/C, Winthrop Publishers, Cambridge, Mass., 1973.

3. Conway, R.W. and Wilcox, T.R., "Design and Implementation of a Diagnostic Compiler for PL/1", Communications of the ACM, March 1973.

4. IBM System 360 PL/1 Reference Manual, Form C28-8201.

5. IBM PL/1 Language Specifications, Form C28-6571.

6. Pollack, S.V. and Sterling, T. D., A Guide to PL/1, Holt Rinehart Winston, 1969.

7. Boulton, P.I.P. and Jeanes, D.L., "The Structure and Performance of PLUTO, a Teaching Oriented PL/1 Compiler System", INFOR, vol. 10, no.2, June 1972, pp. 140-153.

8. IBM: OS PL/1 Checkout and Optimizing Compilers. Language Reference Manual, Form SC33-0009-2.

9. ECMA.TC10/ANSI.X3J1 (European Computer Manufacturers Association and American National Standards Institute), "PL/1 Basis/1-11", February 1974.

10. Wortman, D.B., "Student PL - A PL/1 Dialect Designed for Teaching", Proceedings of Canadian Computer Conference, Montreal, June 1972.

11. Holt, Richard C. and Wortman, David B., "Structured Subsets of the PL/1 Language", technical report, Computer Systems Research Group, University of Toronto, October 1973.

Index

Artificial intelligence, 129
Assembler, 260, 266
Assembly language, 259, 266
Assigning structures, 216
Assignment, 51
   statement, 37
ATAN, 242
Attribute, type, 36, 51
Available storage list, 227
Average, calculation of, 109

B format item, 180, 307
Bank account, 182
Bin, 190
Binary digit, 11
Binary search, 187
Binary tree, 230, 235
BIT, 57, 298
Bit, 11
Blank, 21
   padding with, 100, 301
   as a separator, 130
Body of loop, 58
Bottom-up testing, 200
Branch, 64
   in control flow, 64
   three-way, 65
   of tree, 110, 231
Bubble sort, 191
Bucket, 190
Bug, in program, 202
Building block, 77
Built-in function, 147, 241,
      315
Business data processing, 161
Byte, 11

CALL statement, 143, 155, 303
Calling procedure, 144
Calling a procedure, 135
Card, 16, 318
   punched, 16
   mark sense, 17, 317
Central processing unit, 19
Character, 21, 30, 90
   special, 21, 293
Character string, 24, 293
   fixed length, 215
   reading of, 177
Character string variable, 90,
      301
Character variable, 35
CLOSE FILE, 212, 310
Closing, of file, 212, 216